Robert Mazur has earned glob[...]ng experts concerning the financi[...] [...]orld. There is no one with more first-hand [...]wledge about how international banks and businesses cater to those who own the nearly $2 trillion in criminal proceeds laundered annually. For five years, in the eyes of organized crime leaders, he was thought to be a highly successful mob-connected money launderer who helped manage their illicit fortunes. His clients, some of the most famous and deadly drug cartel bosses, offered a $500,000 price tag for his head when arrests were made around the world and he was revealed to be a highly trained U.S. federal undercover agent.

After completing a decorated twenty-seven-year career as a federal agent Robert Mazur now shares the secrets he learned from senior executives of banks that wielded power around the globe. He is certified in both U.S. and Canadian courts as an expert in money laundering, has published articles in world-renowned newspapers and has appeared on more than 1,000 TV and radio broadcasts, addressing corruption within the financial markets.

ROBERT MAZUR

THE
INFILTRATOR

UNDERCOVER IN THE WORLD OF
DRUG BARONS AND DIRTY BANKS

CORGI BOOKS

TRANSWORLD PUBLISHERS
61–63 Uxbridge Road, London W5 5SA
www.penguin.co.uk

Transworld is part of the Penguin Random House group of companies
whose addresses can be found at global.penguinrandomhouse.com

Penguin
Random House
UK

Originally published in the United States in 2009 by Little Brown
and Company, a division of Hachette Book Group, Inc.

First published in Great Britain in 2015 by Corgi Books
an imprint of Transworld Publishers
Corgi edition reissued 2016

A CIP catalogue record for this book
is available from the British Library.

ISBN
9780552172110

Designed by James Jayo
Typeset in Granjon

Printed and bound in Great Britain by Clays Ltd, St Ives plc

Penguin Random House is committed to a sustainable
future for our business, our readers and our planet. This book is made from Forest
Stewardship Council® certified paper.

MIX
Paper from
responsible sources
FSC® C018179

3 5 7 9 10 8 6 4

*To Evelyn, my wife, whose love and support
are more than I deserve*

CONTENTS

Preface

THE DAY OF RECKONING

U.S. District Court, Tampa, Florida
March 26, 1990

ARMED GUARDS LED ME into a tiny, windowless room in Tampa's U.S. District Courthouse. Through the glossy mahogany walls came the muffled voices of lawyers arguing and the response of an unruly crowd. On the other side of the door, I was about to do battle with some of the best defense attorneys money could buy. For the first time since the unmasking of Bob Musella — my cover as an international money launderer — half a dozen men who had come to realize that I wasn't really one of them were about to lay eyes on me.

As the minutes dragged, I gathered strength for the fight ahead by thinking of my wife and children, who had spent years enduring the hardships of my career. With the operation over, we all looked forward to returning to life as it had been, only to learn that some of the eighty-five men charged in the first wave of indictments had put a $500,000 contract on my head. My family and I had relocated and were living under an assumed name, but I wouldn't be able to live with myself if my role in taking down cartels and their bankers brought any harm to those I loved. The hard work and anguish of the last four years would have meant nothing. I needed every ounce of strength and determination I could muster to get through the next three months on the witness stand.

"They're ready for you now," said a deputy U.S. marshal, opening the door and breaking my reverie. He led me into a courtroom jammed with hundreds of reporters and spectators—and also the wives and children of the defendants with whom I had spent so much time. They said nothing, but their faces all screamed, *How could you?* On the courtroom floor, the six defendants huddled among a constellation of lawyers.

Rudy Armbrecht, a major organizer for the Medellín cartel, had worked with the entire cartel commission to arrange some of their most sensitive operations in the U.S. If they needed to buy fleets of aircraft or assess the feasibility of global laundering schemes, they called on Rudy. He looked like a crazed Jack Nicholson, but he had the extraordinary intelligence and philosophical bent of Hannibal Lecter. Pablo Escobar had hand-picked Armbrecht's boss, Gerardo Moncada—also known as Don Chepe—to control a large part of his cocaine empire. Armbrecht had acted as a conduit between me, Don Chepe, and Escobar. As I glanced toward him from the stand, Armbrecht grabbed his tie and, with a demented look on his face, waved it at me to say hello.

Near Armbrecht sat Amjad Awan, a smooth-as-silk senior executive of the Bank of Credit and Commerce International (BCCI) who laundered money for some of the most notorious criminals in the world. His clients included President Muhammad Zia of Pakistan, General Manuel Noriega of Panama, and high-ranking drug dealers in the U.S. The son of the former head of the ISI—Pakistan's equivalent of the CIA—Awan supported a group then known as the Afghan Freedom Fighters, known now as the Taliban. Awan held himself above stunts like waving his tie. In his impeccably tailored suit, he tilted his head forward and looked down his nose as though he were royalty annoyed by my presence.

Sitting beside Awan was his best friend and co-marketer at BCCI, Akbar Bilgrami, who shared responsibility with Awan to develop business for BCCI in all of Latin America, where they openly sought relationships with the owners of any dirty money they could find. Born and raised in Islamabad, Bilgrami spoke fluent Spanish and had spent long stretches of his career in Colombia, where he met his third wife. Bilgrami stared me down, fidgeting in his seat and rubbing his hands together. Even when I was under-cover, I had trouble putting him at ease. No doubt he knew this day would come.

Ian Howard, a BCCI officer born in India, ran the Paris branch of the bank, doing the dirty work for his boss, Nazir Chinoy. The third-highest-ranking executive in a 19,000-employee bank, Chinoy directed all European and North African branches. After I won Chinoy's confidence in Paris, he brought Howard into our schemes. Chinoy would have been sitting in the courtroom, too, had he not been fighting extradition in London, where authorities there had arrested him and were holding him without bond. The old London jail in which he was languishing made most U.S. prisons look like four-star hotels. His minion Howard glared at me, but neither his face nor his body moved.

Also from Paris, Howard's right-hand man Sibte Hassan found himself tangled in the web of our undercover operation. Hassan's was the hand that pushed money around the globe wherever Chinoy directed. Younger and less experienced than his colleagues, Hassan had never set foot in the U.S. before his arrest. His dependence on his superiors carried through even to the courtroom. He kept glanc-ing at the other defendants, looking to see how he should act.

Last in the line-up came Syed Hussain, a BCCI account execu-tive in the Panama branch. Hussain saw in me an easy means of meeting the bank's pressure to bring in any kind of money, as long as it increased the bottom line of the balance sheet. When agents arrested Hussain, he was on his way to what he thought was my bachelor party. As the cuffs clicked around his wrists, he laughed. Surprised, the arresting agents asked him what was so funny. "I've been to bachelor parties like this when women dress up like cops and act like they are arresting you," he said, laughing. "Where are the women?" The agents shook their heads, and said, "Pal, you need to wake up and smell the coffee. This isn't make-believe. Your ass is under arrest."

I spent years undercover as a money launderer to the inter-national underworld, infiltrating the apex of a criminal hierarchy safeguarded by a circle of dirty bankers and businessmen who quietly shape power across the globe. They knew me as Bob Musella, a wealthy, mob-connected American businessman also living the good life. We partied in $1,000-per-night hotel suites, lived in lavish homes, drove Rolls-Royce convertibles, and flew on the Concorde and in private jets. Bob Musella was their kind of guy. Bob Musella ran a successful investment company, had an interest in a Wall Street brokerage firm, operated a chain of jewelry stores—he had it all. What they didn't know was that I wasn't really Bob Musella. That name and lifestyle were a lie I lived solely to gain access to their secret lives in the criminal underworld.

Under my Armani suits or in my Renwick briefcase, mini recorders captured the damning evidence of our partnerships in crime, which I then passed to my government handlers. After a dramatic takedown staged at a fake wedding (mine), more than forty men and women were arrested, found guilty, and sent to prison. In the year and a half between the end of the operation and the start of the first trial, a handful of dedicated agents and I put in eighteen-hour days feverishly transcribing more than 1,400 clandestine recordings. Those microcassettes became knockout punches in the trials ahead, and Operation C-Chase became one of the most successful undercover operations in the history of U.S. law enforcement.

The story of my role in the sting fed magazine covers and front pages for years: "Breaking the Underworld Bank" (*New York Times*); "BCCI Officials Charged with Money Laundering" (*Wall Street Journal*); "Fed's Playboy Cover Topples Drug Moguls" (*New York Post*); "Narco Bankers—Inside the Secret World of International Drug Money Laundering" (*San Francisco Examiner*). But the value of that exposure paled in comparison to the amount of money pumped into the pockets of the lawyers defending the men I saw from the witness stand. Government officials later calculated that tens of millions of dollars flowed from the shareholders of BCCI—wealthy Saudi oil barons—into the defense's coffers in an attempt to prevent the conviction of bank officers who had catered to my every money-laundering need.

And that figure in turn pales in comparison to the $400 to $500 billion in revenue generated from the drug trade each year, according to U.S. and U.N. estimates. A vast sum, and yet the U.S. government can't track even one percent of that wealth. Banks in Switzerland, Panama, Lichtenstein, and other traditional havens continue to harbor dirty money, but my undercover work gathered intelligence showing that other, less traditional outlets were in ascendance. The cartels were starting to move their money to places like Abu Dhabi, Bahrain, Dubai, and Oman. These banks conduct their business in Arabic, resist investigations by Western law enforcement, and thrive in a dollar-based cash trade.

The dirty bankers in all these places help control multibillion-dollar drug-trafficking empires, running their organizations like public companies. Accountants, attorneys, and financial advisers, their roots run deep in their communities, and they are laundering billions of dollars a year, manipulating complex international finance systems to serve drug lords, corrupt politicians, tax cheats, and terrorists. Subtle and sophisticated, they thrive in anonymity, offering discreet, first-class services no matter how much dirt or blood coats the money they protect. And they are getting away with it every day.

This is the story of how I helped bring some of them down. It is also the story of how undercover agents rise through the ranks, how billions of dollars flow through shell corporations and move across borders, how informants are cultivated and safe houses are made. It is, at its broadest, a shocking look inside the secret world of international drug-money laundering. At its narrowest and most intimate, it is a story of harrowing escapes, near misses, and justice served as my fellow agents and I built our case one piece of evidence at a time.

How it happened is a story I've never shared—until now. It all started with a glass of champagne.

THE
INFILTRATOR

1

IN THE BEGINNING

WHEN I WAS A BOY, my mother revealed—almost as a cautionary tale—that my great-grandfather, Ralph Cefaro, ran a sham moving company on Manhattan's Lower East Side in order to transport bootleg whiskey during Prohibition for Charles "Lucky" Luciano, one of the most notorious gangsters in America.

My grandfather Joe and his brothers worked for the moving company with other guys who belonged to one of Lucky's crews. When Assistant U.S. Attorney Thomas Dewey went after Lucky and his entire organization, one of the guys in the crew with a record got collared—not for bootlegging—and faced stiff time as a repeat offender. My grandfather, truly a stand-up guy, took the rap. After serving his time, he relocated the family from East Eleventh Street to a tiny second-story apartment near the dry docks on Staten Island. Like a lot of guys in the neighborhood back then, he had a nickname—Two Beers—which he earned because, after the yard whistle blew and his shift ended, he went straight to the Friendly Club, a local hangout, and immediately ordered two beers.

My family agrees that I was his favorite, which explains why, when I was only five years old, he started taking me to the Friendly Club to show me off to his friends. Like every good little Italian boy in those days, I played the accordion, and my grandfather couldn't wait to sit me up on the bar so his buddies could see me playing without looking at sheet music. Surrounded by beer taps and billowing clouds of cigarette smoke, he would glance around the club and say with a look, *Hey, shut up. We're going to listen to little Bobby play now.* All the guys in the club snapped to attention and listened while I squeezed out a song. It was awful, but no one dared kid Two Beers Cefaro about how his grandson played.

More than a decade after his death, I landed a summer job at Brewer Dry Dock as a carpenter, painter, and rigger. On my first day, one of the guys who had worked the yard for twenty years asked me, "Hey, kid, how da hell did ya get this job?"

"Well, my grandfather worked here years ago, and he had a lot of friends," I said sheepishly. "One of the guys who knew him helped me out."

"Oh, yeah, kid, who's your grandpa?" he asked, tilting his head.

"Well, he's been dead for a while, but everyone knew him as Two Beers Cefaro."

"You're *kidding*," the guy replied, shocked. "*Everybody* knew Two Beers! He was a great guy."

After word got around that I was Two Beers's grandson, my AFL-CIO union shop steward, Steve, approached me. "Hey, kid, we need your help today," he said. "After you shape up, come see me at the shitter." Shaping up, in dock speak, meant going in the morning to the guy who ran your skill — carpentry, in my case — and finding out what job you had for the day. The shitter was just that: the bathroom building in the center of the yard.

When I showed, Steve explained that I had to hang around outside and bang on the wall if I saw anyone coming who didn't work in the yard. My assignment coincided with visits from the local bookie, who was taking bets inside the shitter on numbers, horses, and games. Steve rotated this lookout job among a chosen few. But before he could ask me to do it again, another union replaced the AFL-CIO, and Steve lost his power. It was an important — and painless — lesson about loyalty and respect.

A couple of years later, at Wagner College on Staten Island,

I stumbled across a job announcement for a co-op position at the Intelligence Division of the IRS. I had no idea what that meant, but it offered full-time summer employment, part-time school-year employment, and a shot at a full-time job after graduation.

Gathering information about the job gave me a chance to speak with a special agent with the division. As he described it, they didn't audit and harass the average Joe. They carried guns and badges and worked shoulder to shoulder with other agencies, including the FBI, on joint task forces. They applied their accounting expertise to criminal tax cases against drug traffickers, mobsters, and big-time tax cheats. He often cited that old saw about the pen being mightier than the sword, ending with, "You know, Al Capone went to prison for income-tax evasion. If it hadn't been for us putting that case together, he never would have seen the inside of Alcatraz."

I was already taking accounting and business courses, and this sounded a lot more fun than becoming a bean-counting CPA. In earlier years, Chase Manhattan Bank and Montgomery Scott, a brokerage firm in downtown Manhattan, had hired me as a paper pusher—and I hated it. I wanted a career that I could be proud of, that kept my interest, that didn't box me into the same boring routine every day. It was no doubt my mind-numbing experience at Chase and Montgomery Scott that drove me to the IRS gig.

That first day on the job at 120 Church Street electrified me with anticipation about what mobster or kingpin we were going to topple by day's end. However, I was in for quite a shock. After I had settled in, Special Agent Morris Skolnick, who didn't look a day under seventy, shuffled over to me and said, "Hey, kid, I'm going to show you the ropes." He grabbed a handful of No. 2 pencils from his desk and slowly made his way to a hand-cranked pencil sharpener. As he struggled to sharpen each pencil, he looked at me with a sigh and mumbled about how important it was to start the day with sharp pencils.

Then he dragged me over to the photocopy machine, placed a schedule on the glass, and pushed START. As the top of the machine slid back and forth, he explained the importance of making "true" copies and always comparing the original to the copier output. My mind spun. What happened to the intrigue and adventure of putting bad guys in jail? This wasn't the super cop job in the ad. It felt like I had been sold a bill of goods.

Later that day, Tony Carpinello rescued me. A young supervisor in the division, he explained that the office had two factions: desk jockeys like Skolnick and guys like himself who got things done. Tony was running what was then called the Strike Force Group, one of a collection of squads that Bobby Kennedy, as attorney general, had established. The agents assigned to Strike Force were working cases on most of the mobsters, drug dealers, and dirty politicians in the city. Tony introduced me to some of the guys, including Tommy Egan, who, along with agents from the DEA and detectives from the NYPD narcotics squad at the 34th Precinct, built the case against the bank that laundered millions for Frank Lucas, one of the biggest heroin traffickers in the state.

Lucas manipulated a ring of corrupt servicemen who were sending back heroin in the body bags of U.S. soldiers killed in Vietnam. His smack destroyed tens of thousands of lives and fed him an endless stream of cash. He and his crew carried huge duffel bags brimming with hundreds of thousands of dollars in small bills into the Westchester Square branch of Chemical Bank. Tommy put the facts together and successfully prosecuted the bank and some of its executives. Chemical Bank paid a several-hundred-thousand-dollar fine; it was a groundbreaking case in its time. But in the end, the fine was little more than a slap on the wrist and the cost of doing business. There had to be a way to up the stakes faced by dirty bankers who played too critical a role. Without their help, Lucas's dirty mountain of cash was a huge liability; it drew too much attention. It dawned on me then that the Achilles' heel of the drug trade was the banks that supplied it with money-laundering services. It was a first taste of my life to come.

My wife and I had our first child while I was working as a special agent in New York City. The baby was fine, but Evelyn suffered severe complications. She underwent months of treatment, during which time I blew through all my vacation and sick leave taking care of them both. She still needed care at home, so I told my bosses at the IRS about the problem, requesting advance leave to drive my wife and son to Tampa, where my brother and sister-in-law lived and were willing to take care of them.

My bosses stunned me the next day when they said, "Hey, you're one lucky guy. There's a three-month detail to Tampa, and we're giving it to you." There had been no detail. They had pulled strings to create one to help me out.

I went to Tampa, worked on some of the cases, and brought my family back to New York three months later. After I returned, the division offered me a permanent transfer to Tampa, which I took.

In sunny Florida, drug traffickers and money launderers were as plentiful as palm trees. To combat the problem, the IRS Intelligence Division had partnered with U.S. Customs in a task force called Operation Greenback that went after drug-money launderers. The cases of the operation often required undercover agents to infiltrate drug- and money-laundering groups, but the Intelligence Division didn't allow its agents to work undercover unless they had gone through an undercover school in Washington, D.C. Now it was getting interesting.

The thought of playing a crook and making split-second decisions that could affect a case—and my life—galvanized me. That position would put me on the front lines, and that's exactly where I wanted to be.

After enduring a merciless campaign of begging, my boss gave in, gave me a chance, and found a slot for me. Imagine my surprise, when I walked into that D.C. classroom, to see that the instructor was Joe Hinton, an old friend from the Intelligence Division in New York City. Joe and the rest of the agents there taught us every trick they knew. Two key pieces of information grabbed my attention and stayed with me.

First: despite the fact that agents at headquarters were helping undercover agents acquire phony identification documents, Joe held that "to the extent you can, don't use headquarters. Develop those documents yourself." If you developed a document on your own, you knew it was solid and no corners were cut. If you received it from someone assigned to an undercover section in D.C. with a connection inside a bank or credit-card company, you could rest assured that a red flag in the company's file identified the government contact in case the account was overdrawn. Those little administrative oversights could kill you if your target had high-level connections.

Second: when you build your cover, stick as close to your real-life experience as possible in order to minimize the number of lies you have to spin. If you're originally from New York City and worked in the Financial District, your new identity should share those same core elements. You can't offer an undercover background that you don't know intimately. The devil's in the details.

Back in Tampa, I started working on my first undercover identity and read stacks of books about how to create new identities and how to check IDs to determine if they were forgeries. With more help from D.C. than I would ever accept on future identities, I created Robert Mangione — just in time for an unexpected assignment and my first undercover gig.

The Tampa Greenback task force had teamed up with the FBI and the Drug Enforcement Administration (DEA) to infiltrate a huge maritime marijuana smuggling ring. The organization was located in San Francisco, but the money launderers were conveniently based sixty miles south of Tampa in Sarasota.

With the help of a snitch, the task force developed a plan for me and two other undercover agents to pose as lead players in a cocaine ring that needed help laundering its profits. Buddy Weinstein, a wiry, outspoken DEA agent from Chicago, played the head of our group perfectly. Jim Barrow, a black FBI agent with a deep voice and the huge build of a defensive end, played the enforcer. I played Robert Mangione, who kept the books and answered to Weinstein.

Weinstein's assignment took him to San Francisco, so Barrow and I dealt in Sarasota with Jack Dubard, an attorney, and an accountant, Charlie Broun. Like many of my future undercover partners, Jim didn't need paperwork and shell companies to convince crooks that he was one of them. He only had to walk through the door. Jim was long on macho and short on paying attention to the details of protecting his identity. More than once, while we were driving around, I caught him about to pay for gas with his government credit card. He also tried to take a gun and his badge with him when we were about to fly to San Francisco to visit the head of the drug organization we were trying to infiltrate. My ass was on the line, and I didn't waste any breath reminding him of same. It must have looked something like Chester the Terrier worrying Spike the Bulldog from the old cartoons.

Jim and I spent a month warming up to Broun and Dubard, who were laundering big bucks for Bruce Perlowin in San Francisco. As a test of their talents, I gave them the opportunity to take me to Las Vegas to introduce me to their casino contacts. As promised, the boys in Vegas exchanged the small denominations — fives, tens, and twenties — that we claimed had been collected from our drug sales for crisp hundreds.

In Vegas, Broun and Dubard also introduced me to Joe Slyman, owner of the Royal Casino — a small operation compared to other casinos like the Dunes — which Broun said also cleaned dope money. Slyman had a great system. He took our small bills, put them in the Casino cage under a phony name, and handed them back the next day as crisp hundreds. To the rest of the world, it looked like some guy no one could ever find was just a lucky gambler. But his system served to make our money compact and a lot easier to smuggle out of the country. Slyman remarkably later beat the federal case brought against him. I guess what he did was business as usual there.

After Broun and Dubard hooked us up with their contacts in Vegas, we needed the help of a lawyer in Florida to acquire offshore corporations to use in order to open accounts outside the United States. It happened in a heartbeat.

Washington National Bank in Grand Cayman opened its arms and its pockets to us and our hoard of hundred-dollar bills. Broun smuggled the money on a commercial flight to Grand Cayman, where he then created elaborate documents as a cover to justify transferring the money back into the U.S. as a seemingly innocent loan to an American company that I controlled. And so fives and tens in a suitcase became financing for a legitimate U.S. company.

Broun and Dubard eventually learned that we were looking for a pot connection for a client in the market for tons of high-grade grass. I told them that, if they helped us find a source, we'd cut them in for a piece of the deal. They soon arranged a meeting among all of us and the head of the San Francisco operation.

Bruce Perlowin, a frail, bespectacled, ponytailed genius, looked more like a psychology grad student than the head of a criminal organization that moved hundreds of tons of pot from Thailand and Colombia to the United States in oceangoing barges, tugboats, and fishing vessels. Hollywood never would have cast him for the part, and, for an instant, when he first walked into a Sarasota hotel room to meet us, he didn't impress. But then he opened his mouth, and when this man spoke he revealed that he thought on levels most people have never even imagined.

"I made my first hundred thousand when I was a fucking kid," he bragged, admitting that, when he operated in Miami, he ran one of the biggest offload organizations the country had ever seen. He owned dozens of speedboats, shrimpers, and trawlers. Just six of the boats in his massive fleet had cost him $3 million. But he had left Miami years earlier because the drug trade in Florida was riddled with killers.

He pioneered a whole new operation in San Francisco, where he spent $500,000 per week on overhead alone — acquiring boats, docks, stash houses, and crews. Since establishing himself in California, he had run seventeen trips, not one of which had been busted. His partner ran a legitimate $30 million business financed from the importation of 40,000 pounds of hashish in the last two years. As Bruce put it, "We know where the Coast Guard is.... I've got all the information. I know where every fucking boat on the West Coast is. Last year we did the 'T' [Thai marijuana] trip. We held the boat offshore for two weeks because there was a massive Coast Guard blockade. It was for a big heroin shipment coming up from Mexico. We knew they were looking for a freighter named the *Cyrus*. We knew where both [Coast Guard] planes were flying. We knew the route they were taking. We knew where every Coast Guard boat was, and there were more Coast Guard boats out than ever before. We couldn't believe they stood out that long. They don't have the money to stay out that long, but they did. And we just waited them out — and then we came in."

Weinstein and I explained how happy we were that we had stumbled upon him. Perlowin countered with the announcement that he felt free to talk to us because he could sense that we weren't cops. Weinstein — who should have been a comic instead of a fed — couldn't help himself. "Do I *look* like J. Edgar Hoover?" he joked. (This was before Anthony Summers's *Official and Confidential: The Secret Life of J. Edgar Hoover* and its allegations of cross-dressing, but still.)

A few of the longest seconds of my life elapsed as Perlowin, legs crossed in a lotus pose on the hotel bed, leaned his head back, looked down through his glasses, and studied each of us, his head turning like the turret of a tank.

"You're not the heat," he finally proclaimed. "It's not that you don't look it; it's that you don't *feel* like it. If you were the heat, I would know it. I'm very intuitive."

Perlowin invited us all to visit him in Ukiah, California, where Weinstein, Barrow, and I spent a few days at his secluded compound. From a perch atop the northern California hills, Perlowin supervised the movement of massive quantities of marijuana hidden inside barges that floated right under the Golden Gate Bridge — and under the noses of cops whose imaginations couldn't compete with Perlowin's.

The little mansion in which we stayed hummed with futuristic electronic gadgetry that could have put CIA techies to shame. Electric grilles hidden under the carpeting could stun intruders. On the top floor of the house sat a command center with steel-plated walls, international toll-free lines, and sophisticated radio equipment used to communicate with captains of the boats that hauled pot from the shores of Colombia and Thailand. Hidden cameras throughout the house broadcast everyone's movements, and sensors everywhere detected everything. In a barn on the property Perlowin kept a motor home packed with electronics that, at critical times, he dispatched to a mountaintop on Skyline Boulevard, on the San Francisco peninsula, where it linked the steel-plated command post with contacts in Colombia and captains in the Pacific and monitored the movements of U.S. Coast Guard vessels.

After half a year of undercover work and dozens of recorded meetings with Broun, Dubard, and Perlowin, we had more than enough evidence to take them down—and a lot of other people in their organization, too. My final challenge in the case was to set up the sting. Broun and Dubard had gone to Biloxi, Mississippi, where they were starting to franchise hotels. I needed to spend some quality time with them, pick their brains about where Perlowin was hiding so he could be collared first, and then set them up for their own arrest.

In Biloxi, Broun and Dubard had literally rolled out the red carpet. They were manning the nationwide headquarters of Red Carpet Inns. They thought I was coming to visit them because my—that is, Mangione's—backers were comfortable enough to meet them directly and enlist their talents in a big way. Broun and Dubard of course believed that I was working for wiseguys in New York who needed their cash cleaned and invested. I told them I'd come first and my bosses would arrive the next day.

At Broun's home, his and Dubard's wives were cooking a feast. Broun greeted me with a hug, and we all sat down to an elaborate home-cooked Southern meal fit for Elvis. As everyone settled into their chairs, Charlie and Jack, seated on either side of me, reached out their hands. Charlie bowed his head and with great seriousness said, "Let's all grasp each other's hands and bow our heads. Lord, we give thanks for Your bringing this wonderful human being, Bob, into all of our lives. We are so blessed with his kind, loving, and loyal friendship. Lord, we thank You from the bottom of our hearts. Amen." As we raised our heads and opened our eyes, it took all the sincerity I ever had to tell everyone at the table that I, too, was blessed and would value their friendships for life.

After dinner, Charlie Broun gave me the goods on Perlowin, who was flying to Chicago the next day. He provided enough detail that agents were able to coordinate his arrest.

The next day, I drove Broun, and later Dubard, to a nearby hotel for what they thought would be secret meetings with my New York bosses. Shortly after I delivered each of them, teams of agents descended and carried them off in cuffs. It came as a huge relief that both Broun and Dubard decided immediately to cooperate. While agents were high-fiving each other and proclaiming victory, search warrants were executed, and we called it a night. But for some reason—a reason I couldn't explain—I didn't feel like celebrating.

The next morning, I called my wife, Ev, and told her what happened. As I spoke, tears rolled down my face and my voice trembled. It wasn't sadness, but I couldn't figure it out. I was feeling something I had never felt before.

Spending the past six months infiltrating the minds and hearts of Broun and Dubard, a small piece of Bob Mazur had become a part of Bob Mangione. These two men had committed crimes and deserved to be prosecuted. The only way to make the case work was for me to lie to them over and over. I had tricked myself into thinking I liked them, and I was paying the emotional price for it. That small piece of me that became Bob Mangione realized that their lives and the lives of their families had changed forever. I had betrayed their deepest trust—which conflicted with everything I had learned from my grandfather.

But I was just doing my job. I never lost sight of who I was and why I was there, and yet the gravity of interacting with them so closely made me susceptible to their pain. To some degree, I did care about them; you can't fake that—not for months or years. Some see this as a weakness, but for me it's the cost of doing the right thing, a kind of collateral damage. It was my willingness to expose myself to that pain that allowed me to win the hearts of my targets.

Bruce Perlowin also cooperated after his arrest, which led to a hundred other convictions. But it was Charlie Broun's help that stood tall. The other agents on the case and I fully supported a reduced sentence for him. His ultimate punishment played out to five years in prison. It could have been a lot worse.

The lawyer who helped Broun establish the offshore corporations and the Grand Cayman bank account was indicted. But after the prosecution presented their case, the judge ruled that Broun and Dubard's testimony about their conversations with the lawyer couldn't be believed. The judge threw out the case, and we learned an incredibly valuable lesson. The witness who delivered testimony about the crimes *had* to be wired to get solid proof of what really happened. And to make the case airtight, the witness who recorded the conversations had to be an undercover agent. Otherwise, the next judge wouldn't believe that a lawyer had knowingly laundered millions of dollars.

It also became clear just how thick the red tape at the IRS was. IRS special agents faced monumental bureaucracy in contrast to a virtual lack of rules at Customs. Agents at the IRS needed five levels of approval to do what customs agents did on their own. So when Paul O'Brien, the agent in charge of the Tampa office of U.S. Customs, approached me about joining his outfit, it was an easy decision. He offered me a job, for which I had to go through training again and for which I had to take a pay cut. But it was worth it, because of the opportunity to do more of what I wanted to do most.

It was an easy decision that changed my life.

2

THE BIRTH OF ROBERT MUSELLA

Crooked River State Park, St. Marys, Georgia
September 26, 1983

HE DIDN'T KNOW the informant was wearing a wire.

Prominent Tampa-area attorney George Meros was backing a massive ring of smugglers bringing hundreds of thousands of pounds of marijuana into the Southeast on oceangoing shrimp boats. Not only was he financing the deals and laundering the dopers' profits, but, after washing money through Swiss accounts, he pumped millions into the development of a major time-share complex on the local beach.

Steve Cook, an old IRS buddy who had also joined Customs as a special agent, looked Meros up in the system and discovered that I was on his trail. Cook called and gave me access to a jailed informant who had some hot intel that cracked the case against the dirty attorney wide open.

We instructed the informant's wife to contact Meros and explain that her husband was about to be transferred from a cushy south Georgia jail to Tampa, where a grand jury was going to ask where he got the money to finance his deals. Meros couldn't rush to Georgia fast enough to reassure the informant, but what he didn't know was that the informant was wired. The case soon became a massive undertaking.

With the help of several agencies and Bill King—one of the brightest assistant U.S. attorneys this country has ever seen—we dispatched agents to secure Meros's law firm while I wrote an affidavit to search Meros's office for records related to his years of crooked financing. Warrant in hand, we seized the most damning evidence you could imagine, including Swiss bank-account records and a complex, step-by-step, handwritten money-laundering scheme. Those records and the testimony of half a dozen terrified dopers earned Meros a forty-year prison sentence.

To keep my workaholic tendencies from getting the better of me during the case, my boss, Paul O'Brien, and I started jogging and socializing together. He loved softball, so he forced virtually the entire office, including me, to play on a team. In fact, the most bizarre episode of my government career occurred one night when we had planned to play a softball game. Two agents on the team couldn't make it on time because they had to make an arrest. They collared their crook, cuffed him, and threw him in the backseat, but they followed Paul's edict that the league had priority. On their way to the local jail, they happened to drive past the ball field, where they discovered that our team was three guys short and about to forfeit the game.

One of the agents turned to the prisoner and said, "Can you play softball?"

The prisoner responded, "Not only can I play, I'm damn good."

"That settles it," the agent decided. "Uncuff him. He's playing." Then he turned to the criminal and added, "Listen, we all have guns. If you try to run, we'll kill you."

They uncuffed him, gave him a team shirt, and had him play shortstop so they had someone along both the first and third baselines in case he tried to bolt. The guy turned out to be one hell of a ballplayer and was the only man on base at the bottom of the last inning when a ball went deep and over an outfielder's head. The guy ran so hard to score the winning run that he pulled his hamstring — you could almost hear it pop. The team helped him into the dugout and joked that his heroics on the field qualified him for a sentence reduction. Then they took him in and booked him.

While we were working on the Meros case, O'Brien and I discussed the benefits of building a sophisticated undercover identity that I could use to portray myself as a money launderer. Impressed by what I'd accomplished since my arrival in his office, O'Brien gave me the green light, and, even though I had already gone to the IRS Undercover School, he sent me to the Customs Undercover School—an agency requirement.

Building the case against Meros and his doper clients took the better part of the three years following his arrest. During that endless march of search warrants, arrests, interviews, hearings, and trial preparation, I began planning for my work after Meros. With O'Brien's approval, I began building the false identity of an Italian-American businessman who controlled companies I could offer as a means through which to launder vast sums of dirty money.

Forging an identity is like aging wine. You can't rush it, and you have to follow certain steps. Most importantly, you need a solid foundation: a birth certificate, and there are only two ways of getting one. First, you can walk through a cemetery, look for headstones of deceased infants, and note names and dates of birth. You need to find one with a birth date close to your own and a name with the right ethnic background. With that information, you contact the Bureau of Vital Statistics in the county of the cemetery and order a certified copy of the birth certificate. If that's not a viable option, a good lab can fake one—but they need to fake it well because the format and stamps, like Caesar's wife, must be above suspicion.

Among the records we had seized from Bruce Perlowin's castle were folders containing documentation on more than two hundred false identities his crew had been developing. In those files lay a perfect match: Robert Musella. He was Italian-American and born within several years of me in the same general vicinity. Most importantly, his first name was Robert. (Under stress, it's hard not to react to your true first name.) And his surname began with an *M*. (Monograms are a dead giveaway.)

So I took advantage of the work that Perlowin's people had done on this identity and augmented it with assistance from FBI and CIA labs in D.C. that did the forgery work for our undercover unit.

A friend in the IRS identified a Social Security number within a few digits of mine that the Social Security Administration hadn't issued. That number helped me land a Florida driver's license. Then, through trustworthy friends at several banks, I opened checking, savings, and credit-card accounts.

Customs regulations allowed me to obtain these documents and accounts, but ironically there were no provisions to fund them. My ass was going to be on the line, so it was worth diverting a few thousand dollars from my personal finances. The deposit in my Musella savings account became collateral for a bank loan, which, along with my use of the credit cards in that name, helped establish a credit history for my new identity. Through another friend, I established a residential address and employment history. Within a year, Robert Musella was receiving more offers for credit cards than my wife and I were.

Agents' careers live or die by the quality of their informants, and informants come from all walks of life. The most reliable informants in my career were turncoats — guys I helped prosecute who decided to cooperate. If they decided to cooperate 100 percent, it formed a bond for life. They cut their ties to real crime, and their livelihoods then depended on the success of the cases they brought me. These men acted as my eyes and ears in the underworld and, a bonus, had access to resources not normally available to agents or agencies.

With that in mind, I developed a relationship with two knock-around guys linked to major New York crime families. Under no circumstances will I ever reveal their real names — and, as the copyright page says, I've changed certain details to protect their identities — but they became invaluable assets. They weren't "made men" — that is, men of Italian descent who have carried out a contract killing as a prerequisite to joining a crime family — but they had worked with different crime groups, dealing drugs, running guns, committing extortion, and doing bodyguard work. They seemed friendly, but beneath the surface these two were calculating and lethal. People around them often developed the habit of turning up with multiple gunshot wounds to the back of the head.

Dominic, a bone-crusher and enforcer, collected unpaid debts for one of the drug groups financed by Meros. Dominic and I met at his bond hearing, staring each other down across a table in the judge's courtroom. A cocky, fearless thug with a thick, hard body, he always meticulously combed his dark hair straight back. Our recordings of the telephone conversations that documented his role in numerous crimes had him by the balls—and he knew it. At the start of the hearing, we told the judge that we had recordings of the real Dominic, not the caring father and devoted family man his attorney was peddling. As the tapes played, the judge heard Dominic say, "You tell little squirt, I swear on my kids—listen to me, before I go to jail, you hear me, I'll fuckin' take everyone out.... I put something to Jeff's head. Do you understand what I did now? I caught him coming out of the fuckin' house. I'd been hiding in the bushes for two weeks.... Tell Jeff I'm willing to meet up at his father's development. We'll go in the pool. I'll go in naked so he doesn't have to worry about me having a gun. 'Cause I'll bite the motherfucker's cock off and spit it in his wife's mouth."

The judge's eyes bulged, and he remanded Dominic into the custody of the U.S. marshal, which gave me a chance to wear him down. It took time, but he won my loyalty when it became clear that he was going to cooperate fully. Underneath his gruff exterior, something about him convinced me that he had more bark than bite.

We got to know each other pretty well as I prepared him to testify against Meros and Meros's "clients." After I learned that Dominic had been craving his favorite breakfast food—Burger King's bacon, egg, and cheese croissant sandwich—I smuggled one in to him each time I came to the prison to debrief him about his life of crime. In exchange, he regaled me with stories more entertaining than anything in *The Godfather*. At one point, he had run a command post from the penthouse of a Fort Lauderdale hotel. From that vantage point, he helped guide freighterloads of marijuana to rendezvous points, from which dozens of go-fast boats buzzed the drugs to offload sites protected by corrupt cops. For his work as a debt collector for drug rings, he carried a Halliburton suitcase that he affectionately called his "hit kit," containing a fully automatic Mac-10 machine gun with silencer, plus a hand grenade, .380 automatic, and surgical gloves.

On behalf of one of Meros's clients, he had once lured a deadbeat distributor to a late-night meeting at Nathan's Restaurant in the Eltingville neighborhood of Staten Island. He led his victim to a nearby Cadillac and, in his deep, gravelly voice — with a heavy accent that revealed that he lived on Staten Island but was born and raised in Brooklyn — he explained: "When we got this fucker near the back of the car, I popped the trunk, gave him a few quickies to the nose, threw him in, and sped off to a cemetery on Todt Hill. My partner and I took the jerk to an open fresh gravesite and threw his ass in the hole. While the guy screamed for us to let him go, we started to throw dirt on top of him. I told the shithead that I didn't want to kill him, but unfortunately the order had been issued."

Needless to say Dom collected the debt. And then he let the guy go.

By the time Musella was about to hit the scene, Dominic was out of jail. He had testified around the country and put a few dozen people away as a star government witness not only in the Meros case but also in a case against some made guys. The man truly had nine lives. He helped put a New York crime-family captain away, yet he didn't get whacked. When pressed, he claimed that the made guys had broken two cardinal rules of their families by dealing and doing drugs and, because of that, he wouldn't have any problems.

You have to become an amateur psychologist to make the informant relationship work. You can't trust someone who isn't emotionally committed to helping you. And convincing someone like Dom to consider you a friend while drawing an emotional line you never let him cross takes skill. He was a source, and everything he said or did needed corroboration. But whatever I said to him couldn't reveal that necessarily paranoid mindset. He had no motivation to make that emotional commitment. So it came as a relief that, when I told him I intended to put a big-time undercover operation together, he said, "Bob, I appreciate everything ya done for me, so if there's anything I can do to help ya, just ask, and it's yours."

I told him I expected to be dealing with some pretty heavy guys out of Colombia. I needed to come across as a connected businessman with mob ties for two reasons. First, those credentials would give me credibility in the eyes of people in the underworld who were looking for a solid laundering outlet. Equally important, I would be handling a lot of money for ruthless people who might try to rip me off. They needed to see that they couldn't fuck with me. I told Dom that it would be a big help if he made some cameo appearances as my cousin and part of my muscle. He reeked of mob crew. After two minutes it was glaringly obvious that he was a connected thug with whom no one wanted to tangle.

As I put it to him, "The desk jockeys in my department don't appreciate that guys like you have a sixth sense about people. Guys like you and these Colombians can smell a cop a mile away. There's nobody in my office who could pull off playing this role the way you could because you won't be acting. You don't have to act. You've been there."

Dom looked at me with disappointment. "Bobby, you don't have to sell me on this. I told you before: I'd do anything for you. Count me in for whatever you need."

Frankie, a friend of Dominic, had worked with him in the pot business. When Frankie and I met, he had already been collared for delivering a truckload of pot to an undercover DEA agent. Out on bond, he was trying to help the DEA in order to get the lightest possible sentence. Unlike Dom, though, Frankie was a low-key, well-educated, sophisticated businessman — the Wall Street–salesman type. His pencil-thin mustache, manicured nails, and trim Mediterranean figure naturally camouflaged his criminality. Besides occasionally delivering, he also maintained Dom's records for the hundreds of thousands of pounds of marijuana that came through their Fort Lauderdale operation.

After he got busted, Frankie moved back to Staten Island and, true to form, worked in a Wall Street brokerage firm owned by his uncle. He had a record, so he couldn't work as a licensed broker, but that didn't stop his family from keeping him on the books as an unlicensed manager. Like Dom, Frankie testified against a couple of wiseguys who pulled the strings of their Fort Lauderdale pot operation. He was pending sentencing, and, with the court's permission, was a good candidate to lend support to Bobby Musella.

I explained to Frankie that I hoped to infiltrate "the big boys in Colombia" and the money-laundering groups that serviced them. After he understood the concept, I said, "Frankie, there's no way this operation can be pulled off with only the tools the government can provide. The people we're going to go after have been successful for decades because they're smarter than the government. If this is going to work, I'm going to need help from people in the real world like you."

"Is Dominic going to be involved?" he asked.

I couldn't lie to him. "Yes," I said, "but on a different level than you, so you won't have contact with him."

"Well," he responded slowly, "let's hear what I can do to help, but I don't want Dominic to know about my involvement."

"Listen," I said, "he'll have to know that you're on the team, but he doesn't have to know details. I'd like you to play the role of one of my cousins, like Dominic is doing. In your case, it would really help if the Colombians and their money guys thought I had a role with the brokerage firm and placed big chunks of my clients' money in accounts. Frankly, if we can convince them to put their dirty money with the firm, it will enable the government to seize the accounts when the operation goes down. Besides, Frankie, this will give us something big to bring to the judge's attention when he considers your sentencing."

"I think I can do that," he said, "but I'll have to clear it with my uncle. I don't think he'll have any problem, since it's going to help me, too."

Not long after, Frankie called and said it was a go. I told him that, in his role as my cousin, there would be plenty of face time with the targets of the operation, but I needed his word that neither he nor anyone else on his end would ever attempt to make independent contact with any of the people I brought to him. If he did, his sentencing judge would hear about it. Frankie was a businessman. Better to explain the terms of a contract than rattle sabers.

Then I approached Eric Wellman, a former bank officer I had interviewed years before while putting together a case against his former employers, the CEO and president of Palm State Bank. The Tampa-area bank had been accepting millions of dollars in cash from customers with mob ties and, of course, not reporting those transactions as required by law. A decent, patriotic, unsuspecting midlevel officer at the bank, Eric despised that we were losing the War on Drugs and, after he realized what his employers had done, testified against them. It was one of many nails in the coffin of their corruption, and it helped lead to their conviction.

After that trial, Eric became president of another bank, then moved on to a new career in management at a company that owned a chain of jewelry stores on the East Coast. He worked in the company's administrative headquarters, located, again, in the Tampa area.

When we started talking about the undercover gig, he told me, "Bob, I'd very much like to help you. You know I've got little kids. I'm really concerned about what life is going to be like for them in the future. Anything I can do to help you do your job is going to help them. I've got a dormant investment company, Financial Consulting, with a documented history. If that'll help you, you're welcome to it. If you need to appear to have roots in the business world, I can help you with that, too. Let's talk about this some more and kick around some options."

He also agreed to lease covertly one of the rooms in his office suite to the government and to bring me — as Robert Musella — on as an officer of one of his companies. He set up a phone line for me on his switchboard and, without informing his staff of my real identity, instructed his employees to do my bidding. He gave me free use of the conference room, computers, and even his Rolls-Royce. Eric and his wife remained on the rolls of Financial Consulting, and he added Musella as vice president. Then, really stepping up to the plate, he formed Dynamic Mortgage Brokers, a licensed mortgage company run by me, him, and his wife.

Next on the list of identity needs came an expensive home with the trappings of a young mobster's lifestyle, a place where I could entertain the targets of our sting. The $400 per month apartment that my bosses at Customs were willing to rent didn't cut it. The best we could do at that price was a roach-infested dive in a low-income rental community near the airport. How the hell was I supposed to convince global drug traffickers to give me millions of their dollars to invest if I lived in a dump?

I explained the problem to O'Brien. Often penny-wise and pound-foolish when it came to government funds, he suggested I tell the targets that it was a safe house and that I didn't bring people to my real home. *Yeah, that'll work. So why will they feel obligated to bring me to their homes and let me get inside their heads?*

While I was struggling for a viable solution, it occurred to me that Dom might be able to help. "You know," I said to him in his Tampa home, "what we need is a house that, by its appearance, is occupied by someone of importance and wealth. To be perfect, it should look like your home, a house that's beautifully furnished, private, and well maintained."

"Not a problem," Dom said as he got the hint and smiled. "It's yours whenever you need it. If you give us a heads up, Anna, I, and the kids can be out of here in a day, and you can put us up in a hotel for as long as you'd like."

Dom's Spanish Colonial Revival house had a tiled roof and a circular brick drive. Inside, the rec room featured a big-screen TV, bar, and pool table. The master bedroom, adorned with statues of saints, sported a huge walk-in safe hidden in the closet. And the overly ornate Mediterranean furniture wore the obligatory clear plastic covers. It may have looked like mafia kitsch, but it reminded me of the mob homes in the best neighborhoods of Staten Island. It was exactly what we needed.

Running 24/7 were a full security system and a camera mounted on a tripod inside the front window, behind blinds. Dom periodically retrieved the tapes and scanned them to see whether anyone had cased the house while he was gone. It was perfect. Dom, my bosses, and I agreed that, when serious criminals earned the right to visit me at home, we'd put Dom and his family in a nearby hotel and use his home for the dog-and-pony show.

To get the evidence we needed to make our cases stick, I needed high-quality, reliable recording equipment that could be hidden inside a briefcase, and I had to know everything about it. Any undercover agent worth his salt needs to know how to operate and maintain recording equipment. You can't call a government tech assistant in the middle of a sting for a minor repair. One of the best private suppliers of covert electronics equipment in the country, Saul Mineroff of Mineroff Electronics, has a shop on Long Island that sells the latest and greatest recording devices available. He's a genius of his trade. Saul and I put our heads together and designed a totally new stereo recording system concealed inside a Renwick buckskin briefcase. The model we chose had an unusually deep lid, which Saul built out from the frame three-eighths of an inch to create a false compartment, behind which we hid a microcassette recorder, a set of stereo microphones, and a remote on/off switch.

Saul recommended we use an SME 700 recorder, capable of running at a low speed of 0.7 centimeters per second, which provided three hours of recording time on one tape. The metal shield casing around this recorder was made of a special alloy that repressed the emission of bias oscillator frequencies emitted from all motor-driven recorders. Sophisticated criminals were using hand-held devices that detected these frequencies and alerted them when a recorder was present. It also had special circuitry and filtering that reduced background noise and enabled optimum recording of multiple voices.

Saul ran the wires of the microphones under the liner, each mike hidden behind a lock opening on the face of the briefcase. With stereo capability, audio techs could later run the sound through a playback system with decibel adjustment filters and further reduce ambient noise. Two separate microphones also ensured optimal placement if people were sitting on either side of the case.

During the prep process, a seasoned informant from Colombia provided one of the agents in our office with information about Gonzalo Mora Jr., a small-time money broker in Medellín. This particular informant usually fed us with intel about crewmen on banana boats who smuggled five to ten kilos of cocaine into Tampa, but he had stumbled across information about Mora's involvement in laundering narco-dollars. When O'Brien heard about the lead, he said, "Hey, this Gonzalo guy might be a good target for the undercover money-laundering operation you want to do. Debrief the informant, and let me know what you think."

My partner in the debriefing was Emir Abreu, an outstanding, seasoned Customs agent from Aguadilla, Puerto Rico. He may not have had as many years of formal education as some, but he has a doctorate from the University of Life. While stationed on an aircraft carrier to Vietnam, he learned that his entire immediate family—both parents and younger brother—had drowned after their car plunged into a canal in Miami. His father, an aircraft mechanic, had given Emir many gifts, but the best of them was an acute ability to get to know people and read them. He mastered that skill beyond belief, which is one of the many reasons he succeeded so well as an undercover agent. And no one in the country can play a street-smart thug better.

He was also the biggest practical joker I've ever met. He and a bunch of other feds once went to a baseball game where the beers were cheap and the sun was hot. As they loosened up, Emir started comparing badge photos with others in the group, including our good friend Mike Miller. Mike unsuspectingly gave his ID to Emir and returned to a conversation with someone else. Emir quickly but carefully taped a photo of a mostly toothless Rastafarian over Mike's and then handed back his credentials. Mike never noticed. A few days later, Mike hit the local jail to interview an inmate. Sliding his credentials under the bulletproof glass, he proudly announced that he was a federal agent and needed to see a certain prisoner. The officer behind the glass opened the credentials and looked back and forth between the photo and Mike.

"That's not you," she said as she handed back his badge.

Mike looked at his creds in disbelief and then turned beet red. "It had to be Emir," he mumbled as he sheepishly removed the Rastafarian.

By now, Emir had made countless undercover dope buys and survived plenty of shoot-outs. With this debriefing, he and I began a close working relationship that deepened into a friendship that has bonded us as brothers for life.

After hearing the informant's story, Emir and I agreed with O'Brien that Gonzalo should be the first target of the long-term undercover operation. Gonzalo was a small-time operator in Colombia, his family selling ten kilos of coke at a time on the streets of L.A. and Miami. Before he met us, Gonzalo couldn't safely move more than $50,000 in drug cash per week because he had no real resources. To convert cash from U.S. dope sales to Colombian pesos, he had family members in the States drive around town using cash to buy cashier's checks in amounts of $3,000 or less—far below the $10,000 maximum that would trigger a report to the government. His family and friends in America deposited those checks into personal bank accounts. Gonzalo held checkbooks for those accounts, so, when his family alerted him that there was $50,000 in an account, he wrote a blank check for $50,000. Then he traded that check to a Colombian businessmen who had pesos but wanted dollars. Tens of thousands of Colombian importers are always looking to buy dollars because they do business in free-trade zones that prefer payment in dollars. With the circle complete, Gonzalo then used Colombian pesos to pay suppliers or buy overhead.

If, through an informant, Gonzalo slowly learned about Musella, a seasoned, organized crime–connected money launderer, and Musella played hard to get, Mora stood to become the perfect, unwitting source to take us inside a major Colombian cartel. Once in, we could infiltrate their entire laundering system.

The timing was less than ideal, though. I was scheduled to take a weeklong vacation with family and friends in the Florida Keys. So, joining the snorkel gear and margarita mix was my briefcase, packed with what I needed to design the undercover operation.

In Islamorada, using two small boats, four of my buddies and I caught about 150 lobsters in a couple of days. Not hard if you know what you're doing. For the rest of the week, in between an endless supply of lobster tails and margaritas, I wrote a proposal for the long-term undercover operation that would capitalize on Gonzalo Mora's needs.

While my family and friends enjoyed the fruits of our lobster hunting, I schemed in a lawn chair with a pen and pad in hand, ignoring everyone and everything but the picture in my mind of how to wheel our Trojan horse through the gates of the cartel. I never noticed the piercing glances of wonder about what could *possibly* be so important to ruin an otherwise perfect vacation.

"You know," Ev said, "we don't get many chances to enjoy time in a place like this. Can't you do this later?"

"Hon, you don't understand," I tried to explain. "We've got to get this proposal in and approved right away. We have an opportunity that will die on the vine unless I get this done. I'm sorry, baby, but I just have to push through this thing and make it happen."

She wasn't happy about it, but she did her best to support me.

One of the problems in formulating the plan was that, at the time, according to the rules at Customs, if we asked for more than $60,000 to finance an operation, D.C. had to review and monitor it. Experience had taught us that involving D.C. bureaucracy meant the kiss of death. Management types would see it as their ticket to a promotion, and they would cease to make decisions based on the facts and needs of the case. And then, when we were ready to grab the brass ring, they would run interference designed to benefit their careers or extraneous priorities. Which meant a maximum budget of $59,000, thereby keeping all operational decisions in Florida. Thankfully, agency policy did allow us to use the profits of our undercover operation to defray expenses. Call it poetic justice that we were going to earn literally boatloads of profit through the laundering business, and the criminals were going to finance their own downfall.

One line item not in the budget was funding for "the look." The government didn't have any problem spending thousands for overpriced equipment, but coughing up more than a dime for appropriate attire didn't sit well with them. Even bringing up the topic could lose you credibility with your superiors. They might suspect you were trying to scam them for personal benefit.

But Dominic had warned me. Experienced criminals eye a newcomer's every feature, and a flaw in the smallest detail could send a budding relationship into cardiac arrest. Those details absolutely included clothing.

"On your clothes, especially your shoes, you need to spend some bucks," Dom warned. "Movers and shakers in the business have money coming out their ass, and spending $1,000 on a suit is an everyday thing for them. And, on your shoes, you have to remember that you'll probably be sitting across a coffee table bullshitting with these guys, and when your leg is crossed your shoes will be staring the guy in the face. You can't have holes in your soles and brands that are sold in Kmart. Remember: if you're traveling with these guys, everything you leave in your hotel room is open to inspection. You have no idea if they have a hook in hotel security or not. Do yourself a favor. Get some nice threads.

"And be careful about your body language. There are certain mannerisms that some cops can't seem to shake. I remember a narc trying to work himself close to me in the old days, and when he got out of his car with his driver's door partly open, he hung his right arm over the top of the door frame and put his other hand on his hip. I'd seen state troopers take that pose dozens of times, and because of that I stopped talking to the guy.

"Oh yeah, and don't use cop talk. You guys use certain words like 'violator,' 'ten-four,' 'roger,' 'vicinity,' and shit like that. Just listen closely the next time you're in your office. You can't do that shit. You know a little Italian. Use it."

At Dom's recommendation, Surreys, a high-end clothing store, outfitted me with several suits by Carlo Palazzi, a pair of Moreschi shoes, pure silk ties, and matching pocket squares. Ashamed of our hand-me-down Samsonite bags, I bought a set of Hartmann luggage. The look cost somewhere between $5,000 and $10,000—at a time when Ev and I were teetering two paychecks away from a zero balance in our checking account and had trouble putting money aside for the kids' college education.

Each time she reviewed a new credit-card statement she went ballistic. I argued selfishly that there was something different about this case, that it was likely to become the case of a lifetime.

"I can't believe you could spend this much money!" she shot back. "*I'm* the one who has to juggle all the bills. When are you going to realize that nobody at Customs will ever care?"

As it turned out, she was right — but Robert Musella was ready to enter the underworld.

3

SETTING THE STAGE
FOR THE COLOMBIANS

Caliber Chase Apartments, Tampa, Florida
September 28, 1986

BUT BEFORE GONZALO MORA ever set foot in the U.S., we almost blew the entire operation.

Through an informant, Gonzalo's brother, Jaime, and father, Mora Sr., met Emir — whom they knew as Emilio Dominguez. In the worst Colombian neighborhoods of Miami, over several months, they passed small amounts of drug money to him that he turned into checks and fed back to them. At the same time, Emir fed the Moras stories about his boss, a mysterious, mob-connected man whose family controlled a small empire of businesses, including a brokerage firm on Wall Street. As they listened in amazement, greed consumed their common sense, and soon Gonzalo was begging to meet Robert Musella.

On a warm fall Sunday night, after I had attended a Tampa Bay Buccaneers game and cooled off with a few beers, Emir called. He was going to meet with Mora Sr. and an informant at an undercover apartment in town. I had helped design the built-in recording system concealed in a false wall inside one of the apartment's closets. Emir didn't know how to activate it, so he wanted me there as fast as possible to turn it on before Mora Sr. gave him $25,000 to launder.

It was the last thing I wanted to do. When I arrived at the

apartment, Emir was vacuuming the rug as though he was preparing for the arrival of the Queen.

"What's up?" I said.

"Oh, I'm just freshening up the place before our guests arrive." He obsessively cleaned like this constantly, like Felix Unger. For him, everything had to be spit-shined.

He reported that he and the informant intended to meet with Mora Sr. for no more than thirty minutes and that they would then drop him off at a nearby hotel. Given the brevity of the meeting and the deadbolt inside the closet door, I told Emir that I would lock myself inside and operate the equipment myself.

The meeting went as planned — or so it seemed, since I spoke little Spanish at the time. After half an hour, Emir, the informant, and Mora Sr. left the apartment. I shut down the equipment, processed the video, and awaited Emir's return. Instinct told me to be careful, though, so rather than wait openly in the apartment, I sat across the threshold of the closet door.

A good hour had passed when the front door opened. Always better safe than sorry, I jumped back inside, bolted the door, and checked the monitor. Emir, the informant, *and* Mora Sr. had returned. I popped another tape into the recorder just in case. It wasn't long before Emir walked to the bathroom next to the closet and laughingly sang, "The old man is staying." He later told me that a convention had filled every spare hotel room in Tampa. And I was trapped.

Minute after minute ticked by, and then Emir left. Mora Sr. and the informant hung out for another endless hour, and — finally — the informant went to sleep. But Mora Sr., some kind of insomniac, read the newspaper for what felt like forever. A couple of empty aluminum cans lying fortuitously in the closet relieved me of the aftermath of too much beer.

At 1 A.M., with almost all the lights out, Mora Sr. stumbled through the apartment. His footsteps approached the closet, and the doorknob turned, his girth leaning into the door. The breath caught in my throat, and my heart stopped cold. The door bowed from the pressure—but the deadbolt held. He found his way to the toilet, relieved himself, returned to the living room, and fell asleep on the couch. He thought the closet door led to the bathroom. At some point I remembered to breathe.

My apprehension subsided, but the waiting game continued. Silence held for another hour until the buzzing of his snore indicated that it was time to go. I peeled off my white T-shirt to blend in better with the darkness and gently opened the creaking closet door. I low-crawled down the hall and past the living room, hanging on the rise and fall of Mora Sr.'s every labored breath. And then I entered the informant's bedroom.

Men with a price on their heads sleep lightly. I closed the door behind me and, as I slowly approached his bed, hoped that he hadn't stashed a gun beneath his pillow. Then, like a scene from "The Tell-Tale Heart," one of his eyes cracked open. He leapt up toward the ceiling, his back arching in midair. His feet landed on the mattress as though he were about to take on a running back. And then came the loudest scream I'd ever heard as he jumped hysterically up and down.

I flew at him, tackling him and covering his flaring mouth with my hand. He slowly calmed down, and I told him that if the old man came in the room he should say that he had had a bad dream. His face registered only confusion. I'd forgotten that his English was as bad as my Spanish. With no time to spare, and fearing that the old man was already on his way, I tried to dive under the bed—but the frame held it only inches from the floor.

We waited, frozen in silence.

The old man never woke.

As I climbed out the window, my mind was racing like a stock car. If anyone spotted me, they'd surely call the cops. My eyes darting in every direction, I crept to my car, cranked it up, and cruised out of the complex.

It was now past 2 A.M., and I called Emir at home from the nearest pay phone. He and his entire family, on speaker, laughed as I described what had happened. Emir realized, though, that I found the situation less than amusing. "Bob, don't worry," he said. "I called your wife and told her you would be home late because you were locked in the closet. Something tells me she thinks you're full of shit."

Great. That's all I need right now, I thought.

My own call to her was short and tense. When I got home, she listened to my story again and conveyed her displeasure with silence. It made for a few tense days, but those only hinted at the tribulations to come.

The sale of huge quantities of cocaine in the United States generates for South American–based drug organizations mountains of cash collected and stored in major U.S. cities. Converting this cash to Colombian pesos often occurs through a network collectively known as the Black Market Peso Exchange (BMPE). Unlike, say, the New York Stock Exchange, the BMPE has no buildings or exchange floors. It consists of a loose-knit group of brokers—some small, like Mora, some much bigger—who try to develop an equal number of supply-and-demand clients, just like any other efficient business. Supply clients are people in South America who have a large supply of dollars and a demand for Colombian pesos. The vast majority of people in this category are drug dealers who sell their dope in the States. Conversely, the demand clients in the BMPE are South Americans who have a supply of Colombian pesos and a need for dollars. Because the U.S. dollar is the currency of preference for legitimate businessmen worldwide, if you are a Colombian businessman and you want to buy something outside Colombia, you need dollars, which gives you two choices. You can buy them through the Colombian government and lose 40 percent to taxes, duties, and fees, or you can go to a BMPE broker and buy them at a cost of 10 percent or less.

This phenomenon has created a lucrative trade in dollars from traffickers and pesos from Colombian businessmen. If a broker like Mora has an equal number of demand clients and supply clients, he simply arranges the swapping of their currencies in exchange for as much as a 10 percent fee from each party, which means a 20 percent return on a deal in which he doesn't put up a dime of his own money. On a typical $2 million deal, that's a $400,000 profit.

Other issues can complicate these transactions, but those who operate the BMPE generally aren't involved in the sale of cocaine — just the purchase and sale of cocaine dollars. This kind of black-market currency trading happens around the world. In the Middle and Near East they call it *hawala* and *hundi*, but in all cases it's really nothing more than an informal association of money brokers who disguise currency transfers through a maze of import-export transactions.

On a brisk night that December, I bought the bottle of champagne that started it all. Emir, Mora, and the informant had spent the day together, and Mora eagerly wanted to meet Musella. I arrived at the modest apartment masquerading as Emilio Dominguez's Tampa home. Emir and I embraced, and, his arm draped around my shoulders, he led me to Mora, with whom I politely shook hands. Mora needed to know that he had to sell himself.

His short, wiry build confirmed his semi-pro soccer career, and he carried himself with the air of a low-level bank official, which confirmed his degree in business from the University of Medellín. He ran a legit business importing lima beans, but his real profits came from his career as a money broker, buying and selling dollars generated from the sale of cocaine in the U.S. As Mora himself put it, "My little business is to launder."

Mora wasted no time telling me about his experience in the BMPE. He had been buying and selling drug dollars for two years, and he had very good contacts because several of his brothers and sisters lived in the States and distributed cocaine for fairly large drug organizations. Mora hinted that he worked his money exchanges primarily with a stockbroker in Medellín, a man he later identified as Juan Guillermo Vargas, who had excellent banking connections in Florida and California. This stockbroker worked closely with drug bosses in Medellín for whom he both laundered and invested roughly a million dollars per week earned in Los Angeles, Miami, and New York.

Mora offered me a fifty-fifty partnership. He wanted my group to handle everything on the American side. We needed to pick up the dope money from representatives of the drug or money groups, get the cash into banks, and then provide him with U.S. dollar checks or wire transfers that he could give to the sellers of the cash, less my commission.

I told Mora to slow down and to enjoy a week in the States, during which he would have an opportunity to understand the potential of our relationship. As Musella, I told him that my primary function was to handle the money from my family's U.S. operations, but they had given me the nod to expand profits by exploring South American connections. Doing business with him was only the cherry on top of a very large cake, I explained. I couldn't afford to jeopardize my responsibility to my family, or I wouldn't be around to enjoy the profits from the business he and I developed. He got the message.

As I tried to explain to Mora in my most serious tone that screwing up meant the end of my life, Emir the prankster stood just a few feet out of Mora's sight, rolling his eyes and making faces. It took everything I had to keep from bursting into laughter. A dangerous move on his part, perhaps, but Emir's antics often brought much-needed relief to business so serious that it could easily have resulted in our being kidnapped and cut into pieces.

The meeting needed to end on an optimistic note, though, so out came the chilled bottle of champagne. We held up our glasses in a toast. "I think at the end of discussing things together for a few days, we will have complete confidence in one another and we will have no reservations about speaking of everything in its entirety," I said. In other words: once Mora proved himself and opened up, we'd do business.

In Spanish, Mora responded to Emir, "Tell him that I congratulate him on the way he handles things and I assure him that my country's financial potential is going to give us lots of profits." He was ravenous for a partnership, and the blindness of that hunger was going to undo him.

. . .

While Mora was in Tampa, he stayed in a condo on Clearwater Beach that he thought I owned. Emir brought him to a pier where we had lunch and then boarded what he thought was my fifty-two-foot Hatteras. Mora glanced at the boat, looked me straight in the eye, and said, "This reminds me of *Miami Vice*."

Little did he know.

Undercover Customs boat handlers, acting as members of my group, piloted the boat on unfortunately choppy seas. After an hour on the water, Mora staggered into the cabin and vomited everywhere. The handlers fumed: the Hatteras was their baby, and they knew that cleaning up the mess would fall to them.

When we returned to the dock, Emir took Mora back to the condo to freshen up. That night, the three of us painted the town. We wined and dined and then hit the infamous strip clubs of Tampa. As the night wore on, Mora relaxed and enjoyed himself with a few of the girls in one of the clubs. He came back to the table with a broad smile and, his bloodshot eyes gone glassy, slurred something in Spanish to Emir and looked over his shoulder. A stunningly beautiful woman stood waiting as Emir explained to me that Mora had paid her to go into a back room and do whatever made me happy.

Panic raced through me. *What would a mob man do?* Many would no doubt go to the back room and enjoy the moment, but that wouldn't play well either in a courtroom or at home. We all had to remember that, despite the importance of adhering to our roles, that need could never overshadow our true identities as federal agents, answerable to a jury for all of our actions.

At the last second, an alibi flashed into my head. I looked Mora in the eye and, translating through Emir, told him that his kind gesture was an honor, but I wanted to share with him that I was madly in love with a woman I intended to marry and that he must have recalled those feelings when he first met his wife. I explained that it was my intention to get married in the next couple of years and that

I hoped he would honor me with his presence at the ceremony. It was a fateful lie for all of us.

"*Entiendo, Roberto, entiendo*," he said with a smile. For all his faults, Mora really was a gentleman. He didn't push the issue, and we enjoyed the rest of the evening joking together and stuffing bills in G-strings.

The next day, Emir and the informant brought Mora to another of my undercover offices—this one near the St. Petersburg–Clearwater Airport. There, thanks to Dominic, I held the title of director of international finance at Sunbird Airlines, an air-charter service that handled reservations for a forty-four-seat commuter jet ferrying passengers and cargo to the Bahamas. Mora also thought I used this charter service to transport money out of the country and into offshore accounts.

While he was there, I arranged for an undercover agent to stage a delivery of $200,000 in cash. We stuffed the money into my briefcase, and Emir, Mora, the informant, and I went to a local bank. They stayed in the car while I went inside and passed the cash to a bank employee. The ease with which I unloaded the cash impressed Mora. I told him that, as part of our cover, we managed high-volume, cash-generating businesses—like the jewelry-store chain I operated with Eric Wellman.

What Mora didn't know was that the bank officer who accepted the cash was Rita Rozanski, whom I'd met five years earlier when I and other members of the Greenback task force were working another laundering case. With the permission of the CEO of the bank, Rita helped me establish accounts, loans, and credit cards in undercover names, including those for Robert Musella.

The next morning, Emir, Mora, and I flew on a commercial airline to New York City. We checked into the Vista Hotel in the World Trade Center and visited the headquarters of Merrill Lynch to see one of my best friends from college, Craig Jantz, an institutional bond trader. He had agreed to provide some window dressing by allowing me to engage him in what appeared to be a serious business discussion while Mora watched. Emir and Mora stood at the edge of the trading floor as I went over to Craig, embraced him, and spoke privately for a few minutes. Mora didn't know that this sideshow was going to lead to a much bigger performance when we made our next visit to the Financial District.

Emir, Mora, and I then walked to Bruno Securities, Frankie's brokerage firm near Broadway and Wall Street. The office treated me like royalty. One by one, about a dozen of the forty employees came up to me and either hugged me or shook my hand while they said, "Hey, Bobby, it's so great you're back from Florida. We really need you here." They did everything but kiss my ring.

Frankie took us to the office of his uncle Carmine, the president of the firm. As discussed before the visit, Carmine, Frankie, and I talked about a few new companies they were taking public and how they wanted me to help. I introduced Gonzalo — first name only — and explained that I expected that he and some of his clients from Colombia would soon be doing business with us. Frankie emphasized to Mora that no one other than me could handle our family's financial affairs with him. When Frankie walked us over to the floor of the NYSE, Mora's eyes went wide as pumpkins. He never imagined that he would be among mafia gangsters so powerful that they had a seat on the Stock Exchange. Through Emir, Frankie explained how the exchange operated, and Mora hung on every word.

At a nearby restaurant, the three of us had drinks. I explained that I had to return to the Stock Exchange to attend an investment seminar about the promotion of a public start-up involved in the exploration of gold and silver mines and the buying and selling of precious metals. Mora needed to know that he wasn't the only act in town and that our venture wasn't going to overshadow my other duties for the mythical crime family. Playing hard to get enticed Mora to open up in order to win me over. It also indicated that I had higher priorities than just keeping him happy.

I told Mora, "You have to understand that I have responsibilities to the organization, and my family's firm has an obligation to put our resources together in a way that preserves the safety of the organization's capital. This gold-and-silver venture is being put together by my family's firm, and I have an obligation to see that everything runs safely. I've been given permission to work with you, but that's just a side venture. My primary job is to clean the cash from our own operations here in the States."

Mora jumped at the chance to attend the seminar with me. We went back to the Stock Exchange dinner club and sat through a truly boring presentation that reinforced for Mora that my family and I were the real deal. Frankie himself spoke at the gathering, which added solid credibility to my cover story. During the post-seminar meet-and-greet, the champagne and caviar were flowing, and Mora worked the crowd like a foreign dignitary, asking questions while swallowing appetizers—and our bait.

The next morning, while Emir and I met with Mora in my room, the tape player was rolling, and Mora couldn't stop talking. Visions of grandeur were dancing in his head, and he threw out any detail that might tantalize me into doing business with him. As we say in the law-enforcement community, he dropped his pants. He didn't have many secrets by the time we left New York: he admitted that 80 percent of the money he could bring to the table came from drug traffickers, and he gave us details about most of his contacts.

After he spilled his guts, I leaned back and acted as though I wasn't sure. After a long, dramatic pause, I told Mora, "I'm willing to do business with you, provided you meet certain terms." I'd continue to work with him for forty-five days, but unless the volume of business dramatically increased by the end of those forty-five days, our marriage was over. I told him that his offer of a fifty-fifty split was unacceptable and that I would do it only for 60 percent. He would have limited time to educate his clients about the importance of getting them to empower me to invest some of their money because simply laundering was far too risky. I needed to hide behind the appearance of being an investment adviser for South American clients, I explained, or the feds would easily figure out what I was doing.

That afternoon, Mora, Emir, and I had lunch at Jeremy's Ale House near the Brooklyn Bridge. When I left the table, on cue, Emir leaned toward Mora and told him that I had my doubts that his contacts in the drug and money world were worth the risks. It was up to Mora to win me over, so he shouldn't hold back. As Emir put it, "If you convince the boss that you're for real, it's going to help you get a bigger piece of the pie." Emir played him like a Stradivarius.

When I returned, Mora couldn't wait to impress me with more details about whom he knew and worked with in the drug world. He spewed more information about the role his brothers and sisters played in the distribution of cocaine in L.A. and Miami. He gave us the names of their bosses and details about the loads of dope that the feds had seized from them. He even gave us details about cops in Miami whom his sister had greased for protection.

That night, in Little Italy, we three had dinner at Casa Bella on Mulberry Street and then cappuccinos and cannolis a few blocks away at Ferrara's. As we strolled the streets, we passed Umberto's Clam Bar, where Crazy Joe Gallo had been whacked in 1972.

I told Mora the story in a somber tone: Gallo had tried to wrest control of the Profaci-Colombo crime family — one of the Five Families, who have controlled organized crime in New York City since the 1930s — from patriarch Joseph Colombo. Gallo had been celebrating his forty-third birthday when two gunmen rushed in and opened fire. Gallo sustained five bullet wounds as he tried to escape, then collapsed in the street. At his funeral, Gallo's sister famously cried over his coffin, "The streets are going to run red with blood, Joey!"

"Is there really a mafia in the U.S.?" Mora asked through Emir.

"The mafia is only for television," I replied with a half smile. "We don't want publicity — only power."

Emir translated for Mora, who looked at a loss for what to say or do. My laughter triggered his, and his eyes indicated that our arrangement satisfied him.

Emir and I dropped Mora back off at the Vista and hit a local watering hole. Over a few beers, we speculated about where the operation might take us. Mora was about to give us access to the big boys in Colombia, and there was no telling how far we could take it after they accepted us.

Emir and I wandered back to my room and ordered two huge

burgers from room service, hardly paying attention to the bellman as he delivered our late-night munchies. We devoured the burgers and then, sated, tried to roll the room-service cart through the hotel-room door. But somehow it was too wide. Our beer goggles firmly in place, we angled the table in every direction, laughing about what a magician the bellman had been to get the table in the room. Totally frustrated, we cleared the cart of everything but the tablecloth, turned it sideways, and angled it into the hall. As we set it down, the tablecloth slid off, and we realized that the table had wings that, with the push of a bolt, dropped the extension leaf. In our beer-soaked haze, we couldn't stop laughing that, although we could engineer secret recording equipment and drug money-laundering stings, we couldn't operate a simple delivery cart!

The next morning we all returned to Tampa and had one last planning meeting before Mora returned to Medellín.

First we established codes to use on the phone for arranging pickups of cash in the U.S. Each city had its own code name. *La Playa* ("the beach") meant Miami; *Los Torres* ("the towers") indicated New York City; and *La Tia* ("the aunt") meant L.A.—the standard industry codes in the BMPE. We confirmed similar codes for Chicago, Detroit, Houston, and Philadelphia.

Mora told us that he would never explain over the phone that he needed a pickup of cash in a particular amount. Instead, he would explain that an invoice—the cash—would be delivered for liquidation in a given location. The invoice number itself would indicate the amount, less the last three digits, which were, of course, always zeros.

Mora explained that he would try to provide Emir with the beeper or cell phone number of the person in the U.S. who had the money that needed laundering—"try" because sometimes Mora's clients in Colombia refused to disclose that information. In addition, he would provide Emir's beeper number to his client—that is, the doper—in Colombia, who owned the money being held for him in the States. That doper would then pass Emir's number to the representative in America who was holding the money, with the strict instruction that the representative put the code "55" after his own number when paging Emir. That code would alert Emir that Mora represented the caller who was reaching out to coordinate a drop-off.

Mora gave his own code name as Bruno and asked me to pick one. I chose Maximo. Therefore, Mora explained, if he wanted to let us know that a $500,000 pickup was ready in Miami, he would call Emir and say, "Invoice 500 in La Playa needs liquidation on behalf of Bruno to Maximo." Not long after, Emir would receive a page followed by the code 55. When he returned the call, the person who had paged him would verify the city, amount of money, and the code—"the delivery was for Maximo and on behalf of Bruno." Emir would then determine the time and place where he or another undercover agent would meet the caller to receive the cash.

Next, in order to pay the clients in Medellín, Mora asked me to sign dozens of blank checks, to be held in his office. If we did a $500,000 deal, he might need to write ten checks that amounted to the total deal, less our commission, because his customers never wanted one check for a huge amount.

Mora and I shared a fee of about 8 percent of each deal, so, on a $500,000 deal, my 60 percent of the laundering fee came to $24,000. When Mora's clients wanted peso checks instead of dollars, he scored more fees, which he wasn't disclosing to me. In these cases, he probably earned about 10 percent more in fees by selling my checks to Colombian businessmen for pesos and then selling those peso checks to his dealers. Mora couldn't know that I knew this because I was supposedly new to this game, but that was fine: I wasn't doing what I did to turn a profit—although eventually I did make millions for the U.S. government.

On each deal, Mora would prepare a ledger detailing the gross amount of the deal, our commissions, a list of the checks, payees on each check, and so on, balancing each transaction out to zero. Each month, Mora would either deliver the ledgers by hand or place them between glued-together pages of a large magazine, mailed to my office.

Before he left, I warned Mora that my life was in his hands and that I was counting on him to treat our business with the utmost professionalism. He thanked me endlessly and promised that he wouldn't let me down, assuring me that he would bring his connections to my doorstep.

Time was about to prove him a man of his word.

4

THE BANK OF CREDIT AND COMMERCE INTERNATIONAL

Medellín, Colombia
December 11, 1986

THE SECOND MORA RETURNED TO MEDELLÍN he started selling us to his clients. Extraordinarily proud to be our partner and exclusive representative in Colombia, he didn't waste any time rolling deals our way. Typical cash pickups jumped from $25,000 to $250,000—which meant developing undercover agents in Miami, New York, Chicago, and Los Angeles who could cameo as workers Emir had tasked to collect cash.

Emir often flew to the city of a given pickup and, with the help of a local undercover agent, received suitcases of cash at a time. Bosses in Medellín often considered the low-level workers running this cash expendable. Typically they earned a few thousand dollars a month to collect, count, stack, and deliver. We called them "T-shirts" because, while they literally handled millions for the cartel, they couldn't afford more than the T-shirts on their backs. Their relatives in Colombia often served as collateral — hostages, really — to assure the bosses that they wouldn't run off with a small fortune.

On the other side of the equation, local Customs bosses made collecting cash from the T-shirts dangerous as well. Customs agents wanted to maximize intelligence developed locally from each pickup by identifying and following the deliverers. Our offices insisted that surveillance agents follow these bagmen after they delivered to Emir or another agent—the idea being that the surveillance agents would follow the T-shirts back to their homes or businesses and later conduct independent surveillance at those locations that would lead to a bust when the mopes were working with some other launderer. It may sound like a good idea—and occasionally it worked—but even when it did work, it put the credibility of Robert Musella and Emilio Dominguez on the line every time.

Agency directors frequently underestimate the intelligence of their adversaries. The men who sit safely at the top in Colombia are not stupid. In fact, they often had operatives conducting countersurveillance, looking for signs that the feds were watching. If counteroperatives detected our surveillance, the drug boss back in Colombia ordered a change in technique and often took business elsewhere. To minimize fallout from bagmen going down, the cartel often kept them totally removed from anything related to cocaine shipments. Since we were planning to gain access to the owners of the money and their advisers through Mora, it was counterproductive to screw with the T-shirts, behavior that would only raise suspicion and hinder infiltration. But the suits in our front offices didn't count patience among their virtues, nor, I suspect, did they believe that Emir and I could get past Mora. It was safer for them to conduct business as usual.

The pickups went smoothly at first. Chicago had two part-time undercover agents picking up cash: Frank Serra, a seasoned agent in his fifties who never put his local office above the greater operation in Tampa, and Tony Macisco, a bright young agent eager to learn from Frank and follow his lead.

With Dominic's help, I started a business selling money-counting machines and marketed them to the Colombians. It passively reinforced that we had enough sense to have a legal front for possessing tools used by the underground banking system. If you're not a bank, casino, or money-service business, why would you have money counters? "Because you're involved in the drug trade," cops would say. But running a retail business legitimately selling these machines neutralized that theory. It also gave our undercover agents an icebreaker topic to discuss other than the details of a suitcase full of cash. And of course it was important that the cash count was accurate—although it rarely was. Counting hundreds of thousands of dollars by hand is tedious, and mistakes happen. Everyone knew our count ruled, but getting money counters in the hands of the T-shirts made for fewer discrepancies.

I sent Frank and Tony a counting machine so they could sell it to a Colombian couple delivering shipments of cash in Chicago. Unlike most of the other T-shirts, this couple was comfortable making the drop at hotel rooms. So the Chicago office rented adjoining rooms: one for the drop and one for a cover team who videotaped the meeting and provided quick and capable security.

When the couple arrived, Tony, dressed professionally in a suit and tie, demonstrated the machine to them, laying a stack of twenties on the feeder tray. Frank sat back and let his apprentice handle the meeting. As Tony delivered his spiel, he leaned over and pressed the start button. But he leaned too close—the machine devoured his tie and almost pulled his neck through the gears. Only a few inches of knotted silk separated him from early retirement. And, since he hadn't read the manual, he didn't know how to get the machine to release him. So he picked it up and carried it around the room like a twenty-pound tie clip while he pondered how to free himself. The Colombian couple were rolling on the floor laughing uncontrollably, as were the agents in the adjoining room, who had watched it all on their monitors. They laughed so loud that Frank heard them through the walls and immediately grew concerned that the Colombian couple would be able to hear them, too. He positioned himself in front of the surveillance camera and, while shaking his head from side to side, ran a finger across his throat to signal to the surveillance team to cut the noise.

Tony eventually extracted his mangled tie—and then, to his credit, sold two machines. From that day on, Emir couldn't resist calling Macisco "Tony the Tie," to which Tony always responded with a curt "Fuck you." It was a light moment in the case, before the increasing volume of money Mora brought us added weight to every pickup.

Mora spent every waking minute planning how he was going to make his fortune with us. He stressed that business would boom even more if we stopped paying out with checks drawn on U.S. accounts and started issuing checks drawn on banks in Panama. Dealers in Colombia largely preferred receiving checks drawn on banks in a country that had strict banking secrecy laws. Mora's friends in Medellín were particularly comfortable with Panamanian banks because they kept General Manuel Noriega on their payroll.

Opening a foreign account presented us with two choices. With the help of Customs, we could contact a bank with branches in Panama and arrange use of an undercover account. Downside: miles of red tape and a definite leak to the Colombians either by bank officials or someone in the Panamanian government. End result? Suicide.

On the other hand, Robert Musella could simply walk into an international bank in Florida and inquire about opening an account in Panama. By now a well-documented businessman, Musella had untold ties in the U.S. business community. My credentials would pass the scrutiny of any banker. As I always told junior agents: when working undercover, sneaky is best.

As I cruised down palm-lined Ashley Drive in downtown Tampa in a money-green Mercedes 500 SEL provided by Customs, a building containing the upscale offices of the Bank of Credit and Commerce International caught my eye. "BCCI" in large gold letters glittered from the second story and screamed of overseas accounts, so I called an officer and scheduled an appointment.

A few days later, in a private conference room of that building, Rick Argudo, vice president of the Tampa branch, was grilling me about my business history and background. As he'd requested when we set up the meeting, he had my letter outlining the involvement of several of my companies in foreign commerce, along with copies of personal and business bank statements. I explained that my associates in Colombia were accumulating wealth in Panamanian bank accounts and they intended to send me funds periodically to invest for them in Florida real estate.

Argudo agreed to open the account. I had passed the test, and apparently it was safe to talk openly with me. As he filled out account forms, he spoke without breaking from his mad pace. Head down and pen scribbling away, he said, "Do you think you'll need to move money in the opposite direction, from the U.S. to Panama? Because we have many clients here who have a need to confidentially place funds in foreign accounts. We can help you with that if the need arises." He continued, "In the past, we often helped our clients get their funds to our branch in Grand Cayman, but I recommend against that now because Grand Cayman has entered into a treaty with the IRS that enables the U.S. government to obtain records of accounts." Argudo explained that he and his bosses now recommended that their clients place their funds in the Panama branch. The U.S. couldn't track it there.

Motionless, I waited for Argudo to make eye contact. When he did, I pressed my lips together, nodded my head in approval, and said, "You know, Rick, that is very interesting. I'd like to talk with you about that when we have a chance to meet in a casual setting, possibly during lunch sometime soon."

Every red flag I had ever learned to detect was flying in a gale-force storm of interest. It was tempting to pump him for more details, but my gut told me that patience would prove more productive — especially since Argudo wasn't mentioning his own experience and capabilities. He was revealing what appeared to be standard global service offered by the bank. I thanked Argudo for his time, gathered copies of my forms, and drove off.

"You're not going to believe the meeting I had with an officer at the local BCCI office," I said the next day to Dave Burris, an IRS agent assigned to our operation who had no interest in working undercover but always dotted his *i*'s, crossed his *t*'s, and wasn't afraid to work. I couldn't wait to tell him about my meeting with Argudo. "I went there thinking that if I was lucky I'd get the chance to open an account for the undercover business without having to tell the world I'm a fed. After this guy was convinced that I was really Robert Musella, I couldn't shut him up about how the bank could hide my transactions from the IRS and every other agency they dealt with. It's unbelievable."

Dave agreed to check with other agencies to see if BCCI had a history of dealing with dopers. Within a week, he reported, after speaking with a Strike Force attorney in Florida, that BCCI had laundered funds for a heroin trafficker and probably knew the money was filthy before they took it. He also assured me that he hadn't revealed why he was asking questions. Only a handful of us in Customs and the IRS knew about Operation C-Chase, and we wanted to keep it that way. Thankfully Mark Jackowski, the one federal prosecutor on the case, was more secretive than any of us. From the beginning, we all agreed not to prepare Reports of Investigation (ROIs) detailing our undercover contacts. ROIs from Tampa routinely made their way to many offices, including D.C. headquarters. Jackowski supported our proposal that reports of our undercover meetings would be prepared only on bond paper and kept in Tampa. It turns out he didn't have the authority to approve this, but he convinced everyone he did.

A bulldog in the courtroom, Mark could have made ten times his salary working for the defense, but he wouldn't hear of it. If he had to stay in his office all night to prepare for a hearing, he did it without comment, and early arrivals at the Tampa Federal Building often found Mark coming out of his office with disheveled hair, in shorts and a T-shirt, a cigarette dangling from his lips and a toothbrush in hand. Mark ran interference whenever it was necessary at this stage of the operation. We didn't yet need his intense determination, though we would soon enough.

Emir continued picking up money around the country, which I converted to checks and wire transfers for Mora, and the clock continued to tick on the ultimatum I had given Mora to convince his clients not only to launder money through my companies but to allow me to invest some of those funds on behalf of the cartel. Mora visited me in Florida again, and it became clear that I could earn credibility simultaneously with Argudo at BCCI and with Mora if they both attended a meeting with me and Emir. To set that up before Mora's arrival, I called Argudo and met with him privately at the posh Hyatt Regency Hotel on Tampa Bay.

Over white linens, blackened grouper, and beef oriental, Argudo and I resumed our game of cat and mouse, trying to reach a comfort level with each other where we could talk more openly. Argudo, a graduate of Boston College, had worked at his family's banana plantation in Guatemala before joining BCCI. He knew the needs of businessmen in Central and South America and how to evade taxes and currency regulations. He already had clients in Colombia.

When I told him that Mora wanted my help to receive currency in the U.S., to deposit it in banks, and to transfer it to Panama, Argudo calmly said, "That's what they call the 'black market.'" He knew all about the illicit trade in dollars and pesos and had great ideas about how BCCI could help minimize risk in those underground currency markets.

Argudo leaned forward and quietly warned, "You have to be careful with the cash because U.S. banks file reports with the government on all cash transactions over $10,000 and even some that are under $10,000." He assured me that I could safely handle deposits for my Colombian clients if I operated a front company that legitimately appeared to generate cash. With a smile and a shake of the head he added, "It's the dumb people that get caught."

To crown his offer of secret banking, Argudo suggested that I open accounts outside the United States for optimum confidentiality. He proposed that I join him in the comfort of his office in Tampa where he could execute the appropriate forms, take my deposit, bundle everything, and send it through the bank's interoffice mail to Panama or the country of my choice. The receiving branch would open the account. Checks, deposit slips, and other documentation would travel back through interoffice mail and then to me in Tampa. The bank in the U.S. would maintain no records of the foreign account, and no government agency could obtain information about the account from any U.S. branch of the bank.

Now, that's service.

Near the end of our lunch, while we looked across Tampa Bay and Argudo sipped from a snifter of Rémy Martin cognac, I told him that I looked forward to our expanding business relationship and that part of that relationship entailed joining me, Emir, and Mora for lunch the following week.

Within a week, Mora arrived in Tampa. Emir and I met him at the airport and started our latest installment of charades. Mora confided to us that his friends in Colombia had warned him to be sure that we weren't DEA agents. He wasn't concerned, but he let us know that these uncertainties might cause delays in his gaining the confidence of his clients.

To counteract some of that concern, Emir and I took Mora to my house — Dominic's, that is — and hosted him there for several days. To give it just the right touch, I had taken pictures with Dominic and his family (my undercover cousins), which we placed prominently around the house. It was a little insurance policy in case Mora's jittery clients checked the place out later and found someone else living there. As I explained to Mora, I was on the road so much that, in order to maintain the house, my cousins lived there when I was out of town.

For every ten minutes Emir spent with Mora, I was able to ask Mora another handful of probing questions. Emir was that good at putting Mora at ease. Emir insinuated to Mora that he was sharing information behind my back and that if Mora didn't give me the opportunity to sit down with any of his clients soon I was going to end the relationship. I couldn't afford only to transfer funds for a fee. The feds could otherwise easily see that I was acting as a conduit for transfers that had no business purpose. These dirty transactions needed a legitimate investment foundation, or it was over. Emir also spun a story that I faced certain danger from mobsters if they thought I was recklessly cleaning cash for Mora's clients. The line to Mora was, "Family or not, Mr. Musella would pay the price."

Mora had heard me say before, "I don't want to hear that you can't convince your clients to invest in our companies. It's your job to give me the audience so I can make that pitch to them myself. If they turn us down, you've done your job." Of course, I couldn't have cared less if his clients invested money with us — although that would be a great bonus. I wanted face time with the men behind Mora so I could identify them and get them on tape.

Mora spewed the names of his closest confidants and clients, including Samuel Escruceria, a Colombian congressman and a big player in the drug business with his father, a Colombian senator. The Escrucerias worked with a man in L.A. known as "the Jeweler." The Jeweler not only moved drugs but also helped the Escrucerias launder their profits.

Then, payday: Mora invited me and Emir to accompany him to the West Coast to meet the Jeweler.

The next day, Mora received the royal tour at Financial Consulting; the headquarters of Tammey Jewels, which controlled more than seventy low-end jewelry outlets in malls throughout the East Coast; and a 250-seat restaurant. Mora saw that these heavy cash-flow businesses provided an ironclad explanation to the authorities for large cash deposits. I even sold him a sample case of gaudy costume jewelry with the thought that he could become the exclusive representative of Tammey Jewels in Colombia. Whenever I offered him the chance to be the exclusive representative in Colombia of anything, yet more dollar signs flashed in his eyes.

After the business tour, Emir, Mora, and I stopped at a small private airport. With the help of an informant who owned a plane, we showed Mora Tampa from a few thousand feet up. As we banked sharply, I pointed out several commercial properties allegedly owned by my group. Emir's eyes rolled as he translated my stories about our so-called empire in Florida. Then Mora's eyes rolled, too — although with the look he had had on the Hatteras. If we didn't land soon, we were going to see his breakfast. The informant, who learned to fly on undersized airstrips in remote jungles, dropped us from the sky and landed at Tampa International before Mora lost it.

We drove across the airport and met Rick Argudo at CK's restaurant, which revolves atop the Marriott Airport Hotel. While we sipped chardonnay and talked about the impending business marriage between the Musella family and Mora's friends in Colombia, Argudo spoke breezily about how BCCI could help us build our coalition. He offered to open accounts around the globe and to keep our transactions secret by pumping them through Panama. He suggested that Mora and I create false invoices to justify money movements across borders. He even proposed—ingeniously—that, rather than simply moving money back and forth, we consider parking millions in certificates of deposit offshore to be used as collateral for loans in like amounts. If the feds tried to trace the origin of our transfers, they would falsely assume that our transfers were disbursements of loan proceeds.

The next morning, before Mora flew to L.A. to set up our meeting with the Jeweler, he met us at Emir's apartment. We needed a gimmick to help us develop intelligence about the dozens of other Colombians Mora serviced in the cartel. Otherwise, we would just be laundering—not infiltrating. I brought a stack of canceled checks that had been written by Mora in Colombia and exchanged for shipments of cash we accepted throughout the U.S. I told Mora that my ass was on the line if the feds ever became interested in any of his clients' Panamanian accounts, so I needed his help reviewing the canceled checks and learning more about the people who negotiated them—my excuse being that, with Mora's help, I would be able to gauge my risk. He knew precisely who negotiated the checks and if any of them was attracting the attention of Colombian authorities.

As he flipped through the checks, Mora confirmed the names of four clients in Colombia, as well as a pseudonym used by a Colombian stockbroker, Juan Guillermo Vargas, who laundered for the cartel. Mora indicated that all these clients would be excited to learn about my relationship with BCCI and the Panama account. He couldn't wait to tell the Jeweler about the opportunities on the horizon with Bob Musella and Emilio Dominguez.

Now all we needed to do was convince Mora's clients that we were for real.

5

THE JEWELER

Bonaventure Hotel, Los Angeles, California
April 13, 1987

BECAUSE MORA DIDN'T KNOW where we were staying—and because
the cartel had both motive and means to monitor federal buildings
in major cities—it was safer for us to meet support agents in rooms
at the same hotel, the Bonaventure in L.A. A half-dozen agents and
managers came for a briefing.

I hadn't expected so many people to show, but the Jeweler—Roberto Alcaíno—had eluded Customs, DEA, and the FBI.
Enforcement circles considered him a primary player in the international drug-trafficking world, and several Organized Crime Drug
Enforcement Task Force (OCDETF) investigations had targeted
him—to no success. But thanks to Mora, in just a few meetings we
had more on Alcaíno than all prior efforts combined.

Mora substantiated Alcaíno as a key player working directly
with Pablo Escobar, Fabio Ochoa, and other members of the cartel.
Alcaíno had already given us cash to launder in New York and in
L.A. A small part of that had been the $170,000 collected recently by
Jessie "Chewie" Ibarra and Conrad Milan, L.A.-based undercover
Customs agents assigned to play Emir's task men. If we could win
Alcaíno over, he would broadcast our credibility to the underworld
elite, and our stock as launderers would soar.

At the briefing, we laid out the plan. Emir and I would record
a meet with Mora and his brother Jaime the next day in Emir's hotel

room, pumping them for details about Alcaíno and his operation. Later that night, we'd take the Mora brothers to a Dodgers game and invite Ibarra so he could establish a rapport with Jaime, who sold dope and moved money in the area. The day after the game, Emir and I, along with Mora and Jaime, would meet Alcaíno and record the first of what we hoped would be many meetings. Then, for the inside scoop, we planned to meet with Mora and Jaime the following day.

As the meeting ended, one of the Tampa agents tossed me a small package. "Mazur, headquarters forwarded your and Emir's undercover passports. You're good to go if you have to travel foreign." When I opened it, the wisdom of Joe Hinton rang in my ears. The geniuses in Washington had given us both passports issued in Washington, D.C., on the same day, and numbered sequentially. There wasn't a single stamp in them showing any foreign travel.

"You've got to be kidding me," I said, shaking my head. "Whoever handled this has their head up their ass. There's no way we're using these! I'll take a trip to Miami and get a passport using my phony birth certificate and driver's license. Then that needs to be sent to our embassies in London, Bern, and San José so we can get our counterparts to put some stamps in it. I can't look like a rookie who never left the country!"

After the briefing, Emir and I brainstormed about how to handle the opportunities on the horizon. We held these conversations on the street or in restaurants to avoid the possibility of speaking in bugged hotel rooms. As we walked past a high-end men's store near the Bonaventure, I said to Emir, "Hey, let's check this place out. Mr. Musella needs some new threads."

I picked out a pair of dark blue wool slacks from Italy, a double-breasted dark blue and white silk herringbone jacket, a crisp white dress shirt with French cuffs, and a navy blue silk Armani tie. But Dominic's caveat rang in my head. I needed a new pair of shoes. I found a pair of dark blue soft leather shoes from Spain. Emir burst out laughing and danced like a ballerina while singing in his thick

Puerto Rican accent, "Oh, Mr. Musella, will you be wearing these blue slippers to the Alcaíno ball?"

"Okay, asshole, you laugh," I said, reddening, "but Alcaíno will be evaluating us from every possible angle. This guy isn't stupid. He pays attention to every little detail—including shoes. If shelling out a thousand dollars of my own money will get me a leg up, I'm going for it. If we make one mistake with this guy, he'll run. If that happens, we're done."

The next day, Emir and I met Mora and Jaime in Emir's room. Mora had spent the previous day priming Alcaíno to meet me. He also verified that the Jeweler was, as Mora called them, "one of the strong ones." Alcaíno had moved $24 million in a recent three-month period, but he was transitioning his operation to the Northeast because cops in L.A. were more aggressive than in any other major city. Mora stressed that my organization, based in New York with elaborate fronts like Bruno Securities, fit Alcaíno's plan perfectly.

Then Mora confided that Alcaíno was concerned about the two guys in L.A. who had picked up money from him recently—Ibarra and Milan. Alcaíno had said to him, "Gonzalo, these guys ask too many questions and parked right in front of my jewelry store in a no-parking zone. Who works like that? They're either sloppy or cops."

My heart almost stopped.

"Gonzalo," I said, trying not to break into a sweat, "be sure to tell me details any time you hear of problems caused by people in my group."

Mora said he thought it wise for us to air the matter with Alcaíno at tomorrow's meeting. As Emir deftly changed the topic, massaged Mora's ego, and got him to reveal more, my mind caught fire. Ibarra had assured us that he would follow our lead, yet he had done exactly the opposite. Emir and I had practically begged them to keep a low profile with Alcaíno—pick up the money, don't engage him in conversation, get out. If we were going to survive this case, no agent involved could act like a cop. Savvy crooks would have parked five blocks away and walked in ten different directions to ensure they weren't being tailed. It smelled like Ibarra was planning to take the Jeweler as a short-term trophy.

We agreed to meet later to head out for the Dodgers game. Shortly before Mora and Jaime returned, Ibarra joined us at the hotel. He downplayed Alcaíno's account as a typical exaggeration.

Hot dogs and beer at the game gave us time to relax and bond with Jaime and Mora, who anchored himself to Emir. I remained slightly aloof, wanting Mora to know that in my organization, like Alcaíno in his, I held a higher level of authority. Ibarra tried to culti-vate a friendship with Mora, but Emir outran him.

The next morning, over a late breakfast, Emir and I discussed how to steer the upcoming meeting. I wanted to come across as a busy executive momentarily tied up at another meeting, so after Alcaíno and the Mora brothers had come to Emir's room and chat-ted for a while, Emir was to call my cell phone to find out why I was delayed. A staggered introduction also allowed Alcaíno to meet and adjust to one new face at a time.

After a brief meeting with the support team, we went to our rooms to get ready. Then Emir called unexpectedly and asked if I could help him with something. I smelled a practical joke, but when I entered his room Emir handed me his tie and said, "Bobby, could you please help me with this damn thing? I don't know how to make a knot in a tie."

As I would dozens of times in the future, I tied his tie and gave him a hard time. "You've got to be bullshitting me! How can a forty-two-year-old man not know how to knot a tie?"

"Hey, what do you want from a kid from Aguadilla, Puerto Rico?" Emir shot back. "There was only one tie in my hometown, and I never got a turn to use it. Just tie the tie, and shut up!"

We both burst out laughing.

At the prescribed moment, Mora and Jaime arrived at Emir's room. Within minutes, Alcaíno joined them and led a perverse philosophical discussion about how it was the fault of Americans that cocaine was entering the country by the ton: if there were no demand, there would be no supply.

When I arrived, Alcaíno wasted no time telling me who he was. He spoke English with a faint Chilean accent, and he spoke both Spanish and Italian fluently. His confidence filled the room, and he led the conversation as though he were conducting an orchestra.

"So tell me—what do you do?" he asked me sharply.

I walked him through the investment company, mortgage company, costume-jewelry chain, air charter service, and brokerage firm, making plain that my first allegiance was to my family and that simply transferring funds across borders was likely to draw the attention of *los feos*—"the ugly ones," an industry term for the feds. It was April 15, so I stressed that, if my future clients didn't keep their affairs in order by reporting enough income to justify their U.S. holdings, I could create a safety net by pushing their dope profits through my mortgage company so that they could be returned to them as what looked like loan proceeds. It would not only bulletproof their financial affairs from the IRS, it would create camouflage for their real business.

Total bullshit, of course. That process would also identify assets to be seized at the end of the operation, and the more contact I had with them the more time I had to gather intel and record conversations.

The IRS worried Alcaíno. They posed more of a threat than the FBI. The IRS was hounding some of his friends in the dope trade because they couldn't justify their wealth. The old Al Capone irony was still hard at work.

Alcaíno sniffed at the notion of investing in the stock market—it was a form of gambling, and neither he nor his partners gambled on anything—but he was willing to promote the idea of making investments through my companies. Then he stared me down, saying, "Investments will be made on trust. I'm trusted, and I trust you, but we don't like mistakes. We don't allow mistakes. Mistakes are costly. Sometimes they cost a lot more than money."

Message received loud and clear: if I double-crossed him and his friends — death. But Alcaíno continued to preach the problems I would face if I failed to keep my word.

"Don't forget," he said, "these people are putting their trust in me. If there are losses, they will look for me. And I will look for you." He went on, "We like to take, not be taken. We don't believe in mistakes. If we're taken to the cleaners, I can tell them I'm very sorry, but two days later I'm pushing daisies."

I couldn't show surprise or concern. I nodded politely while my eyes said, *Tell me something I don't know.*

Then Alcaíno segued smoothly into Ibarra's behavior, which made him uneasy. He repeated the story exactly as Mora had told it: parking, questions, everything. Emir apologized and assured it wouldn't happen again. Ibarra had created a serious obstacle in the road to establishing a rapport.

Alcaíno revealed that his major concern was losing his Colombian partners' money when it was *coronado* — "crowned," or kinged. As Alcaíno explained, getting coke into the U.S. required overcoming many difficulties and was likened in the industry to a game of checkers. When you get a piece — a load of cocaine — to the other side of the board, the money it yields is crowned, and his partners would not take the loss of that money lightly.

At the end of the meeting, we agreed that, if Alcaíno brought in new business, I would share a small portion of my laundering fees with him. We also agreed that, if Alcaíno could orchestrate the placement of funds earmarked for investments, I would split my fees evenly with him on those transactions. Alcaíno in turn felt he could get his friends to do things my way. He intended to spread the word that we offered an interesting service that the cartel should consider seriously. As he put it, it was "a question of education."

Mora then raised the possibility of putting some of our agreements in writing, at which Alcaíno barked that he wanted nothing in writing. I learned later that as he left the room, Alcaíno commented, "Words are words unless this son of a bitch is recording here."

Mora believed Alcaíno would push his partners, and the Mora

brothers themselves were so excited about our prospects that they had already made separate plans to return to Medellín to meet with other clients to educate them about my services.

Finally alone, Emir and I took a walk and found a pay phone. I called the Tampa agents at the Bonaventure who were running interference for our L.A. counterparts. "It's done," I said. "We got the whole thing on tape, and it went well. Emir and I will work our way to your room when we're confident we're alone. I'll bring the briefcase recorder."

We wandered the streets in circles until we were sure no eyes were on us. As we strolled, we agreed that Alcaíno was both for real and within our reach. With this recording and the million or so in cash we'd already received from him, he was ours, but to get him to vouch for us, to gather more intelligence and to climb the ladder, we needed to be patient.

Back at the Bonaventure, we slid into Special Agent Laura Sherman's room. I'd known her for almost a decade, and, since the agency didn't allow agents to work undercover and manage the same case, I'd requested that she handle the administrative side. She didn't have a college degree, but her talents were so extraordinary that she'd made special agent. We gave the tape of Alcaíno to her and the other agents in her room.

For the wrap-up meeting, I taped a recorder to my crotch and the mike wire under my shirt, just over my heart. Better to leave the briefcase behind. It was fine for a meeting in an office or hotel, but we were going to Jaime Mora's house in Ontario, California, which had been exchanged by its owner for a load of dope. Just before we arrived, I flipped the remote power switch that ran from the recorder through a tiny hole into my pocket.

Anti-burglar bars covered every door and window of the house in this comfortably middle-class neighborhood. Obviously a stash house. Jaime proudly showed off a car he used to move drugs and money around L.A. He turned a switch under the dashboard, and a hidden compartment under the backseat dropped forward exposing a storage area that could easily hold twenty kilos of coke. His little game of show-and-tell gave us all the evidence we needed to seize the house at the end of the operation.

As we all discussed the future, Mora warned that Alcaíno wouldn't do much over the next two days. Easter was looming, and Alcaíno, like Mora, was very religious. Despite belonging to an organization that killed people in order to spread contraband around the world, guys like Alcaíno and Mora wore their allegiance to God on their sleeve.

Mora told us that as soon as Alcaíno opened the doors we could expect an unlimited flow of money that needed cleaning. I immediately put my foot down, looking solemnly at Mora and speaking through Emir in a slow, deliberate tone: "The only clients who will be given unlimited help transferring funds out of the U.S. are those who make investments through our companies. Otherwise, we're too exposed. I won't take more than $250,000 a month from those who don't do that."

Mora understood but urged me to reach my contacts at BCCI pronto because "the strong ones" were clamoring to buy dollar checks drawn on Panamanian banks. I agreed to open the account and told him I was also prepared to visit Alcaíno in New York so we could get to know each other better.

By the time Emir and I got back to Tampa, pickups for Alcaíno were already waiting in L.A. and New York. In the Big Apple, a young and very friendly Nelson Chen played Emir's gofer. Like me, Chen came from the IRS and didn't look like a cop. Unlike me, he came from Chinese and Puerto Rican heritage—and he spoke English and Spanish fluently. Because his boss, Tommy Loreto, had worked with me in the Manhattan office of IRS Intelligence, I felt we could trust him to follow our lead.

While Chen was picking up $350,000 in New York under the code name Chino, at our request Agent Ibarra met with Mora and picked up $170,000 from Alcaíno.

A day later, Mora called Emir and got right to the point: "I thought you said that this guy out here in L.A. works for you and that we could trust him?"

"Of course," Emir said, caught off guard.

"Well," Mora said, "he took me and Jaime to a Lakers game, and while we were there he told us that, although you and Mr. Musella are good people, he had a better idea about how our clients could be serviced in L.A. He said that besides Musella's group, he works with a much bigger group that can offer us lower rates and quicker service, and he wants us to bring all the business from our L.A. clients to these other people. I would never do anything to jeopardize our relationship with you and Mr. Musella's organization. I just thought you should know what he said."

Emir turned red with silent rage. "Gonzalo, thank you. I want you to hold off doing anything else in L.A. until I discuss this with Mr. Musella. I'll get back to you soon, brother."

"*That motherfucker!*" he screamed as he slammed down the phone. Then he called me at Financial Consulting. "Bob, we need to talk. Chewie is trying to fuck us. He told Mora to stop using us in L.A. and to let Chewie funnel all the L.A. deals through his people there."

"Damn it, Emilio!"—always undercover names on a line known to our targets—"Let's get together and talk this out." I jumped in my car and raced to Emir's undercover apartment. When I arrived, Emir was working the vacuum so hard it was overheating, and so were we.

"Emir, we'll fix this guy's ass," I said. "All he wants to do is steal this case and screw everyone else. We'll take Alcaíno's lead on this. He told all of us that he's moving his operation out of L.A. because the cops are like cowboys out there. We'll buy into that philosophy and tell Mora that we're beginning to phase out of L.A., too. He needs to know that we'll soon refuse to collect a dime in that town, so he'd better start increasing his business in other cities."

Emir nodded. "That's exactly what I was thinking. It makes me sick that criminals like Mora are more truthful than our own people."

But we couldn't confront Ibarra because no one in the agency had balls enough to call him on his actions. The accusation of foul play would quickly turn into a he-said-she-said debate, and then Ibarra would sabotage us, knowing that we were cutting him out. Better to smile and say we'd get back to him when we needed his support in L.A. We had to lie to one of our own to stay alive. It was the first time — though certainly not the last — that we could trust our targets in the case more than our own people.

It didn't take long for the Alcaíno relationship to blossom. Within two weeks, he wanted to meet me in New York. Emir and I flew commercial, checked into the Vista at the World Trade Center, and invited Alcaíno over. He came the next morning with a briefcase bulging with records.

"Bob, a few friends of mine have a problem. With your resources, I thought you might be able to help us make this go away. They owned two planes, a small one that cost about $100,000 that was caught in Texas with merchandise" — cocaine — "and a second, bigger plane, a Cessna Citation 500 that they bought with a cashier's check for $550,000. Both planes were seized by the feds. My friends are Colombians, but the Citation was put in the name of a California corporation. I'd like you to talk with one of my attorneys. He works for Harold Greenberg, a lawyer who has been a friend of mine for a long time."

When I asked Alcaíno if I could be open with his counsel and let him know we were devising a cover story, he was clear: "He's on our team, so there's no problem. He plays dumb. He's that type of a guy." Alcaíno considered him brilliant and a great actor.

Alcaíno also had a job for me: to legalize about $5 million worth of property "purchased recklessly" — i.e., with cash.

We hardly had to ask him any questions while he rattled off details about his life in the business. He planned to give us between $200,000 and $300,000 a week in New York, explaining that his Sicilian father had old-guard friends in Boston and most of his dope went to traditional organized-crime buyers in Boston or customers in New York.

Then he explained how he ran his enterprise. He hired only older, well-dressed people who could pass as businessmen. Bejeweled young punks need not apply. His workers didn't talk openly on the phone and took time to plan their movements. Many of his key distributors were well-educated Hispanic women professionals in their late thirties who blended into the business world.

The cartel's shipments ran through Mexico because they were paying off government officials and army generals there. "It has the okay of the federal government there. If there's no police or army involved in the contract, you cannot come through. And they tell you point blank, it costs you so much to come in and so much to get out.... When the plane comes in, there's one general in Mexico who has to okay — so you pay the money so the plane can take off. And that's the way it goes, in an airfield owned by the army. If you deal with somebody else, who's not with the government, they kill the people. They confiscate the plane; they kill the people as if they'd resisted arrest. And then they sell the merchandise.... There's not one honest Mexican. They don't make them. They're born rotten."

Alcaíno forecast that our business together would boom. "There are thousands of people bringing millions of dollars in trade into the U.S. per week." But he still wanted to move his operation out of L.A. as soon as possible. "There's too much heat. Every day there are more police, and the cops in L.A. can't be bribed. They have a cowboy attitude. They're brainwashed, and they think they have to catch everyone. It's a lot easier to bribe cops in Boston, New York, and Miami."

I invited him to visit us in Florida and promised that I would call his lawyer soon.

Alcaíno's lawyer told a very different story about the jet. He was trying to get the government to release it, but the hurdles were high. The Cessna Citation had been purchased with $550,000 in currency, and the person who delivered the cash had since been caught in another plane with a shipment of coke. Trying to dummy up anything at this stage wasn't going to work. Period.

A few days later a nuclear explosion detonated inside the cartel. Undercover DEA Operation Pisces went public with sweeping

indictments. Agents had picked up money in the U.S. and transferred it to accounts in Panama controlled by people who worked
with the cartel. Everyone in the drug world went underground and
waited to see whether the indictments would affect their contacts. I
had no choice but to follow suit and wait. Business came to a screeching halt.

Then word came from Medellín that there were concerns that
I might be heading up another undercover operation. Mora's clients
wanted meaningful details about Musella and his companies. At
Mora's request, I prepared a letter with specifics on each company
controlled by my family, along with six verifiable bank references
in the United States. The end of the letter made clear that I would
commit no further details to paper. If this didn't satisfy the bosses,
we could meet to discuss the issue further, or they could take their
business elsewhere.

"When the water gets rough, pull your boat ashore, and take
it easy," Alcaíno said of Pisces. He warned me to stay out of Panama, where all the Pisces agents had done their undercover banking.
Mora, on the other hand, was begging me to open an account there
because he knew it would increase business.

To keep Mora happy, I called Rick Argudo to set up a
meeting—and discovered instead that he was leaving BCCI for
another company. After discussing how Mora and I would be using
the Panama account, Argudo referred me to another BCCI officer,
Dayne Miller, who gave me all the same assurances. BCCI would
keep my transactions confidential; they would help me maintain a
low profile with respect to my black-market money exchanges; and
they would open accounts for me throughout the world in a manner
that would prevent U.S. authorities from discovering them. Miller
opened a checking account for me in Panama in the name of a Panamanian paper company, IDC International S.A.

As Mora passed my checks to his clients, they or their associates would eventually have contact with BCCI Panama to deposit or
cash their checks. It was a perfect arrangement. The dealers saw my
dirty bank connections, and the bankers saw that my clients were

the scum of the earth. Now all I had to do was pressure Mora to pull his clients out of the shadows to deal with me directly.

After Pisces, Alcaíno scaled back sales to $800,000 a week, and through Mora I learned that we were only getting about a third of that because Alcaíno was dishing out the majority to two competing money-laundering groups. Alcaíno anticipated, after the slowdown broke, that he'd be back up to $2 million a week, but none of his clients was stepping forward to allow me to invest. Mora told Alcaíno about the letter I had written, but, with a cold stare, the Jeweler said to me, "We only need to know where your family is."

Some of the agents and managers at Customs took Alcaíno's reluctance and the lull in business as proof that I could never get high-level dopers to let me handle their investments. They seemed to be losing sight that my pitch was a ploy to get high-level meetings on tape. Even if the Alcaínos of the world didn't invest, getting them to the table flushed them out of the shadows. And it was too early in the game to pass judgment on whether this would work. Quality criminals have a lot going on, and newcomers have to have patience. Which of course isn't an easy sell to agency supervisors being asked by their bosses every couple of weeks, "What have you done lately?" Managers are rated and promoted on the number of arrests and seizures made by their agents. If a case isn't producing numbers, managers have to justify why. It is a lot easier to assign agents to many little cases that result in the arrest, prosecution, and conviction of minor criminals. The numbers keep churning, and managers don't have to respond to questions they can't answer. This is one of the reasons why the War on Drugs will always be unwinnable.

I needed advice. Dominic's eyes lit up as I explained my predicament.

"Bob, it's easy," he said. "When I get a guy who I know is for real and won't get off the fuckin' fence on something, I give him a really nice gift, explain to him that I and my people are offering the gift to bless the pact we agreed on, and explain that we're ready to roll. This'll make him feel like it's a done deal and he'll have to produce."

I could just see my bosses authorizing a gift for Alcaíno. They'd see it as a sign of weakness.

"What do you mean by 'really nice'?" I asked. "How much would you spend?"

"*Fuckin' A*," he said, exasperated. "How fuckin' important is this shithead to what you want to do? Are you going to play nickel-and-dime, or are you going to show him you've got balls and give a shit about him? Give him something like this." He brought out a small jewelry box, covered in brown, gold, and black paisley cloth, which contained a solid gold cross four inches high and two inches wide, completely covered in diamonds.

"How much is that worth?" I asked naively.

"At least twenty-five Gs," he said.

There was no way the brass would let me spend $25,000 on a gold cross for a drug dealer worth millions.

"Okay, kid," Dom said, "tell your bosses I'll sign papers loaning this to you guys. When you arrest this shithead, you can give it back. If you can't find it at the end of your gig, you guys can give me a $25,000 reward for all my help. You know I'm doing this for you because I owe you and I don't want money for helping, but that's the way you can get me square if you can't find the fuckin' thing."

There was no way my office would ever endorse Dominic's plan, but something Bruce Perlowin had said echoed in my head: *You can't possibly be a cop because you don't act or think like a cop.* This was an opportunity to get in bed with a man who dealt directly with Pablo Escobar, Fabio Ochoa, and José Rodríguez Gacha.

This was the chance of a lifetime.

6

THE GOLDEN HOOK

Clearwater, Florida
September 2, 1987

GREED DROVE MORA TO BEG Alcaíno to accept my invitation to visit me in Florida and to see my operation in New York City. In August, just three months after we met him at the Vista, Alcaíno agreed.

To satisfy Mora's clients that I had family to hold hostage, Customs assigned two female undercover agents to the case: Adella Asqui played Emir's occasional girlfriend, and Kathy Ertz assumed the role of my girlfriend and fiancée-to-be. Kathy hadn't done any significant undercover work, but she was about to dive in headfirst.

We took Kathy and Adella to all of our undercover residences and businesses. They stayed at Dominic's to learn where everything was in the house. Emir and I briefed them about Mora and Alcaíno, and we exchanged pages of details about our fake backgrounds: address history, employment history, family background, family names and ages, favorite drinks, favorite sports, hobbies, parents' names, political opinions, etc. We all learned one another's cover inside and out. We rehearsed small talk and the topics we'd bring up to keep conversation going and establish rapport. Then we briefed Laura Sherman and the other agents behind the scenes in Tampa so they knew our plans while Alcaíno was in town.

Which reminded me...

"Laura, this case could start moving quickly, and we may need to leave the country. My new undercover passport was sent to headquarters a while back so they could ship it foreign and fill it with backdated stamps. What's up with that?"

"D.C. wants to handle this differently," she said. "The FBI lab has more than enough talent to get that done. They've got the list of countries and dates you want. We should be getting that back soon."

"I don't get why my plan on the stamps wouldn't fly," I said, "but I guess it's too late. Let me know when it comes in."

Mora arrived in Tampa a day before Alcaíno, which gave us an extra day to practice our relationships. We took him for a spin in my—that is, Eric Wellman's—Rolls and ended up in Clearwater Beach, where we partied and drank Dom Perignon until the early morning, eventually wending our way back to the house. The ladies went to bed, and Emir and I took advantage of Mora's inebriation to pump him for more info.

Mora mentioned that some of his clients continued to worry that I might be a fed, but he was convincing them otherwise. My letter had helped, but we really had to win Alcaíno over so he would vouch for me. Mora suggested that we offer Alcaíno a 1 percent kickback for any business he threw our way. No problem. He also noted that it took me around four business days to convert cash to checks, which also troubled some of his clients. Heavy hitters in the money-laundering world have millions of their own money with which they pay clients immediately after a pickup. History had proven that only government narcs didn't have fat accounts from which they could pay clients while cash was being laundered. Problem.

There was no way the U.S. government was going to give me a $5 million bankroll to satisfy the Colombians about turnaround. Emir and I countered that moving swiftly could come to haunt us—unless Mora wanted to accept personal responsibility for counterfeit cash or short counts. Suddenly our method made perfect sense to him.

Then we learned why a small-time businessman like Mora was swimming with the sharks in the drug business. He had attended the University of Medellín with Guillermo Ochoa, a relative of Fabio Ochoa Restrepo, who sat on the board of the cartel. Fabio's son Fabio

Ochoa Vazquez had partnered with Alcaíno. All of which allowed Mora to convince Alcaíno and the Ochoas to do business with us. To cement the deal, Mora suggested that I travel to Colombia to meet the Ochoas and other cartel members. I told him I would give it consideration. I asked, but Customs wouldn't approve it.

Two years earlier, Mexican traffickers had captured and tortured DEA Special Agent Enrique Camarena while he had been working undercover. Customs didn't want a repeat of that horrific tragedy. Not to mention that both DEA and the ambassador in Bogotá had to approve. Too many bureaucrats, and the standing order in DEA at the time was that undercover work in Colombia was off limits.

When Alcaíno arrived in Tampa, we put on a royal show — which made me nervous. Tampa's a big town, but there was always a chance I'd run into someone from my real life. As soon as Alcaíno jumped in my Mercedes, he threw his first test at me.

"You need to come with me to Medellín for a week," he said. "I'll have six beautiful women for you who will travel with us and provide your every pleasure while I introduce you to the big boys."

I told Alcaíno I wasn't sure how my fiancée would feel about that kind of trip. I had announced to Mora the night before, in between bottles of Dom Perignon, that Kathy and I were engaged. Alcaíno promptly turned to Emir and asked if he was married and if he had children. He was hunting for signs that we were feds.

At the home, the Rolls-Royce caught Alcaíno's eye.

"I have a 1979 black Rolls-Royce Corniche. I like your convertible." He opened the back door and peered in. As he turned back, he held up an empty bottle of Dom Perignon from the backseat. "It must run very well, because I see you use the most expensive fuel!"

The next morning, Emir, Adella, Kathy, and I picked up Alcaíno and Mora at the beachfront condo I had arranged and headed to lunch. As planned, my phone rang.

"Yeah, Dom, it's okay. You can come by. We're at the usual place, with a few friends. I'm interested to hear all about it. Come on over."

I told him that my cousin was coming to explain a few details about a new company. "Roberto," I said, "I promise it won't be long but I want you to meet some of the people in my family who are critical to our success. Dominic handles the development of new businesses, but more importantly he watches my back. There's nothing he can't handle, if you know what I mean."

Dominic's booming, raspy voice filled the restaurant as he approached the table with an armful of shirts and a bag full of suntan lotion.

"Hey, boss, how ya doin'?" he said as we did the traditional *Godfather* embrace. "Sorry to intrude. I'll make this fast. This stuff is part of the line we'll be manufacturing under the Caribbean Sol suntan-lotion label. I can't thank you enough for bankrolling this. Here's some shirts for your friends and some of the lotions. Jimmy took your offer, and we now have the controlling interest. We expect to go nationwide within a year."

Alcaíno's eyes and ears trained on Dominic, searching. Dom handed out the gifts and then turned to me with a serious eye. He whispered in my ear, but with his bellowing voice Alcaíno heard every word. "Bobby, we took care of that other thing. You should have seen the look on that fat fuck's face when we showed up. He won't be coming back."

When Dominic left, Alcaíno turned to me and said, "He's Sicilian, from Brooklyn, and was probably stealing cars when he was twelve."

I smiled. "Almost right—except he started when he was eleven."

Alcaíno's belly jiggled with laughter. Dominic's visit had already paid its dividends.

Emir had heard that, since New York City was an operations base for Alcaíno's dope business, the Jeweler was headed there soon. After Dominic left, I mentioned to Alcaíno that Kathy and I would be headed to New York after his visit to announce our engagement officially. He suggested that we three take the same flight to LaGuardia the next evening.

"That would be wonderful," I said, "but Kathy and I will be heading to New York in one of the jets owned by my family's air charter service. Why don't you join us, and we'll get you to New York?"

Alcaíno grinned. "Fantastic. We should have a meeting tomorrow afternoon with Mora and Emilio, and then we can take off for New York. There are some important things we should discuss before we leave."

At that meeting, Alcaíno divulged again that because of Pisces some of the key players in Medellín worried that I was a fed running another sting. He didn't share that concern, and, if he could win the trust of his friends, there was no limit to what we could do.

"But if it is a sting operation," he said, "then Mora's head and my head isn't worth a damn, and neither are our families'." Alcaíno suggested that I join him on a forthcoming visit to Colombia to help him convince his associates that I wasn't a narc. Then he mused about what would happen if I did turn out to be an agent. "You have to take risks sometime. So what, you lose about thirty years. Thirty years will go by in no time. Thirty years passes by fast, you know?"

Total silence.

Then he erupted into laughter that infected the whole room.

When the mirth subsided, he launched into the numbers.

"Some of the big boys are coming here with 3,000 units"—kilos of coke—"every ten days, so let's say 9,000 units per month." Some months, those dopers didn't move anything, but they averaged at least 50,000 units per year. "Let's say only if they wholesale it at $12,000"—per kilo—"So you got 50,000 times twelve. How much is this? You're talking over $600 or $700 million in a year. They have a profit of about 40 percent. So when you're talking about a profit of 40 percent from $600 million, you're talking about $240 million a year profit."

A staggering number, and that was only the wholesale baseline.

After the meeting, Emir drove Alcaíno, Kathy, and me to Hangar One, a private airport service at Tampa International. We hopped on a Cessna Citation elegantly appointed with beige leather seats and teak trim throughout. Two Customs pilots — who had initially resisted the black epaulets and gold stripes of a corporate jet-pilot uniform — flew us to New York.

Halfway through the flight, I told Alcaíno that I had work to complete for a meeting the following morning. I moved a row away and pored over what looked like accounting papers. On cue, Kathy began filling Alcaíno's head with stories about how diligently I worked for my family and how serious we were about building a life together. With her background in art, conversational French, and extensive travel experience, she kept Alcaíno busy with stories about her childhood, her hopes for the future, and the finer details of our undercover story — as she had the night before.

She even read Alcaíno's palm and claimed that his future was filled with great success and achievements, putting him at ease and complimenting him every chance she got when he told his bold stories about his life. Alcaíno liked her, which offered a much-needed respite for me.

By the time we landed, Kathy knew more about Alcaíno's life than he did about mine. He fancied himself an art collector, and he enjoyed fine wines. He had two daughters, one in high school and somewhat rebellious. These details gave me a menu of issues to study and exploit.

The next morning, at Bruno Securities, nearly twenty different brokers embraced me with exclamations that it had been far too long. Frankie apologized that his uncle Carmine couldn't immediately greet us because two SEC auditors had come unexpectedly, demanding to speak with him. We had been waiting only a minute when the door burst open and Carmine shouted the two SEC regulators out of the firm.

"You fuckers are all alike!" he bellowed. "Just because my name ends in a vowel you think we're hoods. Get your asses out of here!" As the doors closed, Carmine took a deep breath, smiled, and said, "Please excuse me for getting a little excited, but I don't give a shit who they are. No one is going to insult me and my family. If this shit keeps up, one of these fuckers is going to get whacked!"

Then Carmine bear-hugged me. "Little cuz! You shouldn't be away so long. The family needs you, and you're working too hard. Let's talk."

He led Frankie, Alcaíno, and me into his office, where, over espressos, he talked about the business and how important I was to their success. Every movement had been choreographed perfectly—even the supposed SEC auditors hightailing it out of the office.

Outside, a sleek black limo took us to lunch at Harry's restaurant in the Woolworth Building. Alcaíno talked about his jewelry business and consignments of diamonds and emeralds to wholesalers across the world—one of the ways he was hiding his drug profits.

But as usual his talk turned to women. "I have three wives," he said, "one in New York, one in L.A., and one in Ecuador." Only one of these ladies was married to him. His theory held that if he had a continuing sexual relationship with a woman, she qualified as his wife.

During the ride back to his apartment near the U.N., Alcaíno said, "I hope to be going there"—Colombia—"in the next ten days to talk with the people. I'll get their reaction and call you when I return." Then he turned to Kathy and said he hoped to see her and me at his home in L.A. in the near future, so he could return our hospitality.

Breakthrough!

We had his trust. No one at Alcaíno's level would invite someone to his home if he thought even remotely that the guest might be a federal agent. We had climbed another rung of the ladder to the big boys.

The limo stopped at the Rivergate, an apartment building on East Thirty-fourth Street where Alcaíno lived when he was in New York, and he started to climb out. The perfect moment had arrived. I followed him outside the car.

"Roberto," I said, nodding in Kathy's direction, "I never speak business in front of her. I don't want her near this stuff." Then I gently grabbed his shoulder, looked into his eyes, and delivered my pitch. "Roberto, I hope you'll soon reach the point where you know we are good people —"

"But I already have," he interrupted.

"I can only then assume that we now consider ourselves partners," I said.

"Yes," Alcaíno replied. "Thank you. I do."

"Well, then," I said, pulling something from my pocket, "I have a gift I want to give you. I don't take important relationships with others lightly. It has been a tradition in my family to cherish these types of relationships. They are lifelong, and we will protect them until the end. That is part of our code. These are the types of relationships that cause people to become part of us, our tradition, and part of our future. I want to bless our friendship and partnership by giving you this gift."

As he opened the small box, the gold bars of the cross encrusted with diamonds glittered brightly beneath the city's dreary autumn clouds. The Jeweler beamed with approval.

"Bob, you shouldn't have. This is wonderful and something that I will cherish all my life." He hugged me, thanked me for my hospitality, and took the bait.

A man of his word, Alcaíno made his pitch for me in Colombia — though it took a little longer than expected. Someone in New York killed one of his workers, and someone in Medellín killed one of his partners. Many thought Alcaíno gave the order. Either way, he delayed his trip to Colombia and lay low for a while.

He always flew first class and packed lightly, so when he struggled off the plane with a whole collection of black leather soft-sided luggage, I knew something was up.

"Bob, I thought of you when I was in Medellín and picked up this luggage for you. Since you travel so much, I thought it would be nice if you had some good Colombian leather bags."

"Thanks, Roberto. That's very kind of you. Welcome back to Tampa. Let's head to my car, Kathy is waiting for us." The cost of the luggage paled in comparison to the diamond-studded gold cross — but it was a start.

Kathy and I brought Alcaíno to a new waterfront home in New Port Richey, where Financial Consulting was, an hour outside Tampa. Customs had installed a state-of-the-art concealed monitoring system that captured high-quality audio and video. To make sure Alcaíno was in the house at all times — and would sing on tape — we had a catering company send over a chef to prepare dinner at the house. After dinner, Kathy took Alcaíno for a walk while I powered and tested the system. When they returned, Emir and Kathy excused themselves and gave me a chance to have a private discussion with Alcaíno.

He recounted what had happened in Medellín. He met with four of the cartel bosses, who pulled him to the front of the line of those waiting for an audience. He explained everything he knew about my operation and my condition that a portion of their money be invested. Nothing was finalized, but, as Alcaíno put it, "The first meeting you have to go slowly with them. It's like it is with Italians."

Since he wanted to cement our partnership, he enumerated the opportunities on offer.

First, he wanted me to know that the cartel had decided to move a lot of their product to Europe. Since the market there wasn't nearly as saturated, they could enjoy an additional kilo profit of $17,000. At the moment, he had 150 kilos stockpiled there and, doing the math, would soon be receiving over $4 million that he wanted transported to Panama or Colombia. And that was peanuts compared to what *los duros* would need moved from Spain, France, and Italy.

He was also working out a deal with an Israeli friend in the States to set up a heroin-importation operation that stood to net millions per month. He had an opening for another investor, and that spot was mine for the asking.

Lastly, he felt he was on the verge of convincing the cartel to allow me to handle $700,000 per week for them. The problem, though, was that "a guy named Molina" was moving $20 million a month for them in New York, and it would take another trip to Colombia to get the $2.8 million piece of Molina's pie. Luís Carlos Molina was the top launderer for the cartel.

I, in turn, told Alcaíno that, though I was pleased with the opportunities, it disappointed me that there were no immediate commitments for me to handle investments. As a result, I was going to cut back my operations for *los duros*. Alcaíno supported that decision.

The next day, Alcaíno bought first-class tickets for himself, Kathy, and me to fly to New York. Before leaving, I phoned my contact there, Customs Supervisor Tommy Loreto, to inform him that we would be flying into Kennedy. Loreto didn't like the idea of Kathy and me on our own with Alcaíno, but I insisted against a surveillance team covering us on arrival. Alcaíno was still feeling out our partnership. If he spotted surveillance, we stood to lose everything. I carried a phone and pager; calling a safe number to report our status seemed adequate to me. Safeguarding my contact with Alcaíno in the U.S., while turning down his invitation to spend time with him in Colombia, looked bad. Loreto acquiesced.

Joaquín Casals, Alcaíno's right hand, met us at Kennedy. Even at a distance the young, burly, Cuban former Marine looked like the strong arm for a dope organization. Before we even left the Van Wyck Expressway, we knew his full name, what schools he attended, where he owned property, and where he had traveled in the past several weeks.

As we dodged New York's infamous potholes on our way to Manhattan, Casals pulled off the expressway onto the back streets of Queens. It looked like he was checking for a tail. As we cruised through Corona—a rough neighborhood—Kathy appeared tense. Trained as a cop, she was already thinking worst-case scenario. At this point, a surveillance team wasn't going to be able to save our lives. They'd only be able to find our bodies quickly.

Like dogs, quality criminals can sense your fear, and, like dogs, if they sense fear, they bite. As we neared Manhattan, I joked about how Queens reminded me of the tough neighborhood of my youth. I played the angle that Kathy had lived the privileged life, a diplomat's spoiled little princess. She ran with the story and filled Alcaíno's head with her tales of her privileged youth spent traveling Europe. By the time we arrived at the Helmsley Palace, everyone was at ease. Before Casals drove him off, Alcaíno instructed us to meet him at 8:30 in the lobby of the hotel, where he would pick us up for dinner.

There was only one bathroom in our hotel suite, so we took turns getting ready. After reporting to Loreto, I headed to the lobby. The elevator doors opened to reveal Alcaíno beaming at me in his tailored, double-breasted suit.

As we waited for Kathy to arrive, our discussion turned to the Helmsley Palace, and Alcaíno asked me whether I thought it was profitable. Which immediately brought to mind a story that Charlie Broun, Bruce Perlowin's accountant and the manager of the Red Carpet Inns, had once told me. According to Charlie, his people often prepared records to show every room occupied, even though the hotel was virtually empty. It allowed them to push dope money through as hotel revenue. With all the hotel's write-offs, no taxes had to be paid, and the dope money was legitimized.

As I was halfway through the story, someone on the other side of the lobby shouted, "Bob!" My head snapped toward the voice, and there before me stood Charlie Broun in a business suit, with his wavy Colonel Sanders hair and a huge smile.

Oh, shit. Charlie had done his time and was now apparently back in action. He started charging in my direction, his eyes glowing with surprise.

Time stopped.

In a split second that felt like a century, I turned to Alcaíno and said, "An old friend. I'll be with you in a moment."

I paced toward Charlie as fast as I could. As I held him in a bear hug, I whispered in his ear, "I'm under again, Charlie. Play along."

As I let go, I saw that Alcaíno had followed me. He was standing at my shoulder.

Did he hear me?

No, he had been too far away, but now I couldn't coach Charlie anymore. Beads of cold sweat rolled down the small of my back. Casals was outside and no doubt packing heat.

To my grateful surprise, Charlie took my lead as though we had been working together for years. In his Mississippi twang, he drawled, "Well, Bob, the boys in Vegas really miss you. Why the hell are you working so hard? You need to come out there and relax with us the way you always have in the past. You're getting too wound up. I know you're doing everybody a great service, but you need to make time for you."

We joked and hugged again before Charlie walked off with my promise to join him the next morning for breakfast at the hotel.

When Kathy came down, Casals drove us to a lavish meal at Il Cortile, a high-end mob hangout on Mulberry Street in Little Italy. Alcaíno introduced us to his favorite meal, *palafitta*: a thin, pie-shaped crust filled with lobster tail, stuffed mussels, jumbo shrimp, stuffed clams, stuffed calamari, and octopus—all smothered in a rich marinara sauce. Casals waited outside, the car running the whole time.

From there we hit the Blue Note, an old jazz club in the Village, where, over snifters of Louis XIV cognac, we soaked up some of the hottest jazz in town and talked for hours about everything but business. At 2:00 A.M., after cannoli and cappuccino with amaretto, Alcaíno dropped us back at the Helmsley Palace with an invitation to lunch the next day before he caught a flight to Paris.

The next morning, at breakfast with Charlie, I gave him a vague overview of the operation. He immediately offered his full support.

"Listen, Bob. I didn't burn you because I'm a different man from the Charlie Broun you knew. I appreciate how you treated me. While I was in prison, I read Watergate burglar Charles Colson's book and became a born-again Christian. My faith in God is more important to me than anything. You're a good man, and you're doing important work. I still have some strong connections in Vegas, especially at Caesar's Palace, so if you'd like me to set you up so you can comp a bunch of these Colombians and show them a good time, you just let me know."

"Charlie, you're a good man," I said sincerely. "I can't thank you enough. Sometime soon I'll take you up on your offer."

Alcaíno took Kathy and me to lunch at Aperitivo on West Fifty-sixth Street, another exclusive Italian haunt where he was well known.

Afterward, as Alcaíno and I strolled along Fifty-sixth Street, I said to him, "Roberto, I'm looking for an honorable and powerful South American connection. I realize we need to get to know one another, but I also recognize that you've done a lot of business without me in the past three months. Why haven't you brought any of that to me?"

Alcaíno smiled. "Anything good comes slowly. We have the capability and opportunity to do big business together."

Time to get serious.

"You and I share a lot of traits. We both have power, loyalty, and compassion. We both hold our families in high esteem. We both respect and reward the women in our lives. Roberto, I have nothing more to show you until we resume the business we were doing and supplement it with the investments. I've let you get close to my personal life, including my future wife, as a sign of trust. You are one of the few individuals who is sufficiently respected by the Colombians and can realistically convince them of the necessity for them to invest through our companies. The Moras in Colombia are driven by profits and unrealistically think they have no risks because they're not here in the U.S. I will either align myself with you or forget about your markets and go back to working for my family."

Alcaíno looked at me like a father. "Bob, this process is necessary, and we will consummate our agreement after I return from Europe. I'll have about $2 million that I will bring to you, some to transfer and some to invest. My cut from what I have going here with the big ones is 200 kilos per month, so I'll be earning $5 million a month here alone. I'll give a good part of that to you to invest, plus I'll talk the big ones into doing the same. I'll also make my people available for you. Joe [Casals] can do more than drive. He's good at other things, too."

He formed his hand into the shape of a pistol and hammered his thumb down. Casals was also an assassin.

When I played Charlie Broun's offer of a stay in Vegas, Alcaíno reciprocated by inviting Kathy and me to stay with him and his family at their mansion in Pasadena.

"Bob, believe me," he said. "We are going to do big business together. Trust me. Your patience will be rewarded in ways you can never imagine."

And it was.

7

THE MAGIC OF PANAMA

BUSINESS WAS BOOMING, but I was being watched.

Tracking money through accounts, examining canceled checks for clues, monitoring tens of thousands of dollars in undercover expenses a month, fielding calls from targets, writing reports, briefing bosses, and strategizing about how to infiltrate the cartel — it was more than a full-time job. Every week I passed reports to agents at out-of-the-way restaurants or safe houses. But no amount of precaution and obfuscation could protect me, as I soon discovered.

The Chicago office reported that telephone records of couriers linked to Alcaíno showed they had been calling pay phones near Financial Consulting in New Port Richey. My car was broken into several times. Someone was tossing it, I suspected, to see if anything in it suggested I was a cop. On the way to my real home, I drove like a doper in fear of being followed by the cops — except I was a cop in fear of being followed by the cartel. I drove down dead-end streets and parked to see if anyone had followed me. I pulled U-turns on highways and ran red lights.

Before leaving the undercover houses, I forwarded calls to a line set up in my home by the phone company's security department and agents from our office. This line rang to a phone in a closet at home that was hooked up to a recorder. I installed a strobe light in the living room to indicate when the closet phone rang.

For a while, I made it to all my family's most important events: gymnastics meets, birthdays, and holidays. But even when I was home, I wasn't really there. Every time my cell or closet phone rang, I dropped whatever I had been doing and answered it. One night, during a holiday dinner with immediate family, as my dad prepared to say grace, the strobe light flashed in our faces and shattered the moment. I shot to the closet. When I returned, ten minutes later, cold silence filled the room. Everyone's body language confirmed that I had made a big mistake.

Our success was creating problems for Emir, too. He and the other agents were picking up millions of dollars a month from couriers in New York, Philadelphia, Detroit, and Los Angeles. But front-office bureaucrats in Customs kept trying to assign surveillance agents to follow the T-shirts in hopes of catching them with money intended for delivery to other launderers. That tactic risked all the credibility that Emir and I were building with the men in the cartel. But Emir's uncanny ability to play his role warded off stupidity that could have cost us our lives.

He flew to L.A. on a cold fall day to meet Sonja, a courier. To please the L.A. office, Emir lured her to a hotel so agents in an adjoining suite could tape the meet. "Sonja, it's best that we meet privately in my room because I don't want to talk in public about our future business together."

Her antenna went up. "It's not that I don't trust you. It's just that I feel very uncomfortable." She was pissing herself at the thought of delivering hundreds of thousands of dollars of drug money to a total stranger in the confinement of a hotel room. Such close quarters offer nowhere to hide and few easy escape routes. Smart couriers like Sonja prefer to drive a beat-up old car no one would want to steal to a fast-food restaurant. They put the keys under the floor mat and join the likes of Emir inside, within sight of the car, and tell him that what he was looking for was inside a duffel bag in the trunk. They tell him where to find the keys and ask that he return the car to where he found it after he finishes his business. They wait in the restaurant until he returns and speak in riddles rather than openly give details. Not much needs to be said anyway, and playing this game keeps couriers away from the money and reduces the possibility of getting caught on tape saying things that offer no defense.

When she balked, Emir convinced Sonja to meet him outside the hotel. She arrived in a beat-up Toyota Corolla driven by her chubby eighteen-year-old son, who looked like he was playing hooky from high school.

"I'm not doing this in the street," Emir said, as the car slowed to a halt under the hotel canopy. "I don't know who is watching. Let's go to my room." When she resisted, he said, "Listen, you're the one who is going to look bad when your people get the word that I wouldn't take this shit because you were unreasonable. You *know* they're not going to be happy."

She didn't know what to say. Emir opened the rear passenger door and picked up one of the two black gym bags lying on the floor of the backseat. Beneath it lay an Uzi machine gun that she no doubt knew how to use.

"Let's go," Emir barked.

Sonja got out. Her son parked, then grabbed the other gym bag.

In the room, Emir tried to make them comfortable, but Sonja's son paced the place like a caged lion. Emir ignored him. But out of the corner of his eye Emir spotted a fatal flaw: on the doorjamb, agents had taped a wired microphone. But the tape had loosened, and the wire was leaning into Emir's hotel suite, about six inches from the top of the door. Emir had to take command of their attention or they might notice the wire.

"Sonja," he almost shouted, "you can tell your people that the money will be in Colombia in a couple of days. Do you know Gonzalo Mora?" She looked puzzled and shook her head. "Well, he'll be in contact with your people in Colombia and will tell your bosses when the money arrives. I hope we will be doing a lot of business together."

Mother and son bolted back to their car as Emir reported the Uzi to the listening agents. When he walked out onto the balcony,

Emir watched as the old Corolla crept from its parking space — and six painfully obvious unmarked police cars fell in line behind it.

"These fuckers are going to get us killed!" he said as he shook his head in disbelief. But he knew no one from Tampa could stop the L.A. agents from taking reckless risks. The commissioners in both regions operated their own fiefdoms and let agents make selfish decisions for local results. Which, of course, didn't bode well for an international case that required large-scale selflessness.

It wasn't long before Mora frantically called Emir. "What the *hell* is going on? The client's people in L.A. say you guys are cops. They claim that *los feos* followed them from your hotel."

Emir knew this was coming. He took a deep breath. "You know, Gonzalo, this woman has a problem. If, in your mind, you think that you're nervous and that everybody watching you is a police officer, you know what, we won't be able to walk half a block because every time that we look there might be a person. That person might be cleaning his car, and we'll think — *Oh, he has to be a DEA agent.*"

Mora bought the paranoia pitch and calmed down.

Then Emir called me. "Bob, we have to be thankful to God if we don't get hurt during this operation. The mighty angels better look over us because I have never seen people like this" — meaning L.A. Customs agents. "They just don't give a shit about us."

He was right, but we both knew that we were traveling a road no undercover agents had ever gone before. We had to see it through.

As pickups increased, Mora continued to pay the cartel in checks drawn on BCCI Panama. Cartel money brokers like Juan Guillermo Vargas, Augusto Salazar, and Bernardo Correa handed our checks to their drug-dealing clients. In turn, some of these thugs were cashing our checks at BCCI Panama City, which raised our profile in the eyes of the bank's officers. Then an innocent mistake turned into one of the luckiest breaks for the operation.

On a crisp winter morning, a receptionist at Financial Consulting buzzed my line to tell me that I had just missed a call from a Mr. Hussain at BCCI Panama — but I didn't know a Mr. Hussain at BCCI, just Rick Argudo and his replacement, Dayne Miller, both in Tampa. What did this Hussain want?

Hussain got right to the point. "Mr. Musella, I am Syed Aftab Hussain, and I oversee the checking account of IDC International, your account with us. There is a problem with two of your checks that have been brought to us by one of your customers. On one check, the payee has been left blank. On the other, the written amount notes 'one hundred ten thousand three hundred thirty dollars,' but the numbers for the amount on the same check note only '$110,000.' Which of these two amounts should I pay to your customer?"

He couldn't know that I had signed blank checks that were smuggled into Colombia. I had to buy time. "I can't answer your question without reviewing some files. I'll do that and call you back with an answer."

"Well," he replied, "I have a suggestion that will avoid these types of problems in the future. When you authorize a check, if you call me and let me know the details you want honored, I'll make sure that any mistakes made on the check are corrected."

The gears in my head spun out of control. Hussain *knew* I wasn't writing the amounts. As hoped, letting the checks flow through the bank sent a signal to officials there that I was a player in the laundering trade. Rather than closing my accounts, they wanted to help me run my business more efficiently!

I called Emir, who called Mora, who clarified the numbers and agreed to provide advance information about each check issued.

After hearing my answers, Hussain almost whispered into the phone, "We are a full-service bank, and I would like to discuss with you how I and BCCI can work with your company to make our business better. We should meet personally so I can explain our capabilities, which will be to everyone's advantage. Let me give you my number in Miami, and let's meet there in early December."

A few days before that meeting, I flew with Frankie to Miami in the undercover jet. Frankie introduced me to two Cubans there who built go-fast boats sold to drug smugglers running cocaine from the Bahamas to Florida. The Cubans were looking for financing to expand their business.

When I walked into the lobby of the Brickell Key Condominiums in Miami on a Saturday morning, Hussain, a portly, unassuming young man from Karachi, was waiting with open arms to greet me. His family had dabbled in banking and insurance there, but a thick Pakistani accent clouded his English — and he wasn't wearing a custom-made Italian suit. We nestled into a remote sitting area on the ground floor, and, as the microcassette recorder in the lid of my briefcase captured every word, he jumped straight to business. He and the bank wanted to protect my clients, and he had a number of suggestions about how we could reach that goal.

He cautioned that people caught by Operation Pisces issued checks to clients like mine, encouraging me to close my checking account at BCCI Panama immediately. It had been very active; too many checks had been issued. He recommended that I place my clients' funds in numbered certificates of deposit that he could establish at BCCI Luxembourg. He also asked for documents on properties to serve as dummy collateral for loans issued by BCCI Panama. Though Luxembourg would collateralize the loans, BCCI would falsify its own records to suggest the Luxembourg accounts didn't exist and the properties were collateralizing the loans in Panama. Loan proceeds, granted in an amount equal to my CD in Luxembourg, could then be transferred to a checking account in Panama maintained in the name of another company. From there, the funds would disburse to clients based on my verbal instructions to him. An officer of one of the world's largest privately held banks was *teaching* me how best to launder drug money!

He warned that when I spoke to him by telephone I shouldn't speak openly. "We talk to the client on telephone only on confidential matters. Only secret language. When we talk, client understand what we are talking." He guaranteed the scheme would prevent U.S. authorities from tracing my transfers. Most importantly, though, he wanted to introduce me to BCCI Miami executives. As he put it, "They know how to talk and when to talk. They don't talk loose."

For maximum confidentiality, he urged me to write a letter of authorization to my client rather than a check. The client would deliver the letter to him, and Hussain would carry out the transfer. That way, authorities had no check they could acquire later and link to my signature. He had every angle figured out.

I told Hussain, "I realize you're just assisting the bank in regard to my interests, but I also feel that it's an unusual luxury to have a person like yourself take the time to look at my affairs." I asked if there was anything he'd like me to do for him personally. If he asked for payments under the table, he was a rogue employee looking to pad his pockets. If he didn't, this was a bank-wide strategy.

"No, thank you," he replied without hesitation. "The only thing I would like you to do is to make a placement of funds by December. It's good for the bank, and then bank can help the clients."

Bingo — bank-wide.

We met again at BCCI Miami four days later. What ensued required two full days of meetings with Hussain.

A tall black glass building on Brickell Avenue — a road lined with huge palm trees and giant office buildings containing hundreds of international banks — housed BCCI Miami. These international banks hold the secrets to the stories of tens of thousands of Alcaínos and have quietly kept hold of drug fortunes for decades.

Huge gold letters on a rose-colored granite wall announced the BANK OF CREDIT AND COMMERCE INTERNATIONAL. On the other side of large clear-glass doors, behind an oversized granite desk, an attractive receptionist greeted me and asked me to wait while she notified Hussain of my arrival. The bank was thrumming with activity. Dozens of rows of identical fine wood desks lined the floor, and phones were buzzing like a beehive.

Hussain escorted me into a gigantic conference room with a central table that looked more like a runway for a small plane. It easily could have seated fifty people around its rich cherrywood expanse. At the side of the conference room was a lounge area with plush chairs and a serving table. This corner of the boardroom became the place of choice where the bank's brass entertained me. It was here that I planned transactions that circled the globe. It was here that I drank imported espresso in fine china while meeting with the bank's inner circle. It was here that the bank's inner circle wove paper webs of confusion to hide the true source of my money.

As I sat in the luxury of one of the plush couches, Hussain whipped up paperwork that hid $1,185,000 in a numbered CD secretly used to collateralize a loan, the proceeds of which went into a Panamanian checking account. He assured me that the "CD will be kept somewhere else, and only the bank and you know." If U.S. authorities ever inquired about the transaction, the bank wouldn't turn over any records of the CD. "They will come and ask, 'Do you have a CD for this?' We'll say, 'No.'"

Hussain brimmed with instructions. He warned me never to use my real name when I called him in Panama, suggesting I simply use the name John. If confusion arose, I should give his last name as my own—John Hussain. When I called him in Panama, we were to talk in general terms to confuse anyone listening. No need to speak the full name of a company or account.

As the papers flew, it became clear that the time was right to prove beyond a shadow of a doubt that Hussain knew my funds came from drug running in the U.S. I knew he knew, but a good defense attorney can twist a steel rod into a knot for a jury in order to create doubt. It was out of character, but I had to do it—and I had to do it in a way that didn't scream *federal agent!*

"There is much more at stake than money," I said solemnly. I gave him a copy of the article about the gangland killing of Rafael (Ráfico) Cardona Salazar, Alcaíno's former partner. "This money comes from some of the largest drug dealers in South America."

"But I think we should keep this money in Luxembourg," Hussain replied without blinking an eye. Then he mentioned introducing me to the manager of BCCI Panama, adding, "but you don't have to mention all this, that the money is involved in drugs and everything. Normally, if you keep the money in Panama, there's only two reasons. Either it's drug-related or it is, uh, taxes. There's no other...any, uh... Panama receives thirteen billion in U.S. dollar deposits a year!"

He was laughing.

When he finished pulling the paperwork together, Hussain shared a name with me and thereby changed the fate of many people for whom BCCI had laundered drug profits — including General Manuel Noriega. According to Hussain, this man was a high-ranking regional officer of the bank and the former manager of the Panama branch. In fact, he still handled Panama from Miami. Unlike with the current manager of BCCI Panama, I could speak openly with him. I could trust this man because he belonged to the bank team that handled accounts like mine.

The man was Amjad Awan.

I flew commercial back to Tampa. As the plane lifted and banked over the glitter of the Magic City, I pondered my next steps with Hussain. He needed to bring Awan into the picture. It would give Bob Musella a confidant in Miami who could serve as a guide and problem solver. It would give me, as a federal agent, the chance to build rapport and record meetings with more members of the bank's team of officers tasked with marketing dirty money. But before I put that plan in play I needed to build more rapport with Alcaíno. It was time to take Charlie Broun up on his offer.

"Charlie, help me look the part in Vegas. I need to come across to a big-time player in the drug world as though I have major connections."

"No problem," he assured me. "I'll lie to the boys at Caesar's Palace that you're a high roller. I'll get you and any of your guests comped by the hotel. Your rooms, food, and anything else you and your guests need will be provided. You'll be treated like kings. All I ask is that you show action on the tables. They don't give a shit if you win or lose. You just have to put money at risk."

On a five-day trip, three rooms and all meals for three couples — Alcaíno and his legal wife, Emir and Adella, and Kathy and me — would have run at least $2,500, so I convinced the bean counters at Customs to put that amount on the tables to look the part. Chump change to the boys at Caesar's Palace, and we'd never be invited back, but to the lunch-bucket workers at Customs it was a fortune.

Alcaíno and his wife Gloria joined us. They enjoyed the luxury of a suite, and anything they wanted was only a phone call away. Charming and sophisticated, she dressed impeccably and was completely at ease among the lavish displays of wealth and risk. Alcaíno didn't gamble, but by now he saw a real future in our relationship.

The first evening, a stretch limo ushered us away from the glitz of the strip to Georges La Forge's quaint, French-country gourmet restaurant, Pamplemousse. While I won over Gloria, Kathy worked Alcaíno, discussing his favorite painter, Chagall, and his favorite wines from the Maipo Valley of his native Chile. We were a well-oiled machine, and the Alcaínos ate up everything they heard.

At the end of the meal, Adella pulled a stunt that reinforced our outlaw status. As I settled the check, Adella, who was wearing an outfit that included a black cape, worked her way toward a rack of fine wine. As the limo rolled from the restaurant, she proclaimed, "Who would like to enjoy one of the finest bottles of red wine Vegas has to offer?" then pulled from under her cape one of Pamplemousse's most expensive bottles. Alcaíno couldn't stop laughing, and I couldn't stop thinking how her disarming behavior had banished any concerns Alcaíno might have had that we were feds. We pulled the cork and enjoyed the best free wine in Sin City.

The next day, Emir and I hit the blackjack tables. Taking Charlie's lead I used only hundred-dollar chips. After an hour I was up a couple of grand, but, in case someone was watching, instead of playing smart I played rich — and lost everything.

We were all smiles, but, when Alcaíno and his wife went elsewhere, we dissolved into pure exhaustion. The front office worried about the cost of the dinner bill, while Emir and I worried about getting every single little detail right. One slip, and it was all over. We played the part of relaxed, close friends, but our wheels turned furiously, anticipating, calculating, and documenting every move around us. The tension behind our smiles is unimaginable unless you've lived this experience. Our internal alert systems shifted from total rest to high alert because of a simple glance or an awkward word that seemed to raise an eyebrow. But no one around us ever knew. Oddly, this became a comfortable sixth sense.

I didn't want to pump Alcaíno too hard for new information, but we had important issues to address. "Roberto," I said, "after you explained the recent fate of your partner, I found this article about Ráfico's murder."

Alcaíno confirmed that it was a report about his close friend, then volunteered that some recent problems had disrupted his European routes but the cartel expected to reopen those routes to Spain, France, and Italy within a month. Shipments would soon arrive in the States, and I had the privilege of handling the money from those sales.

Good news, but now the hard part. The count of the last shipment of cash he delivered was $60,000 short, and I wasn't about to eat that loss. I gave him the check numbers of five checks Mora had given to Alcaíno's partners in Medellín and asked him to call his friends to let them know about the problem.

Alcaíno immediately dialed Casals. "Joe, Gonzalo will call you with details, but there are five checks that will be stopped. Bob tells me we made a mistake in counting. The $360,000 we thought we gave him counted out to $300,000."

After the call, Alcaíno insisted the mistake was ours, but I held my ground. I wondered if he wasn't testing me. After a long discussion, they agreed that they had made the mistake and our count was right. I suggested that Alcaíno buy a few money-counting machines from me to ensure it didn't happen again.

He couldn't wait to tell me that he already had machines in New York that he kept away from his New York apartment. "One time I told my girlfriend Sonja, 'Don't leave the machine here. Take it to the place it's supposed to be.' And she says to me, 'What's the difference?' I said, 'Fifteen years!'"

The room erupted into laughter.

As we flew back to Tampa in the private jet, the success of the Vegas trip sank in. Agents posing as my couriers were picking up suitcases full of cash all over the country. Mora was about to arrive from Colombia. But if we didn't continue to climb new rungs in the underworld ladder, we'd be shut down.

Little did I know that what was about to unfold would end any concerns about climbing that ladder. I was about to meet someone more important than I could imagine, someone whose identity grabbed the attention of everyone in law enforcement from Florida to Washington, D.C.

8

PUSHING BUTTONS

**Holiday Inn Surfside, Clearwater Beach, Florida
January 6, 1988**

IT WAS TIME.

Mora and his family had flown in from Medellín to Miami International at my invitation, to visit Clearwater Beach and Disney World. They stayed at the Holiday Inn Surfside, where nothing but a hundred yards of soft white sand separated their suite from the Gulf of Mexico.

Mora's wife, Lucy, cordial but slow to trust, was watching his back—understandably, since at her side stood their nine-year-old son and seven-year-old daughter. Smiles and horseplay camouflaged the pain I felt for these kids, whose lives were going to change forever. But it was important to remember that it was their father's blind greed that set the stage for that change.

After lunch with the Moras, Kathy, and Adella, Emir introduced Mora to José Cordero, a Tampa-based undercover agent who often traveled with Emir to Detroit, Houston, and L.A. to pick up cash. Emir explained José's role to Mora, and after five minutes of pleasantries, on cue, José, Kathy, and Adella all excused themselves. Emir, Mora, and I settled down to talk business.

Mora had orchestrated our receipt of millions of dollars a week in cash from his clients and expected happiness from me, so my disappointment came as a great shock. He had failed to bring me clients willing to invest. Huge deposits followed by huge withdrawals to Panama were a dead giveaway. BCCI was creating a smokescreen for us, true, but the expense was costing my fair share of profit. My cut had to increase, and in sixty days his clients would have to agree to delivery of only 75 percent of the value of their funds within ten days of our receipt of a cash shipment. The remaining 25 percent would follow six months later, with interest. Mora couldn't sell these terms to his clients, I knew. When he failed, I planned to offer an alternative: the opportunity to pitch this proposal to his clients personally. If they refused, I'd consider backing down. Either way, Mora would campaign on my behalf for face-to-face meetings with the hierarchy of the cartel, whom otherwise we'd never be able to record and prosecute.

Mora gave in. The man in Medellín with the connections was Javier Ospiña, and Mora agreed to arrange a meeting within two months in San José, Costa Rica, to negotiate with him.

Button pushed.

The next day, at the Polynesian Resort at Disney World, as we got out of our cars and Mora tended to his kids, a porter yelled out to Emir.

"*Coño!*" Emir muttered. *Fuck!* "Bob, I have to take care of something. I don't believe this." Emir pulled the porter aside while we checked in. When the porter arrived at our room with our bags, I tipped him $10. He snatched the cash with a trembling hand and ran from the room in a sweat.

I mentioned that the man looked like he was having a heart attack, and Emir shook his head. "That bellman worked at the San Juan airport as a ticketing agent for Prinair in Puerto Rico. He knew me as a Customs agent, and when we arrived he yelled out, 'Hey, Emir! I haven't seen you since you were at the airport!' Who the hell would expect that we would cross paths ten years later at this damn hotel? I pulled him aside and told him, 'Don't mention my name. You don't know me from shit. I'm working undercover and staying here at the hotel with some big-time drug dealers. You could get me killed.' He must have thought you were one of them."

We toured Disney World for the next two days, and everything was going according to plan until Mora pulled out his 35mm camera and insisted he take our picture with his kids. We couldn't refuse — but those pictures would soon get into the hands of Don Chepe, Ospiña, Ochoa, and every other heavy hitter in the cartel. I had to do something. Fast.

"Tell him I'd love to take some pictures of him and his family while we're up in the air," I told Emir as we inched our way to the Skyway. "He should give us his camera."

Swaying, our gondola rose above the park, and I snapped a few shots of Mora and his family behind us. Then, as their gondola lifted from the platform, I held the camera toward the floor, popped it open, and pulled the roll from the casing, exposing the film, rolling it back, and readvancing it. The dial clicked back where it had been just as we entered the opposite station and the attendant approached the door. Mora arrived mere seconds later and immediately retrieved his camera.

On our way to the Tomorrowland Indy Speedway ride, Mora reloaded his camera. *Oh, no, he's not going to take more photos, is he?* Sure enough, Mora clicked away as though we were rock stars. Time to end the threat for good.

"Tell him I'm going to take a break but I'll take pictures of his family on the track," I said to Emir, who snatched the bag and passed it to me. A sea of people allowed me to snake my way to a nearby men's room. One by one, I popped at least eight black plastic canisters, pulled the film, then rewound it. It wasn't until Mora returned to Medellín ten days later that he discovered the poor quality of the film he had bought in the States. It seems that all of his pictures were overexposed.

After our excursion to the Magic Kingdom, it was time to meet Hussain at BCCI Miami so he could introduce me to the inner team who marketed clients like me. They needed to see me as a sophisticated crook with a good front so they had wiggle room for plausible deniability. Undoubtedly Hussain had told them already that I was laundering drug money, but any experienced banker could tell that just by looking at my account activity. They were probably going to weigh the risks of my money. Talking openly would make me look either reckless or like a cop. There would be plenty of time to be blunt later. They had to feel at ease. Which meant I had to feel at ease myself, so in my head I played out possible dialogues, with varying anticipated scripts.

I told Mora that I had important meetings at the bank during the first half of the day. While I was there, I told him, I would receive twenty-five new checks drawn on my account in Panama, and I invited him to join me to get them, scheduling his arrival for half an hour after the meetings started. The bankers would see me interact with a Colombian from Medellín, and Mora would see my status at the bank. No other undercover agent could pull this off. It required a full-blooded Colombian from Medellín. Even though most of the bankers hailed from the Middle East, they spoke Spanish fluently and knew their Colombian accents. Mora was perfect.

Hussain escorted me to the couches. While we were still alone I said to him, "Don't put me in a position where I need to ask enough to know they are on the inner team. They need to say whatever it is that will satisfy me that I don't need to say anything.... Have you had an opportunity to tell them why it needs some very careful handling?"

"Yes. I've — I have told them. You also mention it. Tell them ... that I want it should be very carefully handled, and it should be exclusively handled by Mr. Hussain."

Akbar Bilgrami burst through the door with a nervous laugh like a muffled machine gun. He was wearing huge, heavy, dark-rimmed glasses nearly the size of a diving mask. He looked the part of the brainy commercial banker who had probably been teased as a child for being a rich geek.

Then Amjad Awan glided into the room in an aura of polished confidence. His hair and mustache were as well groomed as his manicured nails.

"That's Mr. Awan," Bilgrami announced, explaining that he and Awan would do my bidding from Miami or anywhere in the world. Hussain had enlightened them, and they were looking forward to assisting in the management of my affairs.

"We're in seventy-two countries," Awan said. "So, you know, whichever country your client has or are comfortable in." Traces of his Pakistani roots mingled with his British accent.

There came a knock on the door, and a secretary broke into Awan's sales pitch to inform me that Mr. Gonzalo Mora had arrived. I told the group that Mora was a colleague with whom I needed to speak before he returned to Medellín. I had taken the liberty of telling him he could find me at the bank if his departure was imminent. As I rose and explained that it would take only a few minutes, Awan and Bilgrami insisted that Mora join me in the boardroom and that they would wait outside.

Even better than expected! Now they would see him face to face, and he would understand my importance when the bankers left the room. Then again, the boardroom may have been bugged, which would give the bankers a chance to hear what I was really all about.

Mora and his nephew, Fabio, entered, and I gave Mora the twenty-five blank checks I had signed. Mora tried to give me contact information for a Chicago pickup for Alcaíno, but I cut him short and asked him to contact Emir, explaining apologetically that I had sensitive matters to work out with the bankers. As they slowly left the room, Mora looked over his shoulder, his eyes soaking up the opulent decor.

When Awan, Bilgrami, and Hussain returned, they conveyed their assent to the plan to hide my client's funds in CDs used to collateralize loans in equal amounts. They agreed to forge documents that indicated the loans rested on pledges of rights to the titles of property. Then the conversation turned to my background as both Awan and Bilgrami asked probing questions. I emphasized my dealings with their Tampa branch, which put them at ease. But then I hit them with my best indication of experience. "There are many things best left unsaid, and, as we mature in our relationship, I'm sure things will develop to the point where we'll all feel very comfortable. I feel extremely comfortable with Hussain and you gentlemen as well. The key to my dealings here is a necessity for confidentiality, and I feel very comfortable with that. My clients are not exactly the greatest fans of the tax system here."

All three men burst out laughing, and Awan said, "We can't really blame them for that, can we?"

I explained that my clients owned the funds I was depositing, and, based on Hussain's recommendation, BCCI could expect to receive about $5 million per month, all of which would need converting to CDs in Europe as collateral for like-value loans. The proceeds of those loans would funnel back to my account in Panama, from which I would disburse the money back to my clients. Each transaction would involve borrowing periods of thirty to sixty days.

"This kind of detail doesn't leave here," Bilgrami said. "The whole idea was for Mr. Hussain to come over so we could meet. And you can rest assured that we'll be ready to handle this…just as discreetly as possible and very intimate."

Awan wanted and received reassurance that the bank would be dealing with me directly rather than my clients. Then he explained how a Luxembourg holding company owned the seventy-two branches of the bank as well as subsidiaries in Grand Cayman and a second holding company in Luxembourg. Through this maze of shells, ruling families in Abu Dhabi, Bahrain, Dubai, and Kuwait owned the bank. Agha Hasan Abedi, president of BCCI and Awan's mentor — who had lured him away from the Bank of Montreal in Canada — had spun this intricate web of offshore companies, happy to accept as much cash as my clients could provide and styled to please.

One block east of the bank was a large parking lot where well-dressed Latin businessmen used the comfortable anonymity of more than a dozen pay phones. They probably worried, like me, that their cell-phone conversations were being monitored — only they worried about government taps, while I worried about the cartel.

From my pocket, I pulled a roll of quarters, thinking of Bruce Perlowin's old saw, "A roll a day keeps the feds away" — only, again, my
concern wasn't the feds; it was Alcaíno's or Don Chepe's people. I
called the managing agent, Laura Sherman.

"Laura, I just got out of my meeting at BCCI. The new guys
I met included Amjad Awan, a senior player at the bank who was
formerly the manager of their branch in Panama."

"You've got to be kidding me!" she said. "That guy is *huge!*"
Apparently major dealers had already identified Awan as the contact of choice for payoffs delivered on behalf of General Noriega.
Awan was one of the top laundering targets in the world. I had
struck gold.

Laura was working on the Noriega case with Mark Jackowski
while he monitored our operation from a distance. As Mark later
put it, we were "deep inside one of the biggest money-laundering
organizations this country has ever seen. Whatever you need, I'm
there for you. This is a once-in-a-lifetime opportunity."

But before I could schedule my next meeting with Awan and
Bilgrami, I had to stoke Alcaíno and keep both sides engaged.
Without the cartel's money, I couldn't feed BCCI. Without BCCI, I
couldn't move millions for the cartel. I had become the middle man.

When in New York, I rented a three-bedroom apartment at
the Sherry-Netherland on the southeast corner of Central Park. The
place came with a full living room, a fireplace, chandeliered dining room, eat-in kitchen, three bedrooms, three baths, and a huge
foyer. Even more over the top, it was fully furnished with high-end
antique furniture. Emir and I welcomed Alcaíno for a catered lunch
there. As we ate salmon with capers, caviar, and an assortment of
gourmet treats, we talked about the cartel's work around the world,
the recorder in my briefcase capturing every word.

Alcaíno assured me that within a week he would deliver
$450,000 to New York City. He had spoken with Pablo Escobar
and other cartel leaders, who wanted to buy properties in the U.S.
It wouldn't be long, Alcaíno said, before he convinced them to use
our services to make that happen. He also disclosed that he and

the cartel board, after spending much time and enormous sums of money, were opening Europe. But then he shocked me with news that he had decided to reopen L.A. and wanted our help moving money from there to Colombia. I agreed, and my mind immediately started spinning ways to work around Chewie Ibarra.

At the same time, Mora had brought Ospiña onboard and increased the volume of our deals with Ospiña's boss, Don Chepe. In just three weeks, Emir and José Cordero picked up nearly $3 million from Don Chepe's primary workers in Detroit, Jaime and Norberto Giraldo, with whom Emir developed a friendship. Polite, humble, and diligent men from Medellín, they and their families lived modestly — but sold thousands of kilos of cocaine and collected tens of millions of dollars for *los duros*, the strong ones.

Emir always treated them as equals and eventually began advising them how to manage their movements more efficiently. Since he was meeting them in hotel rooms, Emir convinced them that they needed to deliver their cash in new Samsonite suitcases. Emir kept the suitcases each time, so the Giraldos had to buy new luggage for each new delivery. Which of course made it easy for surveillance agents in Detroit, who watched the Giraldos go to Sears to buy new suitcases and then knew that money and coke were moving.

On a freezing January day in Detroit, surveillance agents watched the Giraldos go to a McDonald's to meet two men who drove away in Jaime Giraldo's car to an eighteen-wheeler with Florida plates parked miles away. The men put a few large boxes from the truck in the trunk of the car and returned to the McDonald's, from where the car was then driven to a storage rental facility. An agent with no more than a year on the job would know that he had just witnessed a delivery of cocaine. Which is exactly what the Giraldos pulled the next day from the storage facility: two large boxes containing about 220 pounds of cocaine delivered to Khairi "Harry" Kalashol, leader of the Iraq-based Chaldean mafia in Detroit, an organization infamous for its vicious murders, which poured blood on the streets of the Motor City.

The delivery was unbelievably blatant. The Giraldos met the

Iraqis in a mall parking lot. As they stood by the open trunk of Giraldo's car, Jaime Giraldo passed kilo packs of cocaine, one at a time, to Kalashol, who stuffed them into bags. Plain as day. Agents videotaped the exchange, but law-enforcement officers took no action to stop subsequent distribution. It was a realization almost as cold as the weather there.

The Tampa office hosted quarterly meetings attended by all agents, supervisors, and prosecutors on our case. We established clear guidelines: Don't take any action or file documents that might compromise the operation, but do find ways to refer information about crimes of drug trafficking to other federal, state, or local authorities who could take action. The guys in Detroit could have called their buddies in local law enforcement to take these guys down without jeopardizing the operation. But the Detroit office froze at the switch. The special agent in charge of the Detroit office made the decision in conjunction with Tampa and D.C., claiming that letting the dope go was the only way to protect the operation. I didn't buy it. More likely that Detroit didn't want to give up the stats on taking down the Giraldos later. And there was going to be hell to pay down the road.

To prevent a repeat of this fiasco, we hatched a plan to put surveillance on the tractor trailer so the next time that it headed north from Florida it would look like local law enforcement accidentally found the cocaine shipment during a weigh-station inspection.

As the escapades in Detroit were unfolding, I was on my way to see Awan and Bilgrami in order to bounce half a million around the globe and then to Panama. I told Awan that I was late because I had been offered a chance to receive several million U.S. dollars in Toronto, and I was dealing with logistics. I told him that, if I could speed up getting the cash into accounts, I could handle greater volume and bring more money to BCCI.

Awan smiled. "That's your problem," he said. "I don't want to know about it." It was too early in our relationship to talk details, but the bank clearly helped clients by taking large unreported currency deposits.

They arranged to wire the half million to Switzerland for Lamont Maxwell, S.A., one of my Panamanian companies. That money became collateral for a loan from their Swiss branch, and the loan proceeds moved to a checking account for IDC International, S.A., at BCCI Panama. So if checks drawn on the IDC account ever came under scrutiny, tracing the funds would lead feds to a loan in the name of a different company. Because the half-million transfer hadn't yet arrived at BCCI, some of the documents I was signing were still blank.

Bilgrami left the room to take a call, which offered an opportunity to talk privately with Awan. I had to harvest the most critical element of proof in order to prosecute him: his knowledge that the funds he was moving were drug proceeds. Euphemisms wouldn't cut it, but talking plainly ran the risk of scaring him away. Nevertheless, it needed to be so clear that no high-priced lawyer could twist his words.

As the recorder in my briefcase caught every word, I said to him, "You have won my total trust. I don't normally sign blank documents, but I'm quite comfortable with you all, and I rely on that."

"As time goes by," Awan said carefully, "I think we can form a good relationship. We can assure you of pretty good service. I don't think you would have any complaints."

Too vague. Time to hit hard.

"Certain things, I recognize, needn't be said," I said, "and when the few times come when something needs to be said, in my opinion, they need to be said alone. I have more at risk than simply the money that's here. Some of my Colombian clients have less than an appreciation for the business world, and frankly, between you and me, gentlemen in the drug business don't generally have an appreciation for anything other than trust. And when they feel it's been violated, the pressure that they... Therefore, you and only you... I would never have such a conversation in front of the other gentleman—"

The phone rang, interrupting me before I could finish. *Dammit*. I hadn't gone far enough. I needed another opening.

After Awan's call ended, he explained that BCCI's correspondent in the U.S. was First American, a well-known institution based in D.C. "First American Bank is unofficially owned by us. We don't disclose this fact. It is sort of bought by people who are shareholders in our bank."

Interesting. BCCI secretly owned and controlled a large domestic financial institution. I wasn't sure where this was going, but it got my attention. Certainly something to save for when Awan was feeling talkative.

Awan warned me to confine my communication at the bank about my affairs to him, Bilgrami, and Hussain. Maybe that was the opening I needed.

"The things," I said, "that are of most importance to me are just what you've discussed, with regard to keeping the CDs out of the picture. The second important thing is for me to be able to realistically rely on the amount of time that it will take from the time when I meet with you regarding a figure and the point in time when the corresponding amount can be made available in Panama. We'll never discuss this again, but the people with whom I'm dealing are the most powerful and largest drug dealers in Colombia."

Awan winced. "I want to be very clear and possibly blunt with you," he said. "I'm not concerned.... It's not my business who your customers are or whatever. I deal with you. As long as we have a relationship, and we have a straightforward, clear relationship...the funds are legit, clear, and everything, we do it. I'm not concerned further than that because, you know, I'm not really responsible for the morals of your customers. I deal with you. As long as you and I have a clear, straightforward, legitimate business, we will provide you all security, all sorts of security and anonymity. Further than that, I don't want to know."

Before leaving, I suggested to Awan and Bilgrami that we have dinner that night. I had rattled Awan's cage and wanted to calm him down. They suggested a small, trendy Italian restaurant tucked under the canopy of huge banyan trees on Twenty-eighth Avenue in Coconut Grove. Kathy joined me, which made it easier to avoid talking about my clients and douse the fire of concern my blunt remarks might have ignited. I played up my responsibility to my "family," my Italian roots, and the importance of loyalty and respect. At the same time, we talked about sports, travel, anything to put them at ease. Which they must have felt because they picked up the tab.

A bank of pay phones in front of a Winn-Dixie on Key Biscayne became my nighttime base of communications with my supervisor, other agents, and Ev. My old buddy from Georgia, Steve Cook, had become my supervisor, always supporting me in my efforts to get the job done and giving me the benefit of the doubt more than some new bosses on their way to Tampa. Paul O'Brien had taken a promotion to become the Customs attaché in Dublin, replaced by Bonni Tischler, a D.C. staffer with whom Steve ran interference for me.

After briefing, I called Ev to see how she and the kids were doing. I tried to call once a day, but circumstances sometimes prevented me from calling for four or five days at a time. She and the kids were quickly adjusting to my absence. Ev packed her nights and weekends with paying bills, mowing the lawn, getting the car fixed, handling house repairs, guiding the kids, and shuttling them to practices and meets. She was also holding down a full-time job as a grade-school teacher. We were coping, but the strain was starting to show.

"Bob," she said, "I've never stood in the way of your doing anything you thought was important, but this is starting to become a lot more than either of us suspected. How long is it going to continue?"

"The people I'm meeting are at the top of the food chain of crime. I can't say for sure how long this will go on, but I've got to see it through."

"You've said that before."

"Come on, hon, before you know it, things will be back to normal. When I get back tomorrow, I'll be home for a few days, and we can talk it out then."

We talked, which helped, but it didn't solve the underlying problem. When working long-term undercover, I felt I couldn't allow distractions that could cause a fatal mistake. My survival instinct forced me to concentrate solely on the case, which inevitably shut out my personal life. It wasn't that I didn't want to think about my loved ones or talk to them, but doing that posed a challenge because I frequently had to focus a hundred percent on that under-cover world, absorbing every nuance, even if only in body language. I needed to be prepared totally, for anything, and the only way to do that was to think about everything constantly: what these people were likely to do next, how I could stay one step ahead. Each target became an obsession.

At the same time, my loved ones got mixed signals. It increas-ingly appeared that I wasn't the same — which was true, in a way. My mind was always elsewhere. I built a wall around my personal life in order to stay on track mentally while undercover. But even when I was at home, I couldn't shake the habit.

To combat this natural reaction to the unnatural environment of long-term undercover work, you need a lot of help. Awareness of the phenomenon is critical because it provides you with direction about how to try to cope. Physical conditioning was very important. I ran four or five miles almost every day and tried to eat right. Work-ing eighteen-hour days over extended periods of time can lead to disaster if you don't keep yourself in good shape.

It's also critical to build a bond with a contact agent who has little responsibility other than debriefing you, collecting evidence from you, and keeping you grounded. The contact agent becomes your confidant, but at the same time assesses how well you're coping. Obviously that agent needs to have undercover experience because you can't assess another undercover agent unless you've been there yourself. But no one in Tampa had those credentials. Dave Burris of the IRS Criminal Investigation Division filled that role for me some-what, becoming my conduit for passing information along. We'd worked together for years, and he was talented, serious, and reliable.

After Ev and I had talked, I called Mark Jackowski. "I can't believe it. I flat-out told Awan that the money he was moving around the world for me was dope money, and he wasn't fazed. He tried to backpedal a little, but there's no doubt we've got the proof to convict him. The interesting thing is that he is offering to introduce me to other BCCI officers in Europe who work with him for clients like me. This thing could go all the way to the top of the bank."

Jackowski took a long drag from a cigarette, then exhaled in a long, slow sigh that sounded like air escaping from a balloon. "Bob, this is some heavy fucking shit, man. You need to keep pushing buttons. Awan is the key to Noriega."

As Jackowski put it, we were in uncharted territory.

A few days later, on my way to the couches, a young woman selling long-stemmed red roses intercepted me.

"Good morning," I said to the bank receptionist, handing her a rose. "I'm here to see Mr. Bilgrami and Mr. Awan. My name is Musella."

"Thank you very much," she said, smiling. "Very kind, sir."

What cop would do that?

As Awan and I were bantering about the Super Bowl game between the Redskins and Broncos the night before, he took an incoming call.

"Hello. Yes. Friday's okay? Yeah, I know. Well, what is it? What'd he say? No, that's not the point. The point is that under the circumstances — and I told him this last Friday — it will be best if we have the least possible contact because who knows who is listening on the telephone? You know, and I'd offered . . . yeah. Because, you know, you never know who's here, who's listening on the phone. If . . . No, what I told him was that, you know, in future, just get Marcela to call me and not to — and don't call me directly, and whenever you have to say anything to me, tell Marcela to call me, and I'll be there. Okay. Friday night, I'll come, and, ah, you think I can see him Friday or Saturday and leave Saturday? If that's possible, that'd be the best."

He hung up. "My friend is in deep trouble these days."

I knew exactly whom he meant. Marcela Tasón was Noriega's personal secretary and presumed lover. Awan had just been talking with someone passing a message on behalf of Tasón and Noriega. Given the pressure the U.S. was putting on him at the time, Noriega must have been summoning Awan to Panama so they could discuss moving the general's fortune around the checkerboard of BCCI's branches.

"Who is that?" I asked, playing dumb.

Awan smirked. "Noriega."

Seizing the moment, I told Awan that I was postponing my trip to Panama because U.S. influence could jeopardize the secrecy of our transactions there. In reality, I had no choice. I had asked for approval to travel to Panama, but word from the front office was: "DEA says it's too dangerous, and they're not allowing any undercover agents to work in Panama until things calm down."

Total bullshit. DEA had declined our request because Panama was their turf, and they didn't want to deal with supporting an undercover Customs agent there. DEA allowed their own undercover agents to work in Panama at that very time. A shame and an opportunity wasted because Awan offered to take me there to introduce me to his friends, who would have included Noriega or his closest advisers.

We were deeper inside the cartel hierarchy than any undercover agents had gone before, and had made the only covert entry ever into a $40 billion bank operating as the world's largest money-laundering machine. In just one meeting, we were already collecting hard proof about the suspected corruption of Noriega, and we stood to gain solid intel about the location of the millions in payoffs he received from Medellín.

Despite all those expectations, I was in for the shock of my life.

9

POLITICS

WORD HIT D.C. that Tampa had accessed Noriega's banker.

Quarterly meetings expanded to include personnel from Tampa, Miami, New York, Philadelphia, Chicago, Detroit, Houston, and Los Angeles, along with Customs and Justice managers from D.C. and regional offices. It felt like the mob's Apalachin conference in upstate New York: most everyone there was loyal to the cause, wanting what was right for those they served, but factions were plotting—*What's in it for me? How can I take control?*

Agents from each city reported on evidence gathered so far, and everyone agreed not to compromise the operation. Then the bosses from D.C. and each region met privately to mull our fate. Agency guidelines mandated that, as long as operatives were cultivating new contacts and uncovering new crimes, operations would continue for at least another quarter. The cartel's invitation to Costa Rica, the developing relationship with Alcaíno, and BCCI's offers of introduction to key players in Europe, all meant the fate of the operation wouldn't be up for discussion—or so I thought.

After a closed-door meeting, our new boss, Bonni Tischler, convened the Tampa personnel. She and I had disagreed as contending peers on cases overlapping Miami and Tampa in the past, and, apparently because I had had the audacity to disagree with her, she disliked me. She made her decisions, I was warned, based on how a case could best serve her career, not what was best for the case, and (a cardinal sin in law enforcement) she personalized her decisions. If you benignly supported her, she ruled in your favor. If she didn't like you, your case was already over.

Tischler had run the fast track since leaving Miami as an agent, cultivating strong personal friendships with top dogs in Washington like George Corcoran, the godfather of Customs and the assistant commissioner of enforcement, and Customs commissioner William von Raab. Now she was the special agent in charge of Tampa, and I was still working the street. I was no match for her and her friends from D.C.

Tischler gathered the Tampa personnel in one of the hotel rooms, where, in a subtle sign of her disparagement of us, we sat on beds, chairs, or the floor. With no discussion, she pronounced her ruling.

"I monitored this case in D.C., and I'll tell you that I never liked it from the start. If it wasn't for the fact that you've worked yourselves inside the bank, I'd end this thing tomorrow. Against my better judgment, you've got from now until the first week of October to end this case. That's when it's going down." She glared directly at me. "And on the bank, stick to the bank's dealing in drug money, and keep your nose out of whatever else they're doing."

I didn't challenge her, but I sure as hell was going to ignore her. Learning about other crimes would give us either ammunition or leverage against the bankers. BCCI had friends in high places, secret interests in American banks, and who knew what else. It sounded to me like "whatever else the bank is doing" involved the CIA, and Washington didn't want those details getting out.

"Bonni," I said, "given the progress we're making meeting new targets every week and documenting new crimes, would it be possible for us, in accordance with policy, to evaluate our progress every quarter and determine the best course of action based on the facts at that time? Why October?"

Tischler's eyes turned to daggers. "Listen, *Mazur*, you're lucky you're getting that much time. Everything has a beginning, middle, and end. The end of this operation is further off than I'd like, but you're not getting a day past the first week of October. End of story."

No sense in debating. I had nine months to do two years of work, and the only way to do that was to immerse myself completely in my role. Before I even left that hotel room, the gears in my head were spinning.

Around the time of the conference, indictments hit Noriega—and then the front page of every major newspaper. The story led every national news broadcast, and from behind the scenes I knew that Massachusetts senator John Kerry's subcommittee on terrorism, narcotics, and international operations was homing in on the BCCI–Noriega connection.

Less than two weeks after Noriega's indictment, I walked through the large glass doors at BCCI Miami with a smile and another red rose for the receptionist. Bilgrami was always on edge, but, as he processed paperwork routing $1.2 million through Geneva to Panama, he revealed that he was feeling more skittish than ever. He said that the U.S. was pushing European countries to sign amended mutual legal assistance treaties that could lead to sharing bank information from countries like Luxembourg and Lichtenstein that otherwise had strict bank-secrecy laws.

I laughed nervously. "Boy, if those two havens are affected, I would be just shocked. There would be no place left to go. Where would you—what would we do?"

Bilgrami looked at me as though I were a child. He always coughed up more when I played the naive student to his experienced professor. "Unless we go to the Far East—Hong Kong and Bahrain would be sort of... Bahrain is also pretty safe, I would think.... Bahrain, they're good, you know. One thing: the laws are very simple, and there's no laws there basically. I mean, it's a good center."

Good. If he thought I was a narc, he wouldn't suggest that he hide my funds in safer places.

Pushing business out of Panama minimized future BCCI problems there. Influenced by its Saudi ownership, BCCI had substantial branches throughout the Middle East, including the micro-kingdom of Bahrain, nestled between Saudi Arabia and Qatar. I wondered how many other clients moving tens of millions in hot money were getting the same pitch to move their operations to the Middle East.

Then Bilgrami asked me to limit my borrowing of funds in Panama to $9 million at a time because, when my loans went over that amount, "the board will ask all kinds of funny questions... which you don't have any answers for." He also addressed the topic of my clients. "We are not interested in your clients. You are the one dealing with them, so we're doing everything according to the book, as you might say.... It is clear-cut, defined policy of the bank, like all other banks, to keep an arm's length from these transactions."

And then he backed himself into admitting that he knew my clients' funds came from drug sales. "It's very clear," he said. "I mean, the law in the States is that if you're taking cash from a, from an individual, any of your offices... then you have to advise. You have to advise the authorities immediately. Even if it's five thousand, if you have any inkling that the money is somewhat, uh, not clear."

Apparently he was having doubts and hedging his bets with me. I had to put him at ease. "As far as I'm concerned, as far as you gentlemen are concerned, as far as the bank is concerned, you're dealing with me, and that's the end of the line. But I have a lot of responsibilities to some people who aren't as reasonable.... And so when you say some of the things... it scares the hell out of me."

"I, I have to, I have to be, uh, uh," Bilgrami nervously explained himself. "You see, uh, you, later on when we get to know each other better... I have to, uh, also protect the interest, the interests of the institution. And for various reasons we have to be very careful of what we commit and what we say."

He admitted, though, that he was only trying to cover his tracks, so I squinted, offered a small smile, and nodded my head while he went on. "Now, as time goes by, and once we are really in tune, you have enough confidence in us and we have in you, you will have found a fine situation. This be different... But I, I have to, I have to protect the institution at all times, and this is... and, uh, that's what I'm doing."

"I understand." I nodded and smiled. "Well, then I feel better. No, that's all that needs to be said."

Bilgrami laughed. "Very good."

A week later in Miami, Awan helped me bounce another $750,000 from the U.S. through Geneva to Panama, but details needed to change, he said. "For the next few weeks we'd like to slow down a little, if that's all right with you."

Because of substantial loans from the Panama branch, the bank's board had a policy of reviewing such account relationships before authorizing additional loans there. To circumvent that policy, Awan suggested he structure future transactions through BCCI Paris. He knew the top officers in Paris well, and besides, France maintained bank secrecy laws unaffected by the upcoming EEC treaty. Plausible, but something else had to be making him and Bilgrami so tense.

I told Awan that I read between the lines of my last conversation with Bilgrami, and it was apparent that "it would be best for us" — my Colombian clients and me — "to get into a posture of allowing some funds to sit for a period of time with you, so that we aren't dealing with a situation as we have it right now."

"That's exactly right," he said.

In other words, BCCI didn't mind taking millions in dope money as long as I increased the bank's balance sheet and left substantial deposits in their vaults. Easier said than done, though. I was lobbying with Mora to convince the cartel to leave some of their money on deposit, but I couldn't count on that. I'd have to pressure Customs to get authorization for government funds for deposit. If that didn't happen soon, Awan and Bilgrami might discount me. Real international money launderers have a massive bankroll and can accommodate such a request easily, and they know how one hand washes the other. I needed to play that game, especially since the heat was on BCCI for their escapades in Panama.

Awan explained why things were particularly difficult. "You may have been reading the press about this Noriega indictment. And for some reason, BCCI has been named as one of the banks which were doing all sorts of things.... We're in good company because we're named along with Bank of America, Citibank, Chase...you know, the big boys." Given these events, he and Bilgrami thought they "might be asked more questions than usual...that we might slow down for the next couple of months. Let the dust die down a little bit."

I agreed, and he again suggested Europe. "If you happen to be in Paris, let me know. I'd like you to meet some of our people there, because, if you start doing any business from there, their general manager and the manager of the branch, they're both very good friends of mine.... The general manager is an ex-boss of mine, but he's, you know, he's a laid-back sort of person."

I couldn't satisfy Awan with deposits, so I offered him the only other thing I had: my understanding of the game. "All I want to do is see to it that I enhance the clear understanding of the perfectly normal business needs for the matters that we are handling, and therefore I will do whatever it is that I need to do in order to assist you in that regard."

"Thank you very much." Awan smiled. "I appreciate that."

Each time I demonstrated loyalty to BCCI, he rewarded me with new information about the bank's role in the underworld. "One can foresee especially if the bank's name is summonsed. One could foresee a subpoena...you know, and I'm being hauled up before the Congress or before a grand jury, and this, we don't want that to happen." He had just been in New York and was trying to put out a fire related to a subpoena for records of transactions carried out by BCCI Monte Carlo for Adnan Khashoggi, a billionaire Saudi arms dealer allegedly involved with Oliver North in the Iran-Contra affair. BCCI Monte Carlo had wire transferred $100,000 for Khashoggi, but they were attempting to spin the transaction as business as usual.

At the end of the meeting, Awan and I agreed to slow down the pace of our transactions; I would bring no more than $2 million per month to him for Panama accounts controlled by my clients in Medellín. I had to produce stable, long-term deposits before BCCI provided me with the first-class treatment normally offered to the underworld.

On a quick side trip to Philly, after leaving Miami, I called Steve Cook, my supervisor. "Like I told everyone during our last weekly meeting, we need to get D.C. to loosen the purse strings. We need $5 million we can offer BCCI to be placed in safe interest-bearing accounts. That's what they want. Their quid pro quo to launder money is deposits. I never wanted headquarters running this case, but as long as they're now supposedly leading this operation, they need to do the right thing. Between you and Mark [Jackowski], you guys should be able to convince Tischler to sign off on this, and she has friends in D.C. who can make it happen. If we can get this money, the doors at BCCI will open, and we'll get a front-row seat to watch what they do for people like Noriega."

I paused to let the name sink in.

"Besides this $5 million, there are a few other things that would really help. I've been spending a lot of time in Miami, and the cost of hotels is more than it would be for a high-end rental. I'd like the okay to rent something on Key Biscayne so we can wire the house and get good-quality recordings of discussions with the bankers—Alcaíno and anyone else who comes through Miami.

"The other thing that would help a lot is some expensive jewelry. Alcaíno is a jeweler. Wearing a big-ticket watch and ring would go a long way. I understand there's a men's five-carat diamond ring and a Rolex President that were seized, and they're just sitting in our evidence vault. Would you work things out so I can use that from now until the end of the operation?"

Steve took a long hard drag on his cigarette. "I hear you. I'll get Ladow"—Joe Ladow, the assistant special agent in charge in Tampa—"on board. We've already got the support from the regional office in Miami. Between them, me, Ladow, and Jackowski, we'll get it done. But you need to slow your ass down, Mazur. You're not making a lot of friends in the front office."

"I never wanted to be one of them anyway. This case is more

important than a career. As long as friends like you watch my back between now and October, I'll deal with payback later."

As soon as I got back to Tampa, Alcaíno called to say he was coming to Miami and wanted to get together. I hopped a flight, rented a Jaguar, and met with Kathy Ertz and the Miami coordinating agent, Matt Etre. I had discouraged Matt from surveilling our targets when I met with them in the area, but this was an exception. Alcaíno was flying from New York with a contact from Argentina who was going to catch a flight back to Buenos Aires. It was a perfect chance to identify one of Alcaíno's South American connections.

Alcaíno had told me he would be staying at the Hilton Hotel near the airport and to meet him there at 10:30 P.M. Kathy and I arrived, but there was no sign of him. I called Joaquín Casals, Alcaíno's right hand, who confirmed Alcaíno was staying at the Hilton. A tense half hour later, Alcaíno called to say he was at the Marriott Miami Airport because the Hilton didn't have any rooms.

Something was up.

Before Kathy and I got back in the car, I asked the Hilton receptionist if they were booked up.

"No, sir, we have plenty of rooms this evening."

Something's definitely up.

"Okay," I whispered to Kathy, "Alcaíno just lied to us. There could be a reason he wanted us to hang out in this lobby for a half hour. We're headed to the Marriott to meet him. I'll get word to Matt where we're going, but we may be on our own. Matt and the other guys may still be at the airport trying to identify Alcaíno's friend flying to Argentina."

At the Marriott, Alcaíno was waiting outside, all smiles. Every detail, every hair on his head was perfectly in place. You'd never think he had just flown down virtually the whole eastern seaboard. After a warm welcome, I excused myself to make a quick call and asked him to keep Kathy company. At a lobby pay phone, I told Matt where we were, and, by the time I rejoined Alcaíno and Kathy, surveillance had us in their sights.

We hit one of Alcaíno's favorite spots, Cats nightclub at the Mayfair in Coconut Grove. Kathy got him on the dance floor and talked his ear off, showering him with compliments that pandered to his intelligence and wit. Business would come the following day when I pressed him to allow me to manage some of his fortune.

We partied until 3 A.M., then worked our way back to Alcaíno's hotel. Just before parting, I pulled him aside. "Roberto, I value your friendship and wisdom. I'd like to talk privately with you tomorrow about something very important to me. I appreciate our business, but your friends down south are putting me at risk by asking me only to move money from here to their accounts. I know you can help to keep this thing going. Right now I need more from you than promises."

"Don't be so serious, Bob." He smiled. "You have much to be happy about. You have a beautiful and cordial wife and a wonderful future with us. Meet me here tomorrow morning by ten, and I'll bring good news that will have you smiling again."

There was that unorthodox definition of "wife" again.

The next morning, at a palm tree–shaded table by the pool — recorder rolling — I gave him an accounting of the money I had laundered for him during the last month.

"Roberto, I'd definitely like to get more of your business.... It doesn't take a rocket scientist to figure out we did a million dollars last month, divide that by 12.5 per unit" — $12,500 per kilo of coke — "that's only eighty [kilos], and I know that's not where you're coming from....

"Number two, I absolutely have *got* to do something to bring back into balance the requirements that have been put on me by some of my friends, one of the more important banks that I'm dealing with, and so I look to you for some action in the way of doing something on an investment — and not just talking about doing it.... Why don't you leave 20 percent of this money to sit for six months, and then we'll continue to take care of you. Otherwise, I don't know. We're gonna have to close the volume down a little bit."

For a few seconds, Alcaíno stared away, his head tilted. He was weighing my request. "Okay. Let's say, let's start doing — whatever money that I give you, you can put 10 percent aside for that." He would have gone for a higher percentage, he said, but he had $5.7 million of cocaine hidden in Spain because someone in that operation had been arrested, and no one knew if the worker was talking. Even though he had eager buyers, he couldn't risk moving it. "You have to be very careful. Europe is very delicate. That's why the money's better there.... Here it's twelve right now" — the wholesale price in thousands of dollars per kilo. "It's twenty-seven in Europe."

Then more good news. Alcaíno was dumping a lot of his drug money into an apartment project in downtown L.A., and he had decided to funnel all of it through me. He would immediately give me $600,000 to put in certificates of deposit as collateral for a loan to finance the work, with more to follow, as well as another half million to disguise as a construction loan for improvements on his Pasadena Hills home.

And then even more good news. He was funneling money into a professional-boxing promotion company with one of his friends, Tuto Zabala, and he needed some of the money laundered so he could use it safely to promote an upcoming world championship fight.

I asked how he got into the fight business with Zabala.

"All the time I'm thinking crazy things in my mind, you know. The criminal mind never stops." We both laughed, and he continued. "It's very difficult to lose money, because the gate is not that important anymore. TV and tape and closed circuit are important.... They have a convention center here that seats twelve thousand. That's around a hundred and some thousand dollars. So part of the expense goes to the theater, and that's your profit structure right there." It also gave him legitimate cover to travel to Colombia.

Then he asked me to talk to my family to see how much money we could make fixing a championship fight. He had bought my cover — completely. The work of courting him had paid off, and now, like Mora, he would become an unwitting pawn delivering us deeper inside the cartel.

As we talked about the fight, Alcaíno motioned a man to join us. "Tuto, I'd like you to meet my good friend Bob Musella. Bob, this is Tuto Zabala."

A fifty-year-old Cuban exile, Zabala had helped found Alpha 66, the Cuban revolutionary group bent on overthrowing Castro. Zabala fled in August 1961 after ten hard days of interrogation by Castro's security force. He looked like any other hard-working blue-collar Cuban in Miami, except he wore a big gold chain studded with large diamond letters spelling TUTO, and an injury had caused his right eye to drift permanently to the right. After escaping, he'd lived in Jamaica and Puerto Rico, but now promoted fights and distributed cocaine for Alcaíno in Miami — five to twenty kilos at a time to Cuban buyers in Chicago who ran a small grocery-store chain.

The super flyweight world-title fight between Colombian-based world champion Sugar Rojas and Mexican champion Gil Roman was scheduled in Miami for April 8, and Alcaíno wanted me, Emir, and our guests ringside with him. Another chance to build relationships with yet more people in the U.S. who worked with him and the cartel.

Alcaíno had delivered. I was no longer simply passing money through accounts for a fee. He'd greenlighted me to act as his bank, to manage some of his investments, and to pump dirty money into his businesses. When the operation ended, everything he owned would be seized — and all of that from *one* meeting. No need to push him more, especially with Zabala at the table. I thanked Alcaíno for his help, and we agreed to meet in L.A. in two weeks when he next returned from Medellín.

On the same day I met Alcaíno at the Marriott, the Miami and L.A. offices started closing in on couriers who had delivered cash to our undercover agents previously. After couriers were identified dropping money shipments to our agents and a week to ten days had passed, they were fair game as long as they weren't scheduled to drop to us again. So surveillance teams followed them, and, when it appeared that they might be transporting, marked police units working with us made what looked like routine traffic stops.

The bagmen invariably betrayed their nervousness, which gave cops probable cause, allowing them to ask for consent to search the vehicles. The couriers almost always complied, but then denied knowing the money was in the car or who owned it. The cops seized the money and usually let the couriers go. As long as no one filed search-warrant affidavits that could expose our operation, no one else could connect me to the seizures.

No one ever came forward to claim the cash, which then automatically forfeited into the police department's coffers, and which they used to buy cars or equipment. In cop talk, this procedure was called "a rip." At a series of staged traffic stops, about a million dollars of cartel money and thirteen kilos of cocaine were "ripped" in a week.

At the same time the rips were going down, the U.S. government froze all Panamanian government accounts in the States in an effort to pressure Noriega. Because Panama's central bank could no longer obtain U.S. dollars, it closed all of its branches until further notice. Which left $750,000 of Don Chepe's money frozen in my Panamanian account. Don Chepe didn't care why, though. Word quickly came through Gonzalo that I had to find a way to get Don Chepe his money soon — or else. If anyone could release the money and reformulate my system around Panama, it was Amjad Awan.

I called him at the bank, but he wasn't there. Minutes later, he called me with an explanation that he was keeping a low profile because the feds might be monitoring his movements and conversations there. If I wanted to talk business, he invited Kathy and me to his home in Coconut Grove for dinner, after which we could talk.

Awan lived in a beautiful ranch-style house in Coconut Grove, on several acres blanketed by the shade of huge banyan trees. Meticulously kept, the grounds included a full tennis court and pool. He and his wife, Sheereen Asghar-Khan, greeted us with polite smiles. Though technically Muslim, neither of them abstained from alcohol. Awan preferred Johnnie Walker Black on the rocks, but Kathy wisely decided on bringing a bottle of Perrier-Jouet champagne for dinner.

The smell of aromatic spices filled the house with warmth. Sheereen had prepared a rich and savory traditional Pakistani curried chicken dinner. Her humble grace offered no clue that her father had once commanded Pakistan's air force and was now a respected politician. Awan's father, Ayub Awan, former head of the Pakistani police and director of the ISI, Pakistan's CIA, had semi-arranged the match.

Awan's roots in Pakistani Kashmir made clear why he was one of just a few bank officers managing CIA accounts that fed money to Afghan freedom fighters, many of whom later joined the Taliban and Al Qaeda.

Before dinner, we all visited their rec room, which displayed much of Awan's memorabilia, including an autographed, framed picture of Noriega in dress whites. The picture bore an inscription written when the two men had been in Geneva: *A mi amigo Awan con gran aprecio a todo su familia* — "To my friend Awan with great appreciation to all your family."

At dinner, the Awans asked endless questions about our families, my business interests, my employment history, and my travel. He was no doubt assessing just how plausible his and the bank's deniability would be. As often as we could, Kathy and I shifted the conversation to our own curiosity about Awan's prior service with BCCI in Pakistan, Colombia, Panama, and Washington.

After dinner, he and I excused ourselves for a leisurely stroll around the gardens — my chance to elicit help getting Don Chepe's money out of Panama and finding an alternative country. As we walked toward the tennis court, I flipped the remote power switch in my pocket that powered the mic on my chest and the recorder taped to my inner thigh. Awan told me that nothing could be done at the moment about the $750,000 frozen in Panama. He told me to buy time until banking resumed, perhaps a week. It wouldn't be long before Don Chepe came calling, though.

"Tell me something," Awan said, after we debated the merits of other havens. "Where is the cash?"

"Here in the States," I said. "Detroit, Houston, New York."

Awan thought for a moment. "Can it be transported?"

I told him planes owned by our air charter service could move it, yes.

He offered a solution. "If the cash can be delivered, say, to Uruguay...and if there's a general need for cash in Uruguay, which I believe there is...A lot of dollar notes are smuggled from Uruguay into both Paraguay and Brazil because people like to buy dollar currency over there. If we could get the cash transported over there and give you credit in whichever place you want it...because all the consumer items which come into Brazil are paid for with dollar notes in cash."

It was an amazing proposal. The bank would accept planeloads of smuggled cash in South America and exchange it for credits to accounts throughout the world, leaving no link whatsoever between the cash itself and the increased bank balances. But the Uruguayan approvals our office needed would prove far too risky. A great idea, but only for a bona fide criminal. I'd have to find a good reason to decline later.

Since Awan seemed comfortable talking about the dirty side of business, I told him that some of my Colombian clients wanted me to fly planeloads of U.S. currency to them because it "would move right on to Bolivia and other areas because that's where the labs are" — the labs that processed bulk shipments of coke.

Awan didn't so much as blink. He simply offered other banking alternatives to Panama, then said, "Let me give this a little bit of thought and see how I can find out and meet in our various locations, what we can do."

Sheereen opened the door and shouted to us, "Want some green tea or coffee?" We'd run out of time to talk and ended the evening with, tea, coffee, thanks, and plans for Awan and me to meet again shortly.

The next day Steve Cook informed me that Treasury had approved our request for $5 million to place on deposit with BCCI. It was bait I couldn't wait to throw to Awan and Bilgrami.

The day after that, I met Awan for late morning coffee at the

Grand Bay Hotel in Coconut Grove. He had spent the prior evening with the Pakistani ambassador and friends, who had just left for Jamaica. I had his full attention, but he needed to leave for Colombia to reassure his customers about Panama.

"What I would like to suggest," I said, "is that in order for you to get a little bit of a better feel for me, at a time that you're going to go to New York, if there's going to be one in the near future, or if not, I've got a corporate jet which we could use, and it'll cut down time substantially. But maybe if... One, I'd like to invite you to my home for dinner one evening. And then I thought that we might go... if we can complete it in one day, take a quick ride up to New York, and I'd like to introduce you to some of the other people affiliated with the firm."

Awan smiled. "I'd very much like that."

Then the good news. "I'm going to shift some of my personal savings over to some matters with you all, and so therefore I'd say sometime within the next several weeks I'll get with you on the placement of about $2 million, just for me in a, um, anything — a year, whatever it is. It doesn't matter to me. I just think I need to show some good faith here."

Awan almost jumped at the prospect. "Fine. And where would you like that placed?" We decided that the secrecy of BCCI Paris was best and agreed to work out the details as soon as I made funds available.

I told Awan that my Colombian clients had large shipments of U.S. currency backed up in several U.S. cities as well as in Madrid, Paris, and Rome and asked him if BCCI had resources to help me get the cash into the banking system. He asked for time to discuss the issue with colleagues and promised to get back to me with a proposal.

Then I went over my itinerary with him. I was headed to L.A. to meet the client wanting to provide a secret $750,000 deposit as collateral for a construction loan in a like amount. That same client also wanted a similar arrangement for a $500,000 home improvement loan. Then off to San José to meet the clients with the backed-up cash.

Awan liked the concept of the construction loans and asked that I visit Iqbal Ashraf, manager of BCCI L.A. Ashraf could help with those L.A.–based loans and — I read between the lines — was part of the bank's "inner team."

A few days later in Tampa, ten of the personnel and I gathered. I briefed them on what had happened and outlined expectations for upcoming encounters, and they in turn briefed me on what was happening in other cities.

Emir had heard that, the next time the tractor trailer arrived in Detroit, the Detroit office planned to file federal affidavits to execute search warrants for money and cocaine at the Giraldo brothers' home and storage facility. Which totally violated the promises the Detroit agents had made to us when we invited them into our operation. There was no reason they couldn't proceed the same way the Miami and L.A. offices did: let state or local cops orchestrate an accidental find. Detroit was looking for statistics and promotions. Yet another case of being able to trust the targets more than our own people. And, according to Steve, Tischler supported Detroit's approach.

"Hasn't anyone thought this out?" I fumed. "If they file those affidavits, those documents are going to spell out everything Emir and I have done. Even if the affidavits are sealed, you know that simply means that they are placed in a sealed envelope in the office of the judge's clerk. The organizations we're dealing with buy *presidents of countries*. A clerk wouldn't be a challenge. Shit like this is going to get us killed!"

I suggested we force a plan to require surveillance of the semi in Miami, and, when it started moving north, our office could coordinate with highway patrol and agricultural inspectors to orchestrate an accidental discovery of the cocaine at an inspection station near the Florida–Georgia border.

Mark supported our counterapproach, but we had to get the ball rolling with a written request from our office.

"Steve, I have no bridges to worry about burning," I said. "I'll be the bad guy for the front office and write the memo to you. Then you'll have to pass it up the chain and they'll have to deal with it. I can lay out why Detroit's plan will undermine the entire operation."

I churned out the memo that night and had it on Steve's desk the next day. As it worked its way up command, Steve told me that, though he didn't mind, Tischler didn't like my habit of putting things on paper. Probably made it harder for her to lie about what had actually happened. Customs and Justice staff in D.C. eventually refereed the argument between Tampa and Detroit, but I couldn't wait for the bureaucrats to make a decision.

It was time to hit L.A.

10

LOS DUROS AND LOS ANGELES

Los Angeles International Airport, California
March 17, 1988

ALCAÍNO WAS WAITING FOR US as we descended the escalators at LAX.
"Bob and Kathy, it is so wonderful to see you. My car is just outside."

We collected our bags and met him beside his vintage black
Rolls-Royce Silver Shadow, of which he was visibly proud. He drove
us to a local restaurant where his wife, Gloria, joined us. At the
end of the meal, he grandly announced, "Bob, please take Gloria's
Porsche. You can use it as long as you're in town. Tomorrow morning we'd like you to join us at Tiffarri Jewelers, our jewelry store
downtown, where we can talk and look over some of my inventory.
If you're up for it, we can go out to dinner tomorrow evening. The
following day I'll show you around town, and then we'll have dinner
at our home."

He was working hard to impress us.

Kathy thanked the Alcaínos for their kindness, adding, "I
can't wait to see the rings at your store. Bob needs to come through
on his promise of a special gift I can cherish for life to remember
this trip. Something tells me that gift is somewhere in your jewelry
store."

Alcaíno let loose a big belly laugh. "Don't worry, sweetheart. I
promise you we have whatever your heart desires!"

Perhaps, but why would he offer us his Porsche? As we

approached the car, I whispered to Kathy, "Don't talk business in this car. It could be a trap."

As we drove to the hotel, Kathy tossed the car but couldn't find anything. We assumed it was bugged anyway.

The next day, on the eleventh floor of an office building on South Hill Street in downtown L.A. we visited Alcaíno's private and exclusive jewelry store. The Tiffarri Jewelers suite sported thick bullet-proof glass and high-tech security. Very few customers visited while we were there, so we had no problem having an extended meeting, all caught, of course, by the recorder in my briefcase.

Alcaíno wanted me to set up a dummy loan from my mortgage company to Antilles Promotions, the company he and Zabala were using to promote the championship fight in Miami. I had him execute a lien on his multimillion-dollar home as fake collateral, which justified moving $50,000 of his drug money from my mortgage business to his promotion company.

Next order of business was creating corporations, phony loan documents, and fake service agreements to hide Alcaíno's initial half million in the apartment project in downtown L.A. He happily gave me full authority to structure the deal to hide his true ownership.

Before lunch, Alcaíno showed Kathy some diamonds and an assortment of rings, encouraging her to go big. He beamed as he quietly told me he would have the ring sized and the diamond mounted within two days so I could present it to her during dinner at his home.

At lunch, I leaned into Alcaíno's ear. "Roberto, what do I owe you for the ring?"

"Nothing, my friend," he said. "It's my pleasure to bring happiness to you and your lovely bride. This engagement ring is my gift to you."

Back at the hotel, I hit the pay phones, briefed the office, and wrote some notes on critical dates, times, and statements, which I then hid in the false compartment of my briefcase. Those notes became the basis of the memos I would write in Florida about the events of the trip.

A seven-mile jog and some quick sightseeing filled the rest of the day until it was time to get ready for the Alcaínos again. We had dinner, and then Alcaíno insisted we move to a local club, where, on the dance floor, Kathy and I sank compliments and lies into the ears of our dance partners. Easy enough, you might think, but no. The rush of acting, the thrill of riding the cutting edge of crime, eventually numbs your senses, and years of this wear you down because the abnormal environment begins to normalize. You live by your lies. Outwardly at ease, you're burning inside, checking and double-checking whether you've stumbled by offering any sign of your true identity. It's almost easier to surrender to your role, but you can't for even a second because you must also act as a minesweeper, gathering every hint of crime around you while pretending to enjoy the high life.

"I'm going to introduce you to an important friend of mine from Medellín," Alcaíno said in a low voice the next day over lunch. "His wife is the niece of one of *los duros*. I think you'll find him to be very...interesting."

A major player, then. Good.

After lunch Alcaíno suggested the ladies go on a shopping spree while he and I visited a friend — who turned out to be his tailor.

"I want to give you a few pointers," he said. "Your attire is fine, but you should step it up a little. Let's go in this building here, and I'll introduce you to a friend of mine who will fit you nicely in a couple of new suits."

I'd thought the thousands I'd spent out of pocket had dressed me for the big leagues. Apparently not. With Alcaíno's help, I picked out two suits, which the tailor pinned and marked, as Alcaíno proclaimed, "Those look perfect. I'll have someone come by and pick these up for you tomorrow. These have style and look more Miami Beach than Wall Street."

We rejoined the ladies to find that, similarly, Gloria had picked out a number of items for Kathy — but my mind was already training on the evening's meeting. The gift from Alcaíno I appreciated most was the chance to meet another player working with the cartel.

Before dark, Kathy and I put Alcaíno's Porsche through its paces in the Pasadena Hills along Putney Road, a narrow, winding street lined with mansions. As we approached the electric gate at the top of Alcaíno's driveway, it slowly opened and gave us access to a steep hundred-foot path that sloped down to a large fountain in front of their magnificent home. Two Rolls-Royce sedans, a Mercedes two-door sports coupe, and various other cars sat in the driveway. A separate building housed his servants, and a detached garage had become his office. As we got out of the Porsche, two huge Doberman Pinschers dashed toward us. Alcaíno called out, and they stopped cold in their tracks.

"Oh, don't worry," he said, noticing our alarm. "They are harmless."

Yeah, as long as you tell them to be. Otherwise, they'd eat us alive in minutes.

"Bob, this is my very good friend Juan Tobón. He is visiting with us but also has a home in Miami. He is from Medellín." Alcaíno also introduced us to his two teenage daughters, Paola and Claudia, as well as his maid and another servant.

Inside his home — easily 4,300 square feet — Gloria rushed to greet us. "Oh, Kathy, it is wonderful to see you again, and, Bob, thank you for sharing this evening with us."

The Alcaíno home was exquisitely decorated in an oriental theme. Four large jade carvings sat on wooden stands, each more than two feet long. Ivory sculptures filled the house, and on the walls I noticed a Chagall painting and a Miró etching. The back of the house, a sheer wall of glass, faced a huge stone deck and a pool that perched on a hill overlooking the Rose Bowl.

But the architectural detail that struck me most in the home was a four-foot-high safe hidden in the closet of the master bedroom. When the day came for our agents to search the house, that vault would no doubt prove a gold mine.

"I'm going to need your help," Alcaíno confided, "to create a half-million-dollar loan that I can use as an excuse for where I will get the money to renovate this house. I'd like to build an elevated tennis court, underground parking garage, and an additional 4,200 square feet of living space. I can give you the cash to offset that 'loan' soon. Then you can draw up the papers and push the money through your mortgage company."

"*Un pedazo de torta*," I said—piece of cake.

We settled down in the living room to enjoy some fine wine from Chile and hors d'oeuvres. Then to the dining room where we all enjoyed a lavish seven-course meal.

Tobón proudly proclaimed throughout dinner that he ardently believed in Santería, the Afro-Cuban religion born in the Caribbean when African slaves brought to the West Indies were exposed to Catholicism in Cuba. This dark religion thrives in south Florida among many of the men in the drug trade. Until he professed his devotion to Santería, it didn't occur to me that the strange and obvious bulge in Tobón's sock was a charm comprised of herbs, dead animal parts, and other ritual ingredients. Kathy's obsession with palm reading came in handy, and she put it to good use entertaining the room.

Tobón also didn't hide his hatred for *los feos*, who he believed had violated his rights when they seized his twin-engine plane filled with cocaine in Texas and a jet in California bought with $750,000 in cash.

After dinner, Alcaíno, Tobón and I moved to the deck overlooking the valley that cradled the Rose Bowl, Brookside Golf Course, and Foothill Freeway. Under this starlit night, Tobón and Alcaíno opened up about the state of the drug trade.

"Noriega should be shitting in his pants," Alcaíno said. "Jorge Ochoa" —brother of Alcaíno's partner Fabio Ochoa— "sent a mini coffin to Noriega last week that contained a note warning him that he would be able to use the coffin if any of Jorge's money was lost in Panama. The note was signed 'The Ochoa Family.'"

The conversation also revealed, quite plainly, that Tobón's wife,

Clara, was the niece of José Rodríguez Gacha, "El Mexicano," one of the most notorious members of the Medellín cartel.

When talk drifted to credibility, Tobón was quick to challenge mine. "Bob, I own a two-hundred-acre mountaintop ranch in Medellín. We raise horses and cattle. I'd very much like to invite you and your lovely wife to join us at the ranch so you can personally see the beauty of Colombia."

"Let me tell you," Alcaíno chimed in, "that it would make all of us much more at ease if you and your family would enjoy some time with us in Colombia. You know, the men who refuse to come are most often *los feos*. Joining us down there would put everyone at ease and open your business to heights you've never imagined."

A tight spot, but I came prepared.

"Roberto, I love you like a father, so I'll confess like a son: Everything I do is done to protect my family. This business I have with you is a bonus. My core responsibility is to those here that I have served for years. Traveling to Colombia will raise flags with *los feos* and that will jeopardize the responsibility I have to my people. We need to build a sound business reason for my travel there. If I'm managing investments for businessmen in Colombia I have that cover. Until your people show me good faith by letting me manage some of their investments, they'll have to settle for visiting me in a normal vacation spot like San José. I'll be there in a week to meet with Gonzalo and clients from Medellín. Anyone you recommend is welcome to meet me there."

"I understand entirely," Alcaíno fired back, "but on the Colombian side we have everything taken care of. We have most everyone in our pocket. One of my friends, Alejandro, had his bodyguards assassinate the Justice minister in Colombia. Even though his men were caught by the Colombian army with five machine guns, he simply paid them one million dollars, and everything was totally forgotten. We have the power. Juan [Tobón] and I own a resort in Medellín known as San Jéronimo. This place is used for high-level meetings and *los duros* feel safe meeting there. You should come there and I'll arrange for you to meet the people who run everything."

It was the invitation I'd been waiting for, but there was no way Customs would let me accept. Before I could reply, Gloria and Kathy walked onto the rear deck of the house and joined our conversation. As they approached, Alcaíno slipped me an envelope that contained the engagement ring. I proposed, gave Kathy the ring, and everyone bought it. Which gave me the benefit of the doubt on future occasions when Alcaíno might otherwise wonder whether I was one of *los feos.*

Then he started to grandstand. "Bob and Kathy, I would like to invite you to join us in Miami on April eighth when we can all attend the world championship fight I'm promoting. Bob, what can we do special to celebrate this event?"

He wanted something special. We were making millions from the operation, so it made sense to throw $10,000 or so of our profits at Roberto if it got him to bring along his friends in the drug business.

"It would be my pleasure," I announced, "to host a party on the day of the fight for you and twenty-five of your guests. And the night before the fight, I would be honored if you and your friends accompanied me and Kathy to a dinner party in Miami."

That announcement loosened up Tobón, who asked me, "When will you be back in Miami?" and invited me to join him there to meet a friend of his. I wasn't sure where this was going, but I agreed.

A little before midnight, the party broke up. It had been a productive night. Back at the hotel, it was too late to call the East Coast, so for an hour I wrote out notes about the evening's conversations, hid them in my briefcase, and crashed.

The next morning Alcaíno called to say how much he enjoyed his time with us and how enthralled he was with Kathy. "We love her, and we respect her very much.... You know how we are, you know us all the way now."

Before we left L.A., I called Awan's friend, Iqbal Ashraf, manager of BCCI L.A. We met in an airport lounge for a quick meeting before I flew back to Tampa. It was immediately clear why he and Awan got along so well. They looked and acted like twins.

I explained to Ashraf the nature of the transactions I had conducted through the other BCCI branches and that I understood he could help by arranging deposits of funds outside the U.S. used secretly as collateral for loans, the proceeds of which could be made available through his branch. I indicated that my clients were Colombians with large cash-generating businesses in the U.S. and that my clients included Jorge Ochoa, who had just sent a small coffin to Noriega with a threatening note.

Ashraf couldn't have cared less. He simply replied that he hoped I would arrange for my clients' funds, after passing through offshore BCCI branches, to be deposited at his branch in L.A. He was ready to help me hide the funds in haven countries, use it as secret security for offshore loans, and bring it back to L.A. where his branch could manage the funds. All smiles, he urged me to get in touch as soon as I was ready.

Detroit's plan to file federal affidavits to execute search warrants against the Giraldos had been shut down, L.A. had been a roaring success, and now it was time to make some new friends in the cartel.

11

LURING THEM IN

THERE WAS ENDLESS CHAMPAGNE for everyone on Lacsa, Costa Rica's national carrier. Emir and I had planned our strategy before we left Florida, but as we flew over the Gulf of Mexico we quietly went over it again.

"You have Gonzalo wrapped around your little finger," I said. "He thinks you're more loyal to him than me, so let's play that up. If our negotiations with Ospiña get bogged down, we'll take a break, and I'll find an excuse to get away from you guys. While I'm gone, you can let Gonzalo cry on your shoulder and see if you can get some inside information from him that will help. I have to play the hard line. I'm sure they have other sources to do what we do, but with Panama frozen we should look like a good alternative.

"We need two things from this trip. We've got to get these guys to let us hold more of their money for a longer period of time. That will help us seize more money at the end of the case. Besides, that's what the boys at BCCI want. They're hungry for deposits. The other thing we need is to get Ospiña to help us lure his bosses to a meeting in Europe. We've got to get them on tape."

"Ospiña's bosses will try to leave as little money with you as possible," Emir said. "They're going to fight this, but we'll give it a try. The timing is right because Panama is a mess, so maybe you've got a long shot. I hope you brought your wading boots, brother, because you're going to have to throw so much bullshit at them that the floor will be a foot deep in crap."

We laughed.

After getting through Costa Rican Customs, we had a quick meeting at an out-of-the-way restaurant with a Customs agent assigned to the U.S. embassy. The ground rules had been established in advance, but we went over them again.

No more personal contact with law enforcement while in San José unless we needed help. I would call either the local Customs agent or the Tampa office at least once every six hours. An agent in Tampa had my cell phone, so the plan was to call that to report. Nothing more than "Things are fine and going as planned. We're on schedule." Our hotel-room phones were surely tapped, the room was bugged, and the cartel would get access to our hotel records to see what numbers we called. If we needed to have a conversation outside our roles, that would take place somewhere we felt totally confident we couldn't be heard or monitored.

A fifteen-minute cab ride took us to the Herradura hotel and spa in Heredia. A luxury hotel, it had a casino, huge pool with a swim-up bar, fine dining, even a gym. Everything under one roof so we could avoid leaving the property and risk exposure to kidnapping or assassination. Mora, his wife, and Ospiña had already checked in, and after checking in ourselves, we met them near the blue tiled pool, sunning themselves in lounge chairs.

"Mr. Bob," Mora announced, "this is my good friend Javier Ospiña."

"*Buenos tardes, Javier,*" I said. "*Bienvenido a Costa Rica.*" Then to Emir, "Please tell Javier that we appreciate the sacrifice he has made to come all the way here to meet with us. Since we've all had a hard day traveling, let's relax and begin our discussions about business tomorrow."

We sipped piña coladas for two hours and studiously avoided talking business. Shoring up our cover, Mora yammered about the private jet, Rolls-Royce, brokerage firm, trips to the bank, our air charter service, the investment company—on and on. He was the best commercial for our money-laundering services that money almost didn't have to buy.

We met again in the lobby at 8 P.M. While I preferred to eat at the hotel, our Colombian friends wanted to dine at a nearby restaurant. After dinner, a cab took us to La Plaza Disco near downtown San José, an upscale hotspot for the young and beautiful. Emir and I took turns dancing with Lucy, and Ospiña found some women who caught his eye.

He looked like a *GQ* model — short but trim — and carried himself well. Before he became a money man for the cartel, he had worked at a bank in Medellín. Despite dancing with many of the women in the club, he kept coming back to me with a smile, occasionally running his hand up and down my back, feeling for a wire, and saying, "Mr. Bob, we are going to do the big business."

At 3 A.M., we headed back to the hotel, and I told Emir, "This guy must be paranoid. He came over to me at least four times at the disco and while talking to me ran his hand up and down my back looking for a wire."

"Get out of here," Emir said as though I were crazy. "You're exhausted. Go to bed."

First order of business the next afternoon after lunch was signing and giving to Mora forty-six blank checks drawn on the U.S. account of my investment company so he could pay our clients in Colombia while Panama was down.

"With Panama's present situation —" Ospiña started. "Panama has already definitely canceled."

I told him I could understand. "Roberto told me that Jorge Ochoa sent him a coffin."

"That is the system that he has in Colombia," Ospiña replied. "He always sends a coffin to any person that might have a problem with him."

And then Ospiña let me know we had competition from a bank in Panama. "Banco de Occidente, my boss has a deposit, a very high-level guarantee, in dollars deposited in Panama. It gave him an absolute security guarantee."

How could Banco de Occidente provide him with funds seized by Panama while BCCI couldn't? I offered all the excuses that Awan had given and gave the same assurances that Panama would normalize within a week. It satisfied him, but why was Banco de Occidente so cozy with the cartel? Interesting.

Ospiña had come to Costa Rica to hear about my laundering system and to determine its capacity. His boss had a lot of money that could be made available. If I could prove my organization could handle unlimited funds, his group would provide roughly $50 million per month in cash: $8 million in Houston, $10 million in L.A., $10 million in New York, and $20 million in Detroit.

My head spun. At the average wholesale price of $12,000 per kilo, those numbers meant that there were at least 4,166 kilos sold per month in those cities—which didn't even include Chicago, Miami, and Philadelphia. There were probably four or five other laundering organizations operating at the same time, taking in just as much cash. The numbers were terrifying.

During the meeting, Ospiña did something that, had his bosses known, would have gotten him killed. He used my hotel phone to contact Don Chepe—and with the assistance of the hotel operator, he announced the numbers with the recorder in my briefcase just a few feet away. A stupid move on his part, but now our office had four or five numbers in Medellín at which they could find Don Chepe, whom Ospiña finally reached.

"Tell him it is Javier. That I'm calling from up here...Javier *Mina*." Javier the Mine, Ospiña's nickname in Medellín because he handled so much of the cartel's wealth. "What's up, man?...Fine, man.... Listen, man, I'm here right now in a meeting. We're talking about those papers [code for currency].... Yes, about those books [a lot of money]. Yesterday there was a movement in Astros [Houston]. Do you know how much was the amount moved, transferred?...Fine. Of course there still hasn't been an accounting. Therefore I think that negotiation, with which papers are we going to deal with?...That's why, then let's say, that would be, well...in what city? Well, yes...but have you spoken to your father about which future alternative for the location could be more effective? [code for "Where do you want the money sent because of Panama?"] Then it would be best to already settle things here and then talk over there?"

Don Chepe wanted the money received in Houston to be wire-transferred to Uruguay, where he had accounts. Again, interesting. Uruguay had been Awan's first pick as an alternative to Panama, and after Operation Pisces some of his Colombian clients moved their accounts there, too. BCCI and the cartel were thinking alike. Not a coincidence.

I explained to Ospiña that the system our organization offered was unique. Many of our companies were sheltered under a Lichtenstein foundation that owned Luxembourg trusts, which in turn owned other offshore companies that held interests in the many cash-generating businesses managed by my investment company. Our seat on the New York Stock Exchange played a role, as did our mortgage companies. Our air charter service moved money from the U.S. to the Bahamas. I offered him everything I could about BCCI, which created accounts all over the globe that camouflaged the movement of funds that fed money to Ospiña's organization. It took hours.

After all that, Ospiña discussed a proposal to extend the turn-around time for laundering cash. That period would increase from ten days to thirty. Because we would receive no less than $12 million per month, the proposal provided us with a $12 million float the bank could enjoy at all times. This was the cartel's response to my request for holding 25 percent of each pickup for six months.

I told him it had nothing to do with the amount we held but everything to do with our handling funds in a manner that made us look like investment counselors. We couldn't look like a money-laundering machine pumping funds from the U.S. to other parts of the world. We needed to demonstrate, if challenged, that we actually managed money. The only way to do that was to cut 25 percent of the money aside for six months and put it in CDs or other conservative investments.

"I think I would like to take your offer," Ospiña responded, "but not with such a high percentage." He countered with a proposal that his boss allow us to hold 10 percent of each pickup for an investment. I came back with no less than 15.

Ospiña agreed that we were close to a deal, but rather than haggle he proposed a meeting in Paris within forty-five days when he and his bosses would sit down with me to hammer out details. Bullseye! I accepted and suggested we take a break. It was time to change the tape in the recorder.

When Emir stepped outside, Ospiña warned him, "Ever since Operation Pisces, my bosses have decided that they will kill anyone in the money business who steals from them." They weren't playing games.

Back in the room, we spent another two hours discussing how our organization could help the cartel. My mortgage company could finance the purchase of assets or investments in companies. Ospiña liked the idea that all the cartel had to do was give me the cash they would have used to buy a big-ticket item like a jet, and I would make it appear that my mortgage company had loaned them the money they used to buy it.

"Listen." Ospiña shook his head. "From our side, indeed, one can make a lot of commercial transactions through us, buying vehicles and airplanes. Just recently, two months ago, we bought four airplanes with cash. This group has about five or six helicopters. The maintenance and spare parts, the Mercedes vehicles bought in Miami... Man, that's very interesting. That's *very* interesting."

Ospiña also explained that commercial pilots based in Miami were smuggling huge amounts of currency both to Colombia and Uruguay. They were so good that the cartel used them exclusively to move all cash from Miami. In Philadelphia, Ospiña's people had no laundering sources, so they were transporting cash by car to Houston.

Before we ended our marathon discussions, Ospiña made one point very clear. Mora had staked more than his reputation on me and Emir. He had staked his life. If any problems or losses arose from my or Emir's involvement, Mora was dead. Mora knew the consequences long before Ospiña's blunt outlay. He had introduced us to Alcaíno, and now he had introduced us to Ospiña. If we ran or turned out to be *los feos*, he would be killed. As Ospiña made this speech, Mora seemed resigned that it was too late to turn back. In any case, he had all the faith in the world in Emir. After all, there was no way that Emilio Dominguez could be a fed.

After the meeting, Emir and I took a three-hour break before dinner with everyone at the hotel restaurant. On a walk, we stumbled across a cemetery — fitting because the silence and seclusion offered us a safe place to talk openly and because of Ospiña's sobering promise of death for Mora.

"These fuckers are for real," I said. "We're going places no undercover agents have ever been before. We went hunting for the biggest whale in the ocean, but now we've been swallowed, and we're inside it."

"I agree," Emir replied. "My gut tells me that Ospiña is not bullshitting us. This guy is for real, and we are in deep water. I just hope we get the support we need to get through this thing because these guys are not playing. If they ever figure out who we are, no one will ever find us. This shit is getting heavy."

"This meeting in Paris is huge. As we get closer, you'll be the only one Gonzalo will trust with the secret of who will attend from their side. Getting that information out of him in advance will be very important. Let's get back to the hotel and catch a few hours of peace before we're back onstage. I'll write up notes about what we discussed with Ospiña and hide them in my briefcase."

After writing, I barely had time to freshen up before dinner at the Herradura. Mora's mind was surely calculating the millions he was going to make now that he had helped us pass the credibility test with Ospiña. With the first bottle of wine, I offered a toast: "To the marriage of our alliance, loyalty, and friendship and the beginning of a new tomorrow for all of us. Cheers." The clanking of glasses grabbed the entire restaurant's attention, but we didn't care. It was time to enjoy ourselves.

After a magnificent meal, we made our way a second time to La Plaza Disco. Salsa and merengue blared deafeningly from huge speakers, and we had to scream to be heard. Lucy Mora entertained her husband, Emir, and me while Ospiña played the field with more moves than John Travolta. During a break, he came over to me and as he had the first time, he put his hand on my shoulder, then ran it to the small of my back, checking for a wire. He still wasn't convinced.

Ospiña had clearly had too much to drink and through Emir said, "Mr. Bob, do you know a man in your business whose last name is Turk?"

I didn't.

"Well, he is a consul from Finland in Colombia. He arranges the smuggling of millions of U.S. dollars for us from the States and Europe." Followed by another "Mr. Bob, we are going to do the big business together," and another wire check. *Unbelievable*.

At 3 A.M., the Moras returned to the hotel. Ospiña, Emir, and I closed the place an hour later and caught a cab, Ospiña and me in the back, while Emir jumped in the front and told the cab driver, "We want to go to the Herradura, but can you first please drive us through downtown and show us some sights. I've never been in San José before."

Eager to please, the cabbie drove past the Catedral Metropolitana de San José and other buildings that grabbed Emir's attention. Ospiña grinned at me and said again, "Mr. Bob, we are going to do the big business." He patted me on the shoulder, and then a glimmer in his eye confused me.

He put his hand on my thigh and repeated his line in a drunken slur. I smiled back — and then he ran his hand up my thigh into my crotch. It blew me away. All this time I thought he had been looking for a wire when he was actually hitting on me!

A million thoughts from kicking his ass to asking him politely to stop flashed through my head. He was, after all, the key to the cartel. A simple yes or no from him and our fate was fixed in

Medellín. But there was no way I was going to put up with this—not even for my country.

I grimaced, locked my hands together, and shoved him to the side of the taxi with a cold stare. "*Nada más, Javier. No para mi. No me gusta.*"—No more, Javier. That's not for me. I don't like it.

Ospiña put up his hands in surrender. "*Lo siento, lo siento, Mr. Bob. No más, no más. Excusa me, por favor.*"—Sorry, sorry, Mr. Bob. No more, no more. Excuse me, please. Emir was so wrapped up in Costa Rican architecture that he never even noticed.

Back at the hotel, as Emir and I were walking to our rooms, I said, "This son of a bitch started to rape me in the backseat of the cab! Did you see that?"

"What?!" said Emir doubtfully. "You've had too much to drink. Go get a good night's sleep."

"Seriously, I'm telling you, this guy is gay, and we need to talk to Gonzalo and his wife. I don't know how we're going to deal with this from now on, but he was all over me like a teenager on a prom date. I couldn't care less what he does on his own time, but we've got to get this shit under control."

"We'll talk about it in the morning." Emir yawned. "I can barely stay awake. I'll call you when I wake up."

Early the next morning came a knock on my door. "That son of a bitch," Emir muttered.

"What happened?" I asked, still half asleep.

"I was taking a shower, and someone knocked on my door. I had a towel around my waist, and when I opened the door it was Ospiña. He was dressed in a see-through white linen shirt and pants. I remembered what you said last night, and from the look on his face I think you may be right. Get dressed so we can go talk with Gonzalo and his wife to find out about this guy."

With no sign of Mora or Lucy, we had to have breakfast with Ospiña, back to his old cordial self. The three of us caught another cab to downtown San José and did some shopping.

While Ospiña was busy in a store, Emir grabbed me. "Let's get the hell away from this guy. I want to find Mora and Lucy so we can get the bottom line."

We jumped in a cab back to the hotel where we found Mora and Lucy in the lobby.

Emir got right to the point. "Excuse me, Lucy, but I have to ask a personal question so we know how to deal with something. Mr. Bob said that Ospiña came on to him last night in the cab. Is there something we should know about him?"

The Moras both smiled, but Lucy answered. "Why do you think I'm on this trip with my husband? Ospiña is as queer as a three-dollar bill and aggressive as hell. I would never stay behind and let my husband take a trip out of town with him."

They both burst into laughter.

No one cared about Ospiña's sexual interests, but apparently it was funny to everyone else but me that Ospiña thought he could force himself on me because I needed his help to get to the next level of the cartel.

"I couldn't care less what this guy does when I'm not around," I deadpanned to Mora, "but you need to tell him to back off because if I have to deal with this again he's going to regret it."

"No problem, Mr. Bob. I'll take care of it."

We packed and headed back to the lobby to say our goodbyes.

A cold wave of sweat rolled down my back as Lucy pulled a camera from her purse and said, "Mr. Bob, Gonzalo, everyone, stand together and show me a big smile." Disney World all over again, but no graceful way out. Too much had already happened or been said to risk putting anyone on edge, so Emir and I wrapped our arms around Mora and Ospiña and smiled at the camera. Then another shot of me, Emir, and Lucy. Pictures that would soon land in Don Chepe's hands.

The flight back to Miami had a layover in Nicaragua, where anti-aircraft artillery in bunkers manned by the Nicaraguan army lined the runway. They were guarding the airport against the Contras, ready to blow anything out of the sky that wasn't scheduled to land.

On my one night on the home front, the reception was cold.

But trying to sort that out while still undercover was like trying to close open-heart surgery with a bandage. Nothing was going to stop the bleeding.

The next day at Financial Consulting, I entered my office, locked the door, and tossed the place for bugs as I always did.

But this time my heart started racing when under the desk I found what looked like a listening device, taped underneath the middle drawer. I carefully removed it, put it in a box, and walked into Eric Wellman's office. I opened the box and pointed silently to what I'd found.

As we both examined it closely, we began to smile. This listening device was the internal movement of a watch. One of the staff apparently had taken note of my calls from Panama, Colombia, and lands unknown. She and a few other employees joked that I might be a spy and thought it would be funny to tape watch guts under my desk. This harmless office prank that almost gave me a heart attack also warned me that my paranoia must have been more evident than I realized.

That afternoon, undercover Customs pilots flew our jet to Miami, where they picked up Awan and Kathy. As they taxied to the private Page Avjet terminal, Awan pointed to another aircraft. "There's one of the BCCI Boeing 737 jets. It's one of three we had converted from commercial carriers to luxury corporate jets. It has a living area, bedroom, galley, and is manned by a full crew."

Impressive.

Then he drifted to Agha Hasan Abedi, president of the bank. "My good friend, Mr. Abedi, unfortunately suffered a heart attack recently and may not recover sufficiently to return to his job. But I have a better than average chance to replace him as president within the next few years.... At one time, Mr. Abedi operated the largest bank in Pakistan, which led to his establishing relationships with the ruling families in Saudi Arabia and Kuwait."

It was the Saudis who later bankrolled BCCI and gave him the capital to establish branches throughout the world. Not long after, Abedi handpicked and groomed Awan for senior management.

"Welcome to Tampa, Amjad," I said as Awan stepped down the stairs of the jet at Tampa's Suncoast Air Center. "It is so kind of you to visit us. It is a tremendous pleasure to have you as our guest."

And it was the beginning of an extraordinarily important four days. Awan had to see as much of our front as possible, and believe I was a well-polished, mob-connected money launderer working with Medellín. He and Bilgrami had recently shown signs of nerves, probably due to the Noriega affair, but I was a new face in their world. Giving Awan the royal treatment in Tampa and New York would convince him and Bilgrami that I was the real deal.

Awan, Kathy, and I jumped in my Mercedes 500 SEL and headed to Dominic's house. I gave him the tour, and then we visited Financial Consulting and Tammey Jewels. During the drive, I explained that the owner of the $750,000 frozen in my account at BCCI Panama was understandably upset because he was able to get frozen funds out of Banco de Occidente but not BCCI. Awan explained that if Noriega fell the U.S. would control the new regime and ask BCCI to open their books. If the bank violated the freeze, they could lose their banking charter. There were other ways he might be able to get around this problem, and he was working on it, but he didn't have a solution.

Then Awan and I played a long game of revelation tennis.

After hearing about my role as a launderer for my "family" in New York, Awan shared that Senator Kerry's subcommittee was pressuring them for records. One of America's biggest drug dealers, Stephen Kalish, had appeared before Congress and identified Awan and BCCI as the bank to which Noriega had referred him to handle dirty money. No wonder Awan and Bilgrami had started to measure their words. But Awan didn't measure his words enough because he revealed that he was getting closed-door information from the Senate hearings. BCCI had friends in high places feeding them.

I had to relay that leak up my chain of command. The more the subcommittee pushed, the more the bank learned about why

BCCI was a target. We had to get the Senate to back off until October. Their inquiries were only sweating Awan and his cronies.

At Financial Consulting, Tammey Jewels, and Dynamic Mortgage Brokers, phones were ringing, printers and faxes were grinding out paper, and the offices were buzzing. None of it an act. These people were just earning an honest living. They had no idea I was a fed or Awan was a dirty banker. Eric Wellman, always a huge help, told Awan he was a former bank president and explained his long and successful history in the business, something you can't fake. BCCI doubtless had researched the details of both our backgrounds—all verifiable. I explained to Awan how our organization established nationwide cash-generating businesses in order to launder cash through pumped-up receipts. When Awan saw one of the Tammey Jewel outlets, it all made sense.

He in turn explained the relationship with First American Bank. BCCI wasn't licensed to own banks that did business with U.S. citizens in the States, but they circumvented that problem by having BCCI shareholders front for ownership of several domestic banks, including First American and National Bank of Georgia. According to Awan, Clark Clifford, former secretary of defense, had helped arrange this secret ownership. Quite a revelation. How could Saudi and Pakistani interests convince such a respected politician to help them acquire hidden stakes in U.S. banks? BCCI had friends in even higher places than I imagined—and too many people inside the Beltway already knew about our operation.

In exchange, I told Awan that, although Noriega had problems with the U.S., he should worry more if he double-crossed any of the people to whom he had offered protection, like Jorge Ochoa. I explained the coffin. Awan forced a laugh, but then ruminated.

The next morning at Suncoast Aviation at Tampa International we met Kevin Palmer and Craig Morgan, the undercover pilots decked out in braid and epaulets. They flew us in the Cessna Citation to Teterboro, a small airport in New Jersey just twelve miles west of Manhattan. At the terminal, a huge black limo was waiting for us. I'd asked Frankie to arrange transportation to the brokerage firm, but I wasn't expecting this. The chauffeur, an attractive, dark-haired New Yorker, looked more like a model in her black suit and chauffeur's hat.

"Hello, Mr. Musella," she said. "My name is Lydia, and it is a pleasure to see you, sir. Frankie asked me to help you and your party during the next few days."

"Well, thank you," I said, pleasantly surprised. "It's great to be home. This is my fiancée, Kathy, and this is my very good friend Amjad. Let's drop Kathy off at the Sherry-Netherland, and then Amjad and I will be going to the brokerage firm."

"No problem, sir." She handed me a card. "I'll be at your disposal until you leave. Call me at this number anytime you need me, and I'll be back to you within minutes."

The car worked its way to the southeast corner of Central Park, where the Sherry-Netherland offered five-star service and has overlooked the corner of Fifty-ninth Street and Fifth Avenue since 1927. From there, we drove to the skyscraper at 170 Broadway. As he had done when Mora visited, Frankie ran to me as though I was his long-lost brother and embraced me with a warm welcome.

"Bobby, it's so good to see you." He had barely finished speaking when three or four other employees greeted me as though I was a superstar.

"Cuz," I said to Frankie, "this is my very good friend, Amjad Awan. Like I told you before, he and his colleagues at BCCI have been a tremendous help to us with our international banking needs. Amjad has been of invaluable assistance to the alliances we've built down south."

"Thank you very much, Mr. Awan," Frankie grinned. "It's a pleasure to finally meet you. Bob speaks very highly of you and for our family that means we all share that same view. Please, let me give you a little tour of our firm."

Frankie introduced him to about half the employees, explaining the roles they played and emphasizing that our operation specialized in initial public offerings, which take thriving private companies into the world of penny stocks. Risky investments on Wall Street, but also highly lucrative.

From there, we walked Awan to the New York Stock Exchange. Awan held back more than Mora had, but rubbing shoulders with traders clearly scored big points with him. And Frankie was in his glory. He knew exactly what everyone in the exchange was doing, buying and selling and screaming. Awan devoured every word.

"Very impressive, Bob," he said, nodding.

At a nearby coffee shop, Frankie really laid it on thick. He talked to me about various pending business deals as though I were the key to the firm's success. "Bobby, I'd really be indebted to you if you could cover us on another $100,000 in the deal we discussed the other day for Jorge. It didn't turn out quite like we thought it would, but everything will even up within a week."

"No problem," I said. "You know you can count on me."

The brokerage firm so impressed Awan that he immediately announced it was a good opportunity for BCCI. "We don't have personnel versed in the New York Stock Exchange. Although I'd prefer that our clients place their funds with us, in those instances where they are intent on dealing in the exchange, I'd like to refer them directly to you."

"Certainly," Frankie said. "You have my word we'll take special care of them. A referral from you, Amjad, will be treated with our full attention. We wouldn't want to disappoint you or my cousin Bobby."

Back at the firm, as Awan sat outside Frankie's door — but within earshot — Frankie and I ad-libbed a scene about half a dozen big deals pending. Icing on our cake of lies.

Then back uptown to the Sherry-Netherland, during which I invited Awan on behalf of my "family" to dinner at an exclusive club at the Columbus Citizens Foundation on East Sixty-ninth Street. Frankie and his uncle Carmine had said the club's members included politicians and mobsters, which I mentioned to Awan, who was happy to join us.

"Bob, would it be all right," Awan said on a call to my room, "if I invited a female friend to spend the evening with me at the hotel? I'll still accompany you and your family to dinner, but I'd like to leave instructions here for her to be given an extra key so she can await my return. She's in D.C., so she can take the air shuttle and be here by the time we return."

"Amjad, you're welcome to invite whomever you'd like," I said. "It's no problem whatsoever."

At the Columbus Club, Awan, Kathy, and I joined Frankie, his wife, his uncle Carmine, who owned the brokerage firm, and Carmine's wife. For four hours, the seven of us enjoyed a fantastic Italian feast. Everyone at the table except Awan knew that Kathy and I were agents, and they played their supporting roles brilliantly. I was the emerging hero and heir apparent to the family.

At midnight we all went back to the Sherry-Netherland, and everyone except Awan went straight to my suite. Fifteen minutes later, someone knocked. It was Awan.

"Bob, this is my very close friend Rosanna from Washington, D.C."

For more than three more hours, we drank and traded stories. Awan's girlfriend, a stunning blond beauty of Venezuelan and Italian descent, was Rosanna Aspitre. For the past four years she had lived near Embassy Row and Cathedral Drive in Washington. She gave me her number and offered to meet Kathy and me anytime we were in D.C.

The next morning, Awan had an entirely new attitude about me and my problems. Now he wanted to please. "I'm going to find out as soon as I get in what the situation is between Luxembourg and Panama and their interest in doing that.... Would you be in this afternoon, or would you like to give me a call? ... When we restart the situation, will you continue to do it through Panama?"

I declined, suggesting we feed money through Geneva and Paris to Uruguay. Awan was happy to help.

Then we spoke of my client in L.A. — Alcaíno, of course, but no names used — who wanted to finance his own $500,000 construction loan as long as BCCI hid his half-million deposit. No problem. Awan would get his good friend Ashraf, manager of BCCI L.A., to handle it.

"Thank you for everything," Awan said. "It's been a very, very pleasant trip. I really enjoyed meeting Frankie and Carmine...and Rosanna."

Lydia, the beautiful chauffeur, drove Awan to a nearby hotel and picked up our pilots. A few hours later Awan was back in Miami, where at the end of the day he called with news that he and his colleagues had found a solution to my problem. They would have various BCCI branches backdate entries concerning the $750,000 frozen in my Panama account. Within a week, the money would be sitting in Geneva, ready for transfer.

Kathy and I were in a Midtown hotel briefing Laura Sherman when the call came through.

"We need to get the Senate subcommittee to back down," I told Laura, "but we can't afford to give them enough details so that a leak could compromise us. Awan and BCCI have a pipeline to what the subcommittee knows and what they're thinking."

That same day the U.S. Attorney's office in Tampa sent information to Washington, D.C., addressing a plan to inform Senator Kerry's chief counsel, Jack Blum, about our operation. Without specifics, Blum learned that there was an active undercover infiltration at BCCI, and, to further the investigation, the subcommittee was being asked to take a hands-off approach to BCCI temporarily.

The disclosure freaked me out. Subcommittee investigations are still politics, and there was no room in C-Chase for any more politics. The bank was siphoning information from Washington, and now the official response from Washington was that they would abide by Justice's request.

I had done everything I could. Now it was time to prepare for a fight.

12

THE FIGHT BEFORE EUROPE

Miami, Florida
April 5, 1988

THE CLOCK WAS TICKING TOWARD OCTOBER. I had six months left to become a part of their everyday lives and put myself in a position where I could meet with two or three of them a day to speed up infiltration. We needed a house.

Miami sits at the crossroads for Colombia's drug trade and the billions of dollars it generates. With less than a week before Alcaíno and his entourage were scheduled to converge on the Magic City to attend the fight between Rojas of Colombia and Roman of Mexico, we found the perfect place on East Enid Drive on Key Biscayne—just minutes from BCCI Miami, the homes of our Miami targets, and the hotels Alcaíno used for stays between Colombia and the States.

It was perfect. Banyan trees smothered the tri-level unit, offering natural cover. The front door opened onto a split-level staircase, which led down to a sunken living room and up to an elevated dining room overlooking the lower floor. The hollow platform under the dining room offered an ideal spot to install a fake air-conditioning intake-vent cover that concealed a space containing amplifiers, recorders, volume controls, monitors, and other equipment. Technicians wired the dining room for audio and hid a sophisticated audio/video recording system in the living room. They placed separate cameras in both stereo speakers so every square inch of the living room was recorded during meetings. The woman who owned the place was an artist, and she had hung her work along every inch of the walls, which dovetailed nicely with Kathy's cover as a student and art collector.

Though the house on Key Biscayne would serve its purpose from now until October, we decided to use as a base of operation the Doral Beach Hotel, which was much closer to the fight venue, the Miami Beach Convention Center. At the Doral, Emir and I rented penthouse apartments that included a 1,500-square-foot living room in which we could host at least twenty-five guests for Alcaíno's pre-fight cocktail party. We also rented a third room for Mora and his wife to record as many meetings as possible with him. For the dinner party, Kathy found Café Tanino, a small, upscale Italian restaurant in Coral Gables, where she worked out all the details — menu, wines, seating, etc.

Adella Asqui couldn't continue as Emir's girlfriend, so, shortly before Alcaíno and his family arrived, Linda Kadluboski, an agent from Manhattan, replaced her. Her beauty, attitude, and New York street smarts gave her just the right edge, combining grace and strength. Emir, Kathy, Linda, and I spent a full day together going over our cover stories, what we knew about the targets, how we could manipulate private meetings with key players, and our antici-pated itinerary.

At 8:30 P.M. guests began arriving at Café Tanino. Emir and Linda drove Gonzalo and Lucy Mora there, then Roberto and Gloria Alcaíno, their daughter Claudia, and a friend of Claudia all arrived. And joining their table came Tuto and Carmin Zabala; Juan Tobón; Tobón's father, Francisco; and Mexican boxer Gil Roman's promoter.

I offered a champagne toast. "I'd like to thank you all for shar-ing this special night with our guest of honor and very good friend, Roberto, a man we all love and respect. Roberto, we wish you, Tuto, and Antilles Promotions the very best of luck on this momentous occasion, the promotion of your first world championship fight. May this be the first of many."

Half a dozen waiters swarmed around us delivering appetizers, pinot grigio, Gavi di Gavi, and sangiovese. We finished the seven-course meal by 11:30. Alcaíno was sipping his favorite after-dinner drink, cappuccino with amaretto. Some called it a night, but Alcaíno was just getting started.

"Let's go to Regine's and celebrate some more," he suggested. Regine's nightclub, a hotspot for the rich and famous, had locations in Miami, New York, Paris, London, and other major cities. I had bought a membership a few months earlier and had drinks with Alcaíno at their New York location on Park Avenue. Ten of us headed to the Miami Regine's atop the Grand Bay Hotel, overlooking the yachts moored in Biscayne Bay.

We danced, partied, and fussed over Alcaíno until 2:30 A.M., when he had another idea. "Let's end the night with a stop at Club Nu." Another favorite stop for Miami's rich and wild set, Club Nu, in Miami Beach, wasn't far from our hotels. More drinks, dancing, and laughter until 4:15 A.M.

Luckily, Alcaíno had morning meetings, so he decided to catch a few hours' sleep. Before we left, he hugged me. "*Amigo*, this was a wonderful celebration. You and Kathy are like family now. You are with us all the way. I can't thank you enough."

"It's our pleasure, Roberto," I said. "I promise you tomorrow will be even better. We're so grateful that you've invited us to share this experience with you."

After breakfast the next morning, Mora, Emir, and I met privately in the Doral penthouse. He had a lot to be happy about, so we pressed him for names and details. Luckily, he sang.

First, he provided a detailed accounting of all the checks issued during the past month. He explained which checks were issued in phony names and gave us the real names of the people tied to each deal. Then he explained that, after our trip to Costa Rica, Don Chepe had summoned him and Ospiña to a meeting where Mora learned that Don Chepe controlled as much volume in the cocaine trade as Pablo Escobar and Jorge Ochoa.

And then the news we'd hoped for. Don Chepe had "already accepted to do a certificate of deposit, to begin with, for $700,000."

We'd finally worn them down.

He added that, if we were able to get Don Chepe's frozen $750,000 out of Panama, we would be heroes. I couldn't grab my phone fast enough to call Awan, who was confident he'd be able to move the funds out of Panama in a few days. Thrilled, Mora offered his own good news in return. Don Chepe also agreed to have his key representatives meet us in Europe in May to work out details for a long-range relationship.

Mora begged us to put a person like Emir in Houston full time. Don Chepe's organization was accumulating enormous profits from bulk cocaine sales there and needed someone who could react quickly when they wanted to drop off money. "He's giving us a small piece of the cake.... The volume is much bigger.... Houston can move a million per week."

Mora confessed another reason that we needed to put someone in Houston. For the past six years, a Medellín businessman had been handling Don Chepe's money-laundering needs. Upset that we were cutting into his territory, he whispered in Don Chepe's ear every time we were slow to react in Los Astros (code for Houston) that we weren't professional, or — worse yet — that we were *los feos*. It took us six months to identify this competitor: Eduardo Martínez Romero, a chief lieutenant and financial adviser for the senior leaders of the cartel. Romero worked closely with the Panama City branch of Banco de Occidente. They were his BCCI.

Our discussion shifted to Alcaíno. Mora confirmed that Guillermo Velásquez supplied Alcaíno with the cocaine for America and Europe. According to Mora, Velásquez was Alcaíno's partner and worked with Fabio Ochoa.

Mora also gave us insight into Tobón, who worked with a man thought to be even more powerful than Pablo Escobar, a Jewish Colombian named John Nasser, who, according to other sources, was actually Jean Figali. "He's tough," Mora said. "He's a very tough guy. But Tobón confessed to me last night that it's very good to deal with him." Mora planned to have Tobón introduce him to Nasser so Mora could develop him as one of our clients.

After a lunch break, Tobón joined me and Emir, explaining his close friendship with Nasser, the biggest drug lord in Colombia, he claimed. Nasser owned the largest textile import-export businesses in the country and had the complete protection of the Colombian military, police, judges, and politicians.

But then Tobón threw a challenge at me. Before he would do business, he wanted me to visit his Santería priest so the priest could assess my spirit. Luckily, Tobón was leaving for Colombia in a few days, and I bought time by telling him I'd gladly join him when he returned. I needed time to figure out how I was going to handle this.

At the pre-fight penthouse cocktail party, ice sculptures and massive flower arrangements adorned banquet tables filled with mountains of stone-crab claws, oysters, cured meats, cheeses, shrimp, and every hors d'oeuvre you can imagine. Waiters carried trays overflowing with flutes of champagne. Alcaíno and his family arrived first. Not far behind came Tobón, Gonzalo and Lucy Mora. The four WBC judges for the fight attended, along with the referee, John Thomas. Tuto and Carmin Zabala came along with a few other boxing promoters. At 8 p.m. it was time to hit the convention center.

As we approached the doors to the ring, photographers snapped away at our entourage. Excitement hung in the air. This same venue had witnessed Cassius Clay defeat Sonny Liston in 1964 and Richard Nixon at the height of his power at the 1972 Republican National Convention. Thousands of people rose to their feet and watched us as we made our way ringside.

The fight may not have meant much to North Americans, but it was the ticket of the year for Latin America. Television and cable announcers from countries throughout Central and South America focused on every moment of the evening. When the fight began, thunderous shouts flew from every direction. Colombian world champ Sugar "Baby" Rojas seemed to have everything under control during the first half. He pummeled Gil Roman with lightning jabs and occasional hooks.

But as the fight wore on, Gil Roman, the technician, showed his strength just as Rojas seemed to lose his. Round after round, Roman threw surgical barrages of combinations. By the last few rounds Rojas had become a bloody pulp. A river of sweat and blood ran down him — so much so that when Roman landed a hit near our corner of the ring, blood and sweat rained down on us. Both fighters looked like they'd been through meat grinders, and the referee's blue shirt had turned purple.

The arena tensely awaited the judges' decision. When it came, Mexican flags waved everywhere as the referee raised Roman's arm in the center of the ring. Colombia's king had lost his crown.

In the pandemonium afterward, Emir, Linda, Kathy, and I took the Moras to Regine's again, which Mora, a pure businessman, appreciated. He knew it was money well spent because we were winning Alcaíno's loyalty. For the bean counters in the government, though, spending $10,000 to wine and dine crooks for a few days didn't sit well. Then again, we hadn't used a single cent of taxpayer money to finance this or any other part of the undercover operation. We were penetrating deeper into the cartel and money-laundering world than anyone had before. We'd made more than a million in commissions and had already seized more than a million in drug money on the streets. Plus, we were going to seize Alcaíno's fortune and many others'. It wasn't unreasonable to expect that we'd be collecting untold millions in fines and forfeitures from the bank, too. Mora was right. This was a good investment.

The next morning, Alcaíno signed backdated bogus loan documents to cover his stake promoting the fight, and we talked out the mechanics for similar documents to cover his half million into the downtown L.A. apartment complex.

Then talk turned to cartel business. Even behind closed doors we talked in code, a habit developed from speaking in circles on the phone. When someone was arrested, he was "in the hospital." If someone needed a lawyer, he needed a "doctor." Cocaine was merchandise, product, things, or babies.

Alcaíno explained that his workers in Spain had gone to the hospital, but they got out with the help of a doctor. They lost the merchandise, and that was the end of the game. They were already in Italy now, by car and plane. Alcaíno had had someone post $100,000 bond for each of the three arrested. Balancing the cost of the cocaine and Alcaíno's share of the bond, he lost more than half a million. Had the deal gone through, he would have cleared $ 1.7 million. But he was training his sights on the next load to Europe, coming in, this time, through Italy. Despite the Spanish setback, Alcaíno happily had deliveries of cash for me in Chicago and New York.

A few days after the fight, Hussain arrived from Panama. He wanted me to know that, regardless of whether I moved operations to other branches, he would still be involved and get credit for bringing me to the bank's Latin American headquarters in Miami. He knew my clients had doubts about Panama and, if Noriega tried to flee, my clients would have him killed. Yet he still offered to help me move between $15 million and $20 million per month. Awan had said the New York trip had gone well, and his colleagues were impressed. But Hussain wasn't bringing anything new to the table. He was worried that my strengthening relationship with Awan would force him out of the picture.

The next day at BCCI Miami, Awan jumped in my Jag, and we headed to a sidewalk café in Coconut Grove. There were problems getting Don Chepe's $750,000 out of Panama. BCCI now had to apply to the Panamanian authorities for an international banking license before they could move the money, which would cause another week's delay.

My visible disappointment obliged Awan to offer an alternative. If he couldn't surmount this last hurdle, he'd have the bank play games with entries and get the money out, one way or another. On the bright side, he had made arrangements for me in Uruguay. Everything was in order if I wanted to open a Montevideo account, which would replace the BCCI Panama account and serve as the primary disbursement hub. Despite the risks, the Colombians would always keep Panama at least partly in the game; it's hard to teach an old dog new tricks. We would transfer funds from the States to Europe, from Europe to Montevideo, and Montevideo to Banco de

Occidente or any other Panama institution that had a strictly international banking license unaffected by the freeze. We finally had a work-around.

"I would suggest," Awan said, "that whatever we discuss...to be *not* discussed with Mr. Hussain. Not for any other reason but, ah, he's young and somewhat immature. And he tends to talk about his business."

Hussain had blabbed to other bank officers that Awan had gone with me to New York. Awan thought it best to keep his dealings with me more secretive. I agreed.

As we sipped our coffees, nibbled croissants, and Awan smoked a Dunhill Blue, I told him that one of our stops in Europe would be Paris. The general manager of BCCI Paris was his close friend. Things could be done through that branch, he said vaguely. Corners could be cut and arrangements could be made that would please me. He promised to pass word to his friend to greet us with open arms.

Our conversation turned to Noriega.

"His biggest concern," I said, "really has to be people like some of my clients, who, if he were to be out of Panama, he would probably be pursued by."

"I know that," Awan replied. "And I think he knows that, which is why he doesn't want to leave. I don't think he fears as much from the U.S. as he does from other people."

That was my opening. "Yeah, the cartel is, ah, they're not gonna be happy if they lose their money." Then I really poured it on. "I have to admit that the folks that...I'm affiliated with are as professional as Lee Iacocca. You know, it's just that they have a different kind of business. One sells cars, and one sells coke. That's the way it goes."

Awan laughed.

"They really look at it just as an industry," I said.

Recording conversations like these, proving Awan knew the funds came from drug sales in the U.S., provided critical proof. Most dirty bankers would have had a hard time stomaching this type of conversation. They don't like blunt. They'd rather hide behind plausible denial. But Awan had bought my act and thought he was talking to a mob man. He believed me.

A week later, on the couches, Awan, Bilgrami, and I hammered out the details of how to get Don Chepe's money out of Panama. When talk turned to Europe, Awan named his two friends in BCCI Paris: General Manager Nazir Chinoy and Branch Manager Ian Howard. Men on the inner team. Since everything was going smoothly, I decided to push to see how the Senate subcommittee investigation was going.

Awan confirmed that the situation had quieted down and the bank's senior executives expected the matter to blow over. I smiled — outwardly for BCCI, and inwardly that Senator Kerry's staff had kept their word and backed off until we got the job done. My next question opened a whole new door.

"But why would the Senate back down?" I said.

Awan and Bilgrami smiled at each other and shared the secret to BCCI's power. The bank had gone out of its way to build alliances with politicians from both sides of the aisle in Washington. They had Clark Clifford, former secretary of defense and godfather of the Democratic Party, in bed, that much I knew. But Clifford was also CEO of First American Bank, secretly owned and controlled by BCCI, which had retained Clifford's law firm, which included Democratic party bigwig Robert Altman. The bank also made huge charitable contributions to organizations led by former President Jimmy Carter. And Bert Lance, former director of the Office of Management and Budget, was involved in another U.S. bank that BCCI now controlled.

On the other side of the aisle, the bank had alliances with the Bush family. George W. Bush, later forty-third president of the United States, ran a huge company supplying heavy drilling and pumping equipment to companies in Saudi Arabia owned by BCCI's major shareholders. The bank also enjoyed a good friendship with his brother Jeb Bush, introduced to the bank's senior management by George Barbar, a Lebanese multimillionaire businessman in

Boca Raton who had millions in the London, Paris, Holland, and Florida branches of BCCI. At Barbar's request, Bilgrami installed Barbar's nephew as a BCCI official in their Colón office, a branch that took in huge deposits from drug dealers. And there was the close relationship between BCCI's president, Agha Hasan Abedi, and William Casey, director of the CIA. At Casey's request, the bank was secretly moving money to Afghan rebels to finance their war against the Russian invasion.

BCCI had truly hedged its bets. While marketing as much dirty money as they could find, they ingratiated themselves with as many powerful politicians as they could, regardless of party affiliation. The bank could easily quell problems with Kerry's subcommittee through friendships in D.C. The picture of BCCI was beginning to focus. What I'd sensed the first day I spoke with a BCCI officer in Tampa was just the tip of an immense iceberg. The bank *by design* corrupted and seized power by marketing dirty money and building friendships with power brokers.

Back in Tampa, after an internal audit of our operation's books and records, and after almost everyone had gone home, I logged on to a Customs computer to query our Private Aircraft Reporting System, which tracks details about all private aircraft that enter and leave U.S. airspace, including names, dates of birth, and nationalities of passengers onboard. Just who had been jetting around the world in BCCI's 737s?

The results hit hard. President Jimmy Carter and his family. Andrew Young, former ambassador to the United Nations and mayor of Atlanta. Bert Lance and George Barbar, the latter of whom, according to BCCI officers, had big-time connections with government officials in the U.S., U.K., and Jamaica. More queries about Barbar put him on private flights with Richard Nixon and Charles "Bebe" Rebozo and linked him further to American businessmen with alleged ties to organized crime.

My curiosity caught fire. I ran criminal intelligence queries on every passenger on the BCCI jets. Many who weren't politicians were suspected of money laundering, drug trafficking, or other criminal activity.

Awan and Bilgrami weren't bullshitting. BCCI was for real.

Europe was looming, and I still had loose ends with Ospiña, who had to come through. Don Chepe's representatives had to arrive. Despite Alcaíno's promises after the fight, business had slowed down, and I wanted answers. I'd earned the right to pump him for intelligence about the cartel. From Awan I needed rock-solid confirmation that inner team officers in Paris and London would handle me there.

To make sure Ospiña and Don Chepe's representatives showed in Paris, I made a surprise call to Ospiña. He spoke a little English, and I was trying to learn some Spanish. We struggled to communicate, but more than that he sounded drunk. It wasn't even noon. In broken Spanglish, I told him I was looking forward to meeting him and his friends in Paris and I just wanted to make sure everything was on track.

"Bob, uh . . . hey," Ospiña eventually slurred. ". . . I love you."

Christ. Bad enough this guy was bombed, now I had to put up with the thought that he was going to chase me down the cobblestone streets of Paris for a kiss.

"*Javier, Adios—*"

He tried to say something else.

"*Adios, Javier.*"

End of call.

After listening to the story, Emir could hardly breathe he was laughing so hard. I told him to find out why Ospiña seemed so out of it. Mora later reported that Ospiña often smoked bazookas, a combination of coca paste and marijuana. It would have been Ospiña's last Saturday alive if Don Chepe knew. Mora got a good long laugh from the story, too, but claimed I didn't need to worry. Ospiña knew my interests were strictly business.

So much for tying down my first loose end.

Alcaíno took a quick flight from Miami to Tampa and we talked business over dinner at the airport.

"Nothing's been happening," he said about Medellín, "because there was loss, people lost there more than 5,000 kilos.... The government came in and everybody, you know, put all kinds of pressure in there, the army.... We were told about a month ago, we're gonna have this period that we couldn't do nothin' because they're — we're working there with the government. The government says something in particular was going to happen, 'You be careful. Clean your house, and clean everything.' So we did.... Now they [the cartel] are kidnapping diplomats and stuff. They got fourteen guys already kidnapped, from different governments."

Then he whispered details about a secret project in the works. "What I'm trying to do now is set up my own airline. Not only airlines, but a boat. They call it a line. My own line, where I control the transportation.... I tell you, Bob, you have to come. You want to come in with only for ten, twenty, sixty [investing the cost of that many kilos] and then, no problem, because I control it."

Alcaíno's offer beat most other investments on earth. Whatever I invested in a load now, as long as the shipment got to the States, would earn a return three times the original investment within forty-five days. The cartel drew a lot of "businessmen" into the trade with this type of offer.

He used some of the money I laundered to buy a twin-engine Cessna, used to fly cocaine from labs in the jungles of Bolivia to Argentina. Then bulk shipments would be trucked to a commercial facility, packaged, and shipped as freight into the U.S. and Europe.

"We're going to come through New York first," he said. "We're almost there. We've been working for six months."

He'd bought a company that had been shipping to the U.S. and Europe for some time. Outwardly, I showed concerned interest in weighing a potential investment — but my mind was doing backflips. His transportation line could produce a huge prize. If I could get Alcaíno to tell me where this company was and what it shipped, we could intercept a huge coke shipment and shut down one of the cartel's arteries. I just had to do it without scaring Alcaíno underground or causing him to suspect me.

But he had given me a solid explanation about the slowdown and shared sensitive details about his new transportation line. I told him I'd make sure we provided him with whatever he needed. We hugged and wished each other a blessing that God look over us — God's protection, for the devil's work.

Awan and Bilgrami meanwhile had set up alternate routes and had resumed ricocheting money around the world. For our next meeting, I had special news. They had always made it clear that they hoped I wouldn't always borrow against all of the funds I placed with the bank. They wanted deposits. To satisfy that demand, Commissioner of Customs William von Raab had convinced the Treasury Department to provide our operation with a $5 million flash roll, which we could put in bank accounts but not spend. Which is exactly what Awan and Bilgrami wanted. The Colombians had anted up, so in short order I was ready to plop $6 million in the bank's lap.

Over tea on the couches, we reviewed my itinerary.

Zürich first, for meetings with lawyers who had set up new corporations in Gibraltar, Liberia, and Hong Kong in order to open accounts in Geneva, Paris, and London. BCCI could have done it for me, but it was important not to seem like a rookie needing their help at every step. Besides, it wasn't hard to find lawyers in Switzerland willing to turn a blind eye to the companies they sold.

Then Geneva, where at Awan's request, I would meet with BCCI's affiliate, Banque de Commerce et de Placements (BCP). He cautioned me not to be explicit with personnel at BCP. Meet them, open accounts, put them at ease. They were an important cog in the wheel, but they weren't inner team.

Then Paris to see Awan's close friends, Nazir Chinoy and Ian Howard, who would open accounts for us and our clients. And lastly London, where Awan's colleague Asif Baakza would do the same. With these last three, I didn't have to be guarded.

"We had discussions in the past," I said, moving the conversation along, "where you said, well, when we begin to see things happen right, then we'll begin to get comfortable. I'm absolutely comfortable."

"Well, we are," Awan replied as Bilgrami chimed in the same.

"I am prepared to, and I am going to, place at a minimum two...probably five million that will just sit."

Bilgrami beamed. "Oh, good."

Awan took a smoother approach. "Well, what we were looking for, Bob, to be very honest, is something like $25 million."

For a second I thought he was serious, but his smile led a chorus of laughter that filled the room.

Bilgrami admitted that the bank was looking for a little help, and Awan explained why. "We have our figures every half year.... If you could raise some cash, or if you have something spare, if we can have it placed anywhere within the BCCI group on the thirtieth of June, could be even for a day. Of course we'd like it a little more...Our half year figures are very important, because, see, we have a balance sheet brought out every thirtieth of June. So if we have a lot of cash sitting there on the thirtieth of June, that helps a lot. It's window dressing, as I said. I mean, you can take it out on the first of July. That's okay. But, if you can do something for us on that basis, by the thirtieth of June...Five million will be most welcome for us, but you know, that sort of thing, if you can do something for us on that day, we'll appreciate it."

I told Awan he could count on my five million and another million a client just asked me to place in a CD.

No more laughter. Awan and Bilgrami knew this was serious business. This $6 million bought a lot more than just CDs. It earned me the right to ask questions that would otherwise make them squirm. I had anted up, and they had accepted. Reasonable curiosities wouldn't be questioned. That $6 million also bought rock-hard proof of the bank's motive for taking dirty money. This wasn't a scheme by a few rogue officers looking to take money under the table—that happens every day. This was a worldwide scheme by an institution that gave employees promotions and bonuses to bring in big deposits from the shadiest players in the underworld so they could increase the zeros on the balance sheet. A bigger bottom line equaled more power and a bigger wand to wave in every corner of the world — more friendships with world leaders, more money to loan to people who could pay back with hushed favors, more power to corrupt.

And I had it all on tape.

13

THE EUROPEAN PLAN

John F. Kennedy International Airport, New York
May 12, 1988

EVERYTHING WAS IN PLACE as the 747 jumbo jet lifted from the tarmac, soaring toward Zürich. Awan had his colleagues in Europe waiting for us with bated breath. Mora and Ospiña had Don Chepe's people packing to join us. Customs had come through with the $5 million flash roll.

Just when I thought it couldn't get any better, Steve Cook delivered more good news. My request to use high-end jewelry from our evidence vault came through. The five-carat diamond ring and Rolex President nicely complemented the thousand dollars' worth of new clothes I picked up. Well, the Mazur family picked up the tab for the clothes, and it was starting to look like I needed all the help I could get.

It was late morning when Emir, Kathy, Linda, and I arrived in Zürich, too exhausted to appreciate fully the Savoy Baur en Ville, a luxury hotel in the heart of Zürich's financial and shopping district overflowing with marble walls and dripping with crystal chandeliers.

Dieter Jann was the examining magistrate for International Mutual Assistance in Criminal Matters for the canton of Zürich — a mouthful of a title that would stretch any business card. Swiss cantons are like states in America, except federal authorities have less power over what occurs in each canton, so we couldn't so much as sneeze in Zürich without a nod from Dieter Jann. More layers of government than you can count had coordinated our work in Zürich, including Customs agents at the U.S. embassy in Austria who coordinated with Swiss authorities, but they couldn't so much as sneeze either without approval from the DEA special agent in Zürich. Despite knowing our itinerary, our Austria personnel didn't greet us. They would get there when they could, they said, but in the meantime, "Call DEA Agent Greg Passic in Zürich. He'll get you a quick meeting with Jann, and you'll be cleared to have your undercover meeting with the lawyer in Zürich who's setting up companies for you."

Passic had disappointing news: "Bob, I'm going to be tied up at the airport for at least the rest of the day, but hopefully I can introduce you to Jann sometime tomorrow."

"We've got targets waiting for us in Paris and London," I said, incredulous, "and my office back in Tampa thinks I'm yodeling in the Alps. We'd really appreciate it if you could help us get our meets done in Switzerland so we can get out of here."

Hurry up and wait.

Emir and I began to worry that agency wars were causing the problem.

"Gosh, I'm really sorry," Passic said the next day. "I'm still overwhelmed with this unexpected matter I can't leave. I'll get back to you later today."

Our offices in Tampa and Austria were working on it, but the only new piece of information I learned from Roger Urbanski, the Customs agent assigned to Austria who was supposed to be "coordinating" for us, was that he had an elevator in his house and was living like a king. And he'd get to us just as soon as he could.

By now my blood was boiling.

On prior trips to Switzerland, chasing witnesses and drug money, I had had the pleasure of developing a wonderful friendship with Urs Frei, a Swiss magistrate in Horgen, a district in the canton of Zürich.

"I've got an idea," I said to Emir. "A good friend is a prosecutor in Zürich. If he knows Jann, maybe he can introduce us."

"Can we do that?" Emir squinted in thought.

"Our only other choice is to sit here and wait for these bureaucrats to cancel cocktail parties so they can find the time to get off their butts. I guarantee you Tischler will think we're on vacation, and we'll have hell to pay if we don't get things off the ground fast. We've got appointments in Geneva and Paris that can't wait. I'd much rather ask for forgiveness later than permission now."

Frei lit up like a Christmas tree. "*Bob*, how are you? It's wonderful to hear your voice.... No problem, Bob, I know Dieter Jann. Let me make some calls, and I'll get right back to you."

In a few hours Urs, Jann, Emir, and I were sitting on the outdoor patio of a remote restaurant in Horgen, atop the Albis Mountains. The view of Lake Zug and the distant Swiss Alps offered a postcard-perfect backdrop as we raised our steins and thanked Jann for the chance to brief him about what we wanted to do here. Customs and DEA had already briefed him, so there were no surprises. By our second stein of beer, he gave us the go-ahead.

Six months earlier, in Miami, I had played the same game with Credit Suisse as I had with Rick Argudo at BCCI Tampa. Just like Argudo, the Credit Suisse officer had no problem opening accounts for me. But before I could pursue them, BCCI, Mora, Alcaíno, and their contacts had me on overload. But when the need to have a slew of offshore companies arose, my Credit Suisse account officer in Miami referred me to Samuel Sommerhalder in their Zürich branch.

Initially Sommerhalder had me call a Swiss lawyer who asked a lot of questions, wanting me to disclose the names of people who owned the money I was managing, to ensure it wasn't dirty. When he realized I was looking for a lawyer who would acquire offshore companies and prepare powers of attorney without asking questions, he prevaricated, saying he didn't know any lawyers like that, but then suggested I discuss the issue further with Sommerhalder, who might introduce me to someone else. Sommerhalder then gave me the name of a different lawyer in Zürich. This second attorney had all the documents I needed — for about $50,000. Without those documents, we couldn't open new accounts with BCCI branches in Europe, controlled by me and Don Chepe's representative, Rudolf Armbrecht.

When I met him in Zürich, the second lawyer handed me a stack of Hong Kong, Gibraltar, and Liberian corporation papers empowering me to conduct business on their behalf around the globe. I had asked him to form a Lichtenstein foundation that could serve as the owner of all the companies, but he warned against that. A prior client had had him link companies under the ownership of a single foundation, and, when authorities uncovered drug proceeds in one, they seized the assets of all the companies on the basis of common ownership. The second Zürich lawyer's advice: keep the companies separate, and my Colombian clients wouldn't lose everything if one went down.

The next stop in Zürich brought me to Samuel Sommerhalder, whom I thanked and told that I'd contact him again when ready to open new accounts in the names of the companies I'd bought from his friend. A lie, as it turned out. There wouldn't be enough time; it was already the middle of May, and we had less than five months left.

From Zürich, a sleek, spotless Swiss train sped Emir, Kathy, Linda, and me to Geneva. The Hotel Bristol, a four-star luxury hotel, lay in the medieval section of the city, a short walk along narrow cobblestone streets from the Jardin Anglais, an immaculate park filled with statues, fountains, and a rainbow of flowerbeds along Lake Geneva. Hard to imagine that this picturesque setting helped sling billions in drug money around the world.

At Banque de Commerce et de Placements, Emir, Kathy, Linda, and I met Franz Maissen, head of BCP's private banking division, and Azizulah Chaudhry, the bank's general manager. The Zürich lawyer had prepared powers of attorney that, if presented at BCP or BCCI, authorized Kathy to move funds in the accounts. That tactic is a kind of insurance policy if criminals land in jail and can't move money to new hiding places while cops figure things out. It also sent a signal that I knew how to play the game. With that out of the way, Kathy and Linda excused themselves from the meeting, citing an uncontrollable urge to shop at Geneva's most exclusive jewelry stores.

This gave Emir and me time to talk business. We shared details about our management of funds for South American clients, but I didn't tell them outright that our clients were drug dealers giving us suitcases of cash. Hard to imagine that experienced bankers like Maissen and Chaudhry couldn't surmise that on their own, though, just from the transactions they'd already handled.

One of the first-class services provided by banks that cater to crooks like Bob Musella is holding all mail generated by accounts. This prevents law enforcement from linking a bank to a criminal through mail monitoring. At BCP, I picked up the last five months of that mail, crucial records that contained a road map for the money routed by Hussain, Awan, and Bilgrami—and something we'd need at trial.

Criminals also open safe-deposit boxes at banks in havens like Switzerland to hide bank records and other information about their financial affairs. Maissen and Chaudhry opened a box for me and Emir, for which I prepaid with cash to avoid any link to my account. In the privacy of the vault, I pulled a stack of notes from my briefcase and stuffed them in the box. The notes contained bogus passwords, codes, account numbers, names, and contact information. If the bank ever accessed the box, everything would look normal.

As I slid the box into its place, Emir grabbed my arm.

"I'd like you to put this piece of paper in that box for me," he said.

Emir had drawn an outline of his fist on a sheet of paper with his middle finger extended.

"That's what I have to say to these assholes," he said. "They make me sick."

I laughed, folded the paper into my pocket, and gave Emir the bad news. "We don't know if someone else will get into this box.

Plus, I'd hate to be shown that someday on the witness stand by their lawyer."

The vault might be bugged, so I couldn't say more, but Emir knew what I meant.

We had all the paperwork we needed and made our courtesy visit to BCP. Time to go to Paris.

Gare de Cornavin, a dark and crowded old station, made even the brightest day in Geneva seem drab. It was rush hour, but the insufferably polite Swiss orchestrated their escape from the city like a well-practiced drill.

It should have been easy enough to get our tickets, but Linda took the lead and asked the agent in rapid-fire colloquial American English for four tickets to Paris. The agent stared and said something in French. Linda tried to force the conversation. Unfortunately, she was operating under the common misconception that speaking English slowly in a very loud voice would make her understood to a smart person without a hearing problem who didn't speak English at all.

Linda also suspected that the ticket clerk was pretending not to speak English. So Linda did what a streetwise *cummara* from New York would do. She stuck it back louder, again and again.

Emir of course played dumb and urged her on after each chorus, whispering, "I think this lady is bullshitting you. She speaks English." Then he stepped back and rolled his eyes in silent laughter.

"Let me try," murmured Kathy, who spoke French and easily returned with four first-class tickets on the bullet train to Paris.

We settled into our seats, and Emir set down a brown grocery bag from which he pulled a couple of bottles of wine, a loaf of bread, cheese, and prosciutto we'd picked up at a charcuterie near the station. Before long, we were warmly sharing our Gallic meal with two conductors and a passenger who sang songs and joked with us about the ugly Americans who were about to invade Paris.

Little did they know.

Though I felt relaxed, my mind stayed focused on the Chinoy meeting. There weren't going to be any second takes. Stumbling could set us back months, and I didn't have months to lose. As the train sped west toward Paris, through the Jura Mountains, along the Rhone River, and north through Burgundy, scripts churned through my head as they always did before critical undercover meetings.

Unlike the military, the rule in banking circles has always been "Don't ask, don't tell." Too much information made for sand in the gears of international commerce. Anyway, I had already had blatant conversations with Hussain and Awan about the source of the funds. Word would get back to them about my conversation with Chinoy, which could arouse suspicion if I wasn't completely careful.

But the first rule for undercover agents is "Get them to talk, and get it on tape." If you can't take your case to a jury, what's the point? Chinoy needed to confirm verbally that he wanted in. A nod wouldn't cut it. The jury needed to hear him say yes, preferably in enthusiastic terms. If I came away without hard proof that he knew what was going on, that he was already in the game, and that he intended to engage in a criminal conspiracy to hide drug profits, I was wasting my time. But if I pushed too hard, he would smell a setup. France itself offered the perfect solution: boil him like a frog. If you dunk a frog in hot water, it hops out. Put it in cold water, though, and you can heat the water so gradually that it doesn't realize it's cooking. That's the way I had to handle Chinoy.

The TGV pulled into Gare de Lyon in the center of Paris at midnight. The five-star Hôtel de la Trémoille lay just off the Champs-Elysées. The sheets on the enormous bed smelled as if they'd been dried on a line in the sun. I tried to run through one more scenario with Chinoy, but I was out before I got past the handshake.

In what felt like only a few minutes later, a maid in a traditional black dress and white apron, carrying a tray with coffee and croissants, knocked on my door.

It was time. Chinoy was expecting my call. We made a date for lunch.

I shook out my best suit, a black, double-breasted Carlo Palazzi, a white polished cotton shirt with French cuffs, and gold cuff links. My scarlet tie matched the silk square in my breast pocket.

When Emir spotted me, he sashayed across the room, one hand on his hip and the other extended to be kissed. "Oh, Mr. Musella, you look like you're going to a wedding," he gushed.

Better a wedding than a funeral, I thought, and left well enough alone.

While Kathy and Linda were dressing, Emir and I loaded fresh batteries and blank tapes into the recorders in our briefcases.

At the BCCI office on the Champs-Elysées, a few blocks from the Arc de Triomphe, we met a well-dressed, balding man with goggle-thick glasses. Nazir Chinoy introduced himself first, then Ian Howard, the BCCI Paris branch manger, and Sibte Hassan, his executive assistant.

After small talk, he led us outside to where three large Mercedes sedans, chauffeurs standing at the ready, waited to whisk us to lunch at Cercle de l'Union Interalliée, one of the most exclusive clubs in the heart of Paris, housed in an eighteenth-century mansion, and the club of choice for France's most distinguished political, cultural, and business figures.

We dined in the Salon Duc de Luynes, replete with ornate clocks, wall-length tapestries, and ceiling frescoes. When waiters had popped the corks from bottles of fine champagne and filled our glasses, Chinoy raised his flute aloft.

"I would like to welcome you to Paris," he said. "Please join me and raise your glasses to the beginning of what I'm sure will be a very wonderful friendship."

How many others like us had received such regal treatment?

Bottle after bottle poured as Chinoy held forth. He claimed descent from royalty and boasted that his father had been a top General Motors executive in Bombay. His forebears, he said, had been cabinet members and were knighted when India was still part of the British Empire.

In little more than a whisper, while conversation swirled around the table, I filled Chinoy's ear with my own "family" history.

"They came to America from Naples with nothing but the shirts on their backs. We fought our way to where we are today, and we like to think that we have won the respect we deserve in the financial community. My grandfather ran a moving company on the Lower East Side of Manhattan. With the help of 'special friends,' he built up the power and resources we have today.... My primary responsibility is to manage our group's money, but my friends in Colombia have provided us with a new, unique opportunity that I would like to share with you after we enjoy this wonderful lunch."

"I am one of a handful of our executives," Chinoy smiled, "who work closely with our president to shape the direction of our nearly five hundred branches worldwide. I'm sure we can be of assistance."

In fact, Chinoy was third in command at the bank, which employed 19,000 people. He spoke for the company. And on the company's dime, for two and a half hours, waiters brought an endless feast of caviar, foie gras, salmon, oysters, shrimp, escargots, cheeses, rabbit, lamb, and the finest French pastries.

After that amazing feast, Chinoy, Emir, and I settled down in the privacy of a small living room adjoining Chinoy's office. The courtship began. I told Chinoy that my company had developed several South American clients during the past several years and, under the watchful eye of Awan and other BCCI staff in Tampa, Miami, and Panama, the bank had enabled us to service our clients well. But we were growing concerned about Noriega's notoriety. He was destabilizing Panama as a banking center.

Chinoy nodded silently.

"So, we've restructured the whole thing all over again," I continued, "which is part of the reason we're here for two weeks. We are looking to Luxembourg, Paris, London, Uruguay, and Lichtenstein as the centers through which it would be most advantageous for the funds of our clients to be placed.... And we're quite interested in placing the funds, but of utmost ... interest to them is the sensitivity and the security of their funds in that there really can be no trace between the placement of the funds and them."

In seconds he had a solution. "I believe I can be very useful to you," he said, his face barely moving. "The link will be directly here without anybody being aware of it. No one need know who the real owner of the funds is.... Furthermore, you want that confidentiality. I think I can give that to you."

I explained that our clients had accumulations of large amounts of U.S. dollars in the States. "Although there is a certain degree to which I can and have handled those matters, anytime there's an opportunity to handle it to a greater degree, it will do nothing other than increase business. Currently, with no help, I'd say we're somewhere in the range of between $12 and $20 million a month. We could be substantially in excess of that if there were some means through which we could complement what it is that I accomplish."

Chinoy paused, running the numbers and options. "There are difficult factors, and this...that could make it trip up.... You establish your center goal first. Then let's sit down and make adjustments you'd like. We on both sides have to gain a certain amount of confidence."

Not what I expected to hear. Had I gone too far? Chinoy's reaction could be trouble or caution, but it was the first time he had suggested I didn't yet have his full trust—that there might be a limit to conversation he was willing to have. Time to throw him a carrot.

"Confidence? It's taken me two years to sit here and speak with you today.... At the very least, what I'd like to be able to accomplish between today and Monday—I want to transfer some funds from BCP here and place some funds of a very trusted friend of mine. We'll start with a million dollars for a period of six months in a CD, of which there's no need to make any borrowings. It can just stay. I have also decided, since we've had the pleasure of knowing Amjad for as long as we have, that I'm going to transfer some of my personal funds here. I'd say that that'll be somewhere between—about two million. Again, no need to borrow against that. And the same thing would go for Mr. Dominguez. We can take things as they develop from there."

There it was. If a $5 million carrot didn't earn his candor, nothing would.

Chinoy nodded in approval. "You've made an evaluation of Howard. You made the evaluation of Hassan. Every one of us makes an evaluation. Let's be honest. Do you feel these two people meet — you would be confident for them to be assigned as your account executives?"

"My gut reaction would be yes," I said. "What would be your recommendation? Because you've known them much longer than I."

"I know Hassan's family in Europe," Chinoy said. "I know these guys. I know I trust this boy implicitly."

He gave Howard even greater praise and explained that his faith in his two assistants was such that he let them independently manage more than a billion dollars of client funds at the Paris branch.

I explained how for the past year other BCCI branches had taken millions in funds, placed them in CDs, and let us borrow the bulk of the value of the CDs in another name, and that we'd like to continue that practice.

"No problem," he said.

Chinoy asked Hassan to join the meeting to handle the paperwork, which I handed to him. Hassan quickly assured me that he would prepare the signature cards and other forms to get the accounts up and running.

"You will find," Chinoy said after Hassan left, "that we will be much more understanding. If some of your clients have a problem, we will try our best to hide it from the authorities, to give you as much cover as we can. It is in our interest to assist you and your clients."

As important as it was to bring in big-dollar accounts, Chinoy explained, it was equally important to manage accounts like mine to minimize the risk. He had experience doing just that at Bank of America and Citibank.

Convinced we were approaching the final hook, I gave Emir a prearranged sign for him to leave so Chinoy wouldn't spook when I went in for the kill. Emir announced that he needed to make a call to Colombia. If anyone was listening or followed up on the call, Emir did in fact call a bona fide money broker in Medellín.

"Nazir," I said when Emir had left. "The sensitivity with which the funds must be handled, and the confidentiality, is of the most extreme nature. I don't have to talk any of this, you know, drug dealers in Colombia are the types of people that —"

"Yes, I understood you," Chinoy interrupted. "I didn't ask, okay, but I followed the deal."

For a terrible moment, I sat stupidly trying to remember what I had been saying before he cut me off. Chinoy knew the source of the funds, but a jury had to assess that there was no mistake, that he was willingly laundering drug money. Had he said enough? I wasn't sure.

"Listen, Nazir, we're big boys, and you need to know how sensitive these things are. My clients are professionals. The only difference between them and Lee Iacocca is that Iacocca sells cars and they sell coke." I stressed that I'd like my discussion about their business to remain confidential.

"That's how it should be," Chinoy said.

And we had him.

"Well, what do you think?" Emir asked as we walked back down the Champs-Elysées.

"The guy never blinked," I said. "He admitted that he already realized our money came from Colombian dopers." As we turned down a narrow cobblestone street, we quietly high-fived each other. We had done it, and we both felt the rush of success — but a dark undercurrent of anger surfaced.

"Those motherfuckers," Emir snarled after a while. "If it wasn't for them, the cartel would be powerless. Those assholes are bigger crooks than Escobar and the other killers we're dealing with. At least *they* don't hide behind a lie and claim they are something other than what they are. These guys make me sick."

"That's why we've got to see this thing through," I said, visually sweeping the area. "As bad as what this bank is doing, their officers didn't invent this; they learned it while they worked for other big banks in the world. This is just the beginning."

Back at the hotel, I took the tape out of the recorder, marked it with my initials and date, and popped the tabs so it couldn't be erased. Then I loaded a new cassette in case someone decided to pay me a surprise visit.

In an attempt to escape the tension, Emir, Kathy, Linda, and I changed and headed out to see a few sights. We had dinner at a quaint café in the shadow of Sacré Coeur, that strange, beautiful church standing sentinel over the City of Light. This same tiny patch of Montmartre had played host to Modigliani, Monet, Picasso, and Toulouse-Lautrec. As a street musician wandered past playing his tattered accordion, we all exhaled. I couldn't help but wonder at our luck.

The next day, we took a quick tour of the Louvre. Kathy was resolutely passionate about the art, but by the second hour Emir and I began to flag. As we walked through a collection of Egyptian artifacts, Emir disappeared behind a large statue of Anubis and emerged, serenading us with a distinctly Puerto Rican version of the Bangles' "Walk Like an Egyptian," flailing his hands like Steve Martin. We all doubled over laughing.

Chinoy had invited us to drinks that evening at his home, a high-end loft in the heart of the city. It was Chinoy's weekday home. He and his family spent weekends at a house in the countryside. Chinoy's teenage son, who had the manners and presence of a man, answered the door and escorted us to the living room. While Chinoy was running late, his son engaged us in a conversation about Paris that you would expect from a diplomat.

Five minutes later, Chinoy emerged, sporting a blue-and-red silk paisley ascot and a scarlet silk shirt. He introduced his wife and two children and opened a bottle of wine while asking how we were enjoying our stay. As casual conversation took over the living room, I signaled to Chinoy that I wanted to speak with him privately. We strolled to an adjoining room.

"Some important clients of mine will be arriving tomorrow from Colombia," I said. "It is possible that I may need a little help to convince them to join the BCCI family. Would you be willing to meet with me and the clients, if I feel they are on the fence?"

"Of course I will help," he said, as though I had asked a foolish question. "You should know that I have an account executive in my Paris office whom I routinely assign to manage affairs for clients in Colombia. He travels there once every three months and slips into the country with account records that detail the status of client accounts. We encourage the client to allow us to hold those records after they're reviewed, for their own security. Otherwise they run the risk of their financial picture being discovered by the authorities. If you'd like, I will assign this person to assist you and your clients."

"Thank you, Nazir," I said — and I meant it.

No wonder BCCI Paris attracted more than a billion dollars in deposits. The bank not only laundered money but took extra precautions to prevent the feds from intercepting or seizing incriminating records.

As we departed later, Chinoy and his wife asked us to join them, Howard, Hassan, and their families for dinner the following night. We had to accept. He was the key to our new system around the logjam in Panama and the man who would open new doors at the bank.

Time to hit the pay phones. I needed to brief Steve Cook and call home.

Ev was tired of hearing about the case of the century that warranted endless sacrifice. Like Tischler, she was counting the days until October. Government agents prepared for this work in undercover schools, but no one prepared our families, and in the War on Drugs the families of undercover agents often become collateral damage. We had infiltrated the underworld at a level never seen before by undercover agents, and nothing could stop me from doing as much as I could before headquarters pulled the rug out. Silence, pain, and frustration often filled our calls.

"I miss you," I said.

"I know," she sighed. "When will you be back?"

"We'll be in Paris for a few more days, but then we're off to London. I'm not sure—but we should be back in the States in a week or so—but then I've got to hang out with some guys in Miami for a while. How are you and the kids?"

"We're okay. We're doing our usual things—work, school, gym meets, dentist appointments, car repairs, and everything else.... Plus, it's near the end of the school year, so it's pretty crazy.

"Listen," she continued after a pause. "I'm done with this case. When you get back, Scott will be at the regional gym meet with the team, and Andrea will be staying with friends. I won't be here. I'm going to a hotel on Redington Beach for a few days. When I decide which hotel, I'll let you know. You can meet me there if you want to and if you have the time."

"Of course I'll meet you at the hotel. I'm sorry I'm putting you through this."

"It is what it is," she said. "When this is over, we'll see if we can put things back together again."

After a long silence, we said our goodbyes and hung up.

I stared at the phone for what felt like hours, then shook myself from the sadness overwhelming me. I had to. I was about to face the biggest test of Robert Musella's credibility yet. What happened next could redefine the War on Drugs.

14

MEDELLÍN INVADES PARIS

Hôtel de la Trémoille, Paris
May 22, 1988

THE SMELL OF SCOTCH POURED INTO MY ROOM as Mora and Ospiña burst in, all smiles and bloodshot eyes. They had celebrated all the way from Medellín to Paris. Despite the fact that I'd partied with them before, this was behavior hardly fitting two men guarding the gateway to a deadly cartel. Which didn't stop Ospiña from asking to attack my minibar — the man needed more.

In slurred Spanish, as he rummaged, Ospiña explained that Don Chepe's people would invest a million dollars at BCCI Paris and four more at a German bank controlled by Armbrecht's uncle. These investments were little more than a drop in the bucket. The Scotch had lowered his guard, and Ospiña was wagging his tongue, announcing that it was important I convince Don Chepe's representatives that I had the resources to clean and invest the organization's money securely. He warned that Armbrecht had a lot of authority. The other man to participate in our meetings on behalf of Don Chepe, Santiago Uribe, a lawyer and consigliere, oversaw much of the cartel's operations.

Ospiña planned that we all join Armbrecht and Uribe for dinner that night, but Chinoy had already asked us to join him, Howard, Hassan, and their families for dinner. Meeting Armbrecht and Uribe would have to wait. Ospiña fumed. How could I keep Armbrecht waiting? I'd flown to Paris for many reasons, I told him, but he shouldn't have assumed that I traveled 8,000 miles exclusively for their business. Ospiña needed to know he wasn't the only act in town.

The Colombians had balls but not scruples—a dangerous combination. But we couldn't show fear. I had to be as confident, cold, and calculating as them. They sensed fear, always alert to signs that a person wasn't what he seemed. But at this point friendly fire was more likely to kill us than they were.

Because most of the cartel's money that was in banks normally flowed through Panama, *los duros* direly needed alternatives. Money was backing up, and Noriega's fight with the U.S. was creating a banking logjam. If we could sell our alternate system, we could get a big chunk of their business. It all made sense, but Ospiña was drunk, and we had plans.

Emir took Ospiña and Mora back to their hotel and returned with Mora and Lucy. Other people from the cartel, including Don Chepe, Mora said, would join Armbrecht and Uribe. An important detail. We would be outnumbered, and I needed more intel on their entourage. Don Chepe wouldn't be traveling without muscle.

Mora also worried that Ospiña's behavior didn't sit well with Armbrecht and Uribe. We had to distance ourselves from his stupidity. Mora helped us develop a strategy to deal with Don Chepe's men. Although Armbrecht, a pilot, normally didn't involve himself in money matters, his opinions carried considerable weight with the cartel, who held his integrity and intelligence in high regard. His report on our operation would go a long way. We needed to win Armbrecht as we had Alcaíno.

A competitor—a man known as *El Costeño Mama Burra*—was also arriving with Don Chepe tomorrow. Emir burst out laughing. Roughly translated, the nickname meant "Donkey-Fucker from the North Coast." The man, known to the DEA at the time as Eduardo Martinez, was considered one of the most influential launderers servicing the cartel. In return for payments to Banco de Occidente officers in Panama, Martinez was laundering tens of millions of cartel money. And he was surely going to try to undermine Don Chepe's confidence in our every move. According to Mora, if we could convince Armbrecht to keep $1 million at BCCI Paris, then we had become a trusted source for Don Chepe and a threat to Martinez. Mora had put everything on the line for us — including his head. He needed me to win Armbrecht's trust.

Seven of them and only two of us. Not a good ratio. But we couldn't afford to ask for backup. If they detected surveillance, we died. We had no guns, no badges, and no authority in France. Only a handful of people at our embassy and French Customs even knew we were in Paris, and they weren't keeping tabs on us. We had to feel our way through it, one meeting at a time.

While Ospiña passed out at his hotel, Emir, Kathy, Linda, and I joined Chinoy, Howard, Hassan, and their families for dinner. As with every other feast, Chinoy arranged a five-star meal in one of the many exquisite restaurants in Paris. Between courses, Chinoy whispered, "I intend to travel to the U.S. in two months, and I would very much like to meet with you and whoever you think would be appropriate in your group. I think we can do good things for one another."

"I'm sure we can," I said. "I would very much like to introduce you to a few members of my 'family' who share the responsibility I have with our organization to maintain the security of our financial affairs.... It would be a pleasure to have you as our guest. You've been so kind to us.... I feel like we've known each other for years."

"Thank you, Bob." Chinoy smiled. "The feeling is mutual."

Time to test a plan Kathy and I had been discussing. We eventually needed to get all our targets to Tampa to end the case. If we didn't grab them on our turf, they'd run beyond the range of extradition — to Colombia or Pakistan. We didn't have to set a date now, but we could test the reaction to an event planned for five to twelve months out. All the targets seemed to like us. They thought we were engaged....

"We're beginning to make plans for our wedding," I said to Chinoy. "It will be a lavish celebration over a couple of days, and every important person of authority in my family will be there. This will include all the members of our board, if you know what I mean. I know we've just met, but I see you not only as a friend but a very important person in the life of our organization. I would be truly honored if you and your family would accept our invitation to join us at this celebration. We haven't set a date yet, but it could be as early as October."

"Why, thank you very much," he replied, seeing a golden opportunity. "We would be honored to attend and wouldn't miss it for the world. Munira, the children, and I will be there."

That was easy. Perhaps staging a fake wedding made sense.

After dinner, Howard drove us on a short tour of Paris and through the Bois de Boulogne, the 2,100-acre park on the western edge of central Paris. As we cruised along narrow roads, he pointed out dozens of hookers, who smiled and waved. After an extra long drag on his cigarette, in his proper British accent, Howard said, "You'll find this amazing, Bob. These are transsexuals, and they migrate to certain areas of the park based on their nationality. So if you're interested in a he/she from Venezuela, this is your section. Over there, you can find them from various parts of Africa and so on. Utterly amazing, isn't it?"

Indeed.

The following day, Mora informed Emir that Armbrecht was ready to begin discussions with me. Best to meet him privately first. Ospiña had created a lot of distractions, and Armbrecht needed to focus on the issues most important to us. Six people in a room pushing the conversation in their direction wasn't going to work. And naturally cautious people tend to withdraw even more when they meet new people in a crowd. Armbrecht needed to know that I, too, was cautious. If he was a real player, he would understand. With Mora's help, I coordinated a rendezvous in the lobby of the George V hotel, where Armbrecht was staying, a seventeenth-century palace a few blocks from the Trémoille.

Mora had warned me that Armbrecht dressed simply, but he still deserved my best business outfit. Armbrecht knew what I would be wearing, so it was up to him to find me. I found a secluded alcove on the first floor, turned on the recorder, and waited, studying the massive ceiling-to-floor seventeenth-century tapestry a few feet from the Victorian couch on which I was sitting. Armbrecht would have to sit on my right, facing open space. I didn't want us opposite one another — too confrontational. On the loveseat, my body would be open to him, no legs or arms crossed, nothing to hide.

An unassuming, confident man dressed in blue jeans, cowboy boots, plaid shirt, and brown suede jacket strolled toward me. He sat down next to me wordlessly and offered a smile and a nod of his tilted head.

"I'm sorry we had so much confusion that prevented me from meeting you sooner," I said.

"Nothing personal," he replied, after a long pause. "They're making things a little difficult to get here.... It's somebody that's, like, in the middle, and I don't like him over there."

He meant Ospiña. His English offered a hint of an accent from his German and Colombian heritage.

"I apologize," I said. "There was a lack of communication by the people between me and you...but thank goodness we are together now, and that's what counts."

"There is somebody that has been in the middle, that's been in the middle of Mora...and the guy who I wish wasn't, he has some big personal problems, at best. But he's letting that go in the middle of the business, and I came over here not to look around, I came over here to get to business."

"Hopefully we'll have the pleasure of your company this evening for dinner," I said. "If you haven't got plans already, we'd love to——"

"Wonderful," he said.

"Emilio works with all my South American clients," I said, diving in. "He helps in translation, as well as for assisting in actually receiving those things we need to receive and ultimately get for the client's benefit back in the States" — code speak for money for wire transfers.

"Well, Bob, I would like to know a little bit more of the type of arrangement your financial corporation has over there. What are the mechanisms that function, how do they function, and what are the guarantees that could be given to us, one way or the other? Because, if the arrangement is good, and it seems to be very good, the amount of money that we can generate and remove is quite considerable."

"That would be very good," I said after a measured pause. "I think this gives us the opportunity to see whether we can move forward or not. I have no reason to believe that we can't. I recognize that you need to know more about me personally and I think you deserve to. I have no hesitancy in discussing whatever it is that needs to be discussed."

"I didn't want to ask that, but if you propose it, yes, great. It could be very interesting."

"I think it could be good for both of us to be a little more familiar with each other. Therefore, as we say in the States, I'm prepared to drop my pants first and tell you about me."

He laughed. "Bob, you have to understand a little bit my position. I'm very cautious and...certain things, I like to get all the facts."

"Neither of us would be sitting here, in the business that we are in, if we didn't have that mindset. And that's the way we both are."

"Good."

Armbrecht explained that the lawyer, Santiago Uribe, would attend our meetings. *Los duros* also weighed Uribe's opinions heavily. Then he returned to complaining about Ospiña, which might have caused problems if he didn't know I knew him.

"I'm very appreciative of having developed, through Gonzalo, a friendship with Mr. Ospiñ—"

"Oh, shit!"

"—but Gonzalo in fact is our representative in Colombia."

"Good," he said, relieved.

"Gonzalo is the one with whom we've dealt for years," I continued. "He's the one in whom I have utmost confidence."

I briefed Armbrecht on the history I had with BCCI. I explained in detail how I had been persuaded about three years ago to deal with South American clients. I invited Armbrecht to join me in the States, where I could give him the full dog-and-pony tour. I explained how the accounts of the many front businesses enabled us to make cash deposits in the U.S. and how our air charter service smuggled cash out of the U.S. to offshore banks.

Armbrecht worried that I was requiring his group to place a million dollars in a CD as a prerequisite to handling large volumes of their money.

"Why do you characterize it as a requirement," I countered, "as much as it is 'You scratch my back, I'll scratch yours'?" We couldn't survive without the help of the banks, so we had to do what made them happy. I gave him a full overview of the system, adding solemnly, "If I accept the responsibility, I accept it not only with my reputation but with my life. If I put it any other way, you wouldn't do business with me."

"The problem is cash," he said, "and we have a lot." They had cash in many places and wanted as much of that cash in CDs, but they also wanted Occam's razor. "The best solution to any problem is the simplest of all solutions, so we try to keep this very simple. And that's why I do so many things personally. I go and buy the airplanes myself. I have them repaired myself. I fly them myself. I do transactions across my accounts over here in Europe.... Never do I pay in fucking cash, *never*.... Nobody else knows what I do. We try to keep things simple, simple by not getting many people involved."

"From the standpoint of the streets," I replied, "Dominguez is responsible. After it leaves the street, it's on my shoulders."

"Good," he said. "Aside from the million we are currently dealing with, which is no big deal, we're going to have another operation that is a lot of money sitting just for the security of the organization.... We don't want anybody to take it. We have $30 million sitting now in Louisville, Kentucky, and I don't have any more because I don't know any more. But we could have, I don't know, fifty, a hundred million dollars or more. It's an immense amount that we want to place simply as insurance money for the organization. If we can develop a good machinery, it could be renewing.

I could get many other people interested in this system.... We are big businessmen who don't like to buy huge homes or buildings. This is an organization and we like to have it more concealable to deal with it, and we like cash. It's very available."

"I've done a lot of talking about myself," I said. "I'm eager to know a little bit about you." His response would reveal whether he was comfortable with me.

He paused. "I'm a professional pilot.... I used to fly for Avianca. For seven years I've been flying 707s and 737s.... I studied medicine for a few years. I didn't like it.... My father is German, and I've lived in Europe, the States, and Latin America.... I have a very open mind because I have had the opportunity to appreciate many different cultures. I'm also a compulsive leader; I'm leading all the time, and learning, and learning.... I'm in the middle of all this because you find throughout life you can trust very few people, and I have this problem that people trust me very much.... I'm extremely analytical.... I don't make big mistakes."

You're about to, I thought.

"I would like to have Mr. Ospiña out of all, out of everything," he continued. "I don't like him.... I think he handled things so that we could not get together.... His sexual preferences can be whatever, and I don't care about them. But he tried to get me involved in his experiences. I don't like it.... I don't like him knowing anything.... I think he's a person that's very subject to pressure, and it's very easy to get something on him."

He asked that we return to my hotel, and if Ospiña was present we'd cut our meeting short and resume later without him. If Ospiña wasn't there, we'd meet at length with Uribe and resolve any unanswered questions.

In the room, Emir, Mora, and Uribe were waiting—all business, no greetings. Armbrecht went right to his biggest concern. He stared into Mora's eyes and with a driven tone said, "I want to know exactly what role he has played in the transactions."

Again, he meant Ospiña.

"Right, right, uh," Mora stammered. "Uh, I met that individual in November. In Medellín, they introduced him to me, um, um. They spoke to me about having potential clients because he was a middleman. He hasn't been any more than that...and he tried to make those deals without talking about Don Chepe."

Mora was distancing himself while still offering enough so that Ospiña wouldn't be killed before he left Paris. He credited Ospiña with introducing him to Don Chepe, but that didn't matter to Armbrecht and Uribe.

"I don't want him," Armbrecht decided.

"No, neither do I," Uribe said.

Ospiña's many vices made him vulnerable. He'd been drunk the night before, and he talked too much even when sober. On top of that, he exaggerated his own importance.

"This is a man who is dumb, besides being vulgar and an ass," Armbrecht said.

Uribe whispered in Armbrecht's ear.

"Violence doesn't solve anything," Armbrecht replied.

Ospiña's life might soon come to an end, it seemed.

Their frustrations vented, it was time for me to explain the system to Uribe. I laid out how BCCI helped us hide the true sources of funds, and then I reviewed and explained the documents the lawyer had prepared in Zürich for the Gibraltar company, Nicesea Shipping Ltd., a company established to maintain the account holding Don Chepe's million at BCCI Paris. To reassure Armbrecht and Uribe, I told them I had arranged a meeting for us with Nazir Chinoy.

"I would like to have made a little graphic of how things are functioning so we can all make this graph of what's happening," Armbrecht said.

"No problem." I drew a step-by-step diagram of how our process worked, which impressed him.

At the end of my presentation, I played a card that a cop never would. "You have an open invitation to come to Tampa, to stay with me at my home, to come with me to New York and, in the case of New York, certainly since it's my cousin, I have no doubt that we're dealing with a situation where you can be there but not be known in any way, shape, or form. You needn't even be introduced by name, if you would like. I think sometimes it's helpful to actually see the operation and maybe spend a few days so that you can satisfy yourself that things are being professionally run. That invitation is open at any time that you should so choose to think it's advisable."

"Thank you," Armbrecht said coolly.

Mora chimed in and supported my arguments. He stressed that I was concerned about jeopardizing the security of our operation, set up originally for our clients in the U.S. Ours was a complete package that didn't just move money but invested it.

"That's why we are here," Armbrecht said, "to be able to examine all this and eventually to be able to establish a complete mechanism that will benefit us for a long time."

Years of planning were paying off. We were not only becoming one of their primary money-laundering sources but also one of their banks. Then Armbrecht offered a sign of trust. He wanted me to obtain powers of attorney for Nicesea Shipping so someone else could control the account with him.

"Since I've messed up names before," I said, "if one of you would write down the name..."

Armbrecht wrote "Gerardo Moncada."

Bingo. Another high-ranking member of the organization hit the radar screen. We didn't know it yet, but Moncada was Don Chepe, the man in charge, Pablo Escobar's underboss.

Armbrecht stroked his chin. "What happens if you disappear?"

Everyone laughed but me. I knew he was serious. "That's why you have power of attorney. Everyone knows where I live. Everyone knows where I work."

My response surprised him a little. "I'm not talking about that," he said. "I'm talking that if, you know, something, an accident. You know you have to think about it."

I had issued two powers of attorney on his accounts for just that reason. If Bob Musella died, Armbrecht and his organization could take control.

"That's right," he said. "That's very, very good. Yes. Basically it's questions and questions and questions. Good, good, good."

Then a knock on the door. It was Ospiña. Armbrecht lied that we had met by coincidence and that he had just begun to test me on the security of our system. We talked in circles for half an hour. Ospiña couldn't realize he was being cut out, but he also couldn't learn any more details.

Dinner and the night's entertainment were on me, so I picked the centuries-old Le Grand Véfour restaurant on rue de Beaujolais. In the heart of Paris, next to the gardens of the Palais Royal, Véfour formed one of the ideological centers of the French Revolution. Its guests over the years had included Napoleon and Josephine Bonaparte, Victor Hugo, Jean-Paul Sartre and Simone de Beauvoir. Huge stone columns lining the entrance made a runway for the red carpet that led to the front door. An army of doormen and waiters fell all over themselves to cater to our every wish. The famous interior mirrors made it seem much bigger than it was. *An apt metaphor*, I thought. We feasted for almost four hours, running up a tab of about $2,000.

Unless you live with high rollers like Armbrecht, you don't realize that the refined luxury of Le Grand Véfour represents nothing more than a credibility prop to make your job a little easier. You don't think about whether you're drinking Dom Perignon or jug wine. You're so intent on maintaining your cover and getting information that the decadence of Le Grand Véfour is the last thing on your mind. You develop tunnel vision.

As she had with Alcaíno, Kathy lavished her attention on Armbrecht. They discussed French art and philosophy. She read his palm and filled his head with predictions of his greatness and talent. He ate it all.

After midnight, at L'Escalier, an exclusive nightclub, more champagne flowed and everyone, including the stiff professor, Santiago Uribe, danced to the hottest beats Paris had to offer. While they danced, Uribe told Kathy he wasn't feeling well. She asked if he had a fever and tried to touch his face. He grabbed her wrist and warned her not to touch him again. I was listening to Armbrecht saying that three important people from Medellín were arriving the next day, with whom he planned to travel to Austria and Germany. I never noticed Kathy's incident with Uribe. Better not to, in any case—I didn't want to create a scene.

At L'Escalier, Armbrecht apologized for Ospiña's conduct. "He's a big liability. He drinks too much, has a big mouth. He's rude, and he's disruptive in meetings. His sexual escapades draw attention. His coming on to me was a big mistake; that will never happen again. He will not be in our meetings anymore. Santiago and I are bullshitting him that he needs to go back to Medellín to brief one of the bosses about the status of our negotiations. It's best that we compensate him fairly, but he needs to be disassociated from Don Chepe's financial transactions. We'll keep an eye on him, and, if it appears that he is not being loyal, we'll do what we have to do."

"Your call," I nodded. "However you see fit to handle this I support you one hundred percent."

"Emilio, I would like your help," Uribe said. "We'd like you to do Ospiña, take him out, while we're here."

"Are you crazy?" Emir said. "Here in Paris? No, man, that's too risky. If this needs to be done, it should be done someplace safe. Ship his ass back to Colombia. Your people control everything there."

"So be it," Uribe said. "You won't see him again."

Through the blaring music, Emir shared what Uribe had just said. Armbrecht and Uribe were looking right at us. I nodded as a sign that I understood.

We never saw Ospiña again.

We returned to the hotel at 4 A.M. to find that Kathy had contracted food poisoning, which put her out of commission for the next few days while Emir and I continued negotiations with the Colombians and work with the bankers.

The next day, Mora marched into our room, full of energy. We needed to pump him before our meeting with Armbrecht and

Uribe. Two of the three men from Medellín arriving tonight worked with Armbrecht, and one of those two was Gerardo Moncada. The third was the younger brother of a board member of the cartel who worked with Uribe. Armbrecht and his two buddies belonged to the same organization that sent tons of cocaine to the people in Detroit who gave us suitcases full of cash. We had gone deep. This was management.

Uribe, impressed with what we had to offer, wanted to introduce the younger brother, but Armbrecht killed the idea. If we handled major money for another group, that group's mistakes could taint me and my companies, creating collateral damage for Armbrecht and his bosses if they were tied to us. Armbrecht had big plans — but a knock on the door cut short our discussion. It was Armbrecht and Uribe.

"I told him," Armbrecht said of Ospiña, "that I didn't want him near these things. That he had been very kind and a very good person and that it had been nice of him to introduce us to Gonzalo and to Robert and to Emilio. That basically his task in relation to us had finished, and that as far as I knew we didn't have any obligation to him. That anything —"

The telephone rang. Emir answered and turned to Armbrecht.

"He is asking me," Emir said of Ospiña, "what instructions are you giving him, if you want him to go there to wait for those people at the airport."

Ospiña was seeking permission to make another move. Armbrecht issued his order. Ospiña would pick up the three men from Medellín and bring them to the Trémoille.

Dammit. They were staying at our hotel. Three of Armbrecht's people, none of whom we could recognize, staying under our noses and possibly in the next room.

Armbrecht pulled out a pad full of questions, which we covered one at a time. He had done his homework — and thoroughly. We had been out late the night before, but he had studied all the documents I had given him.

One of his sticking points involved establishing a means

by which, at any time he chose, he could take total control of the corporations and bank accounts we established on behalf of his group. To be in total control, he had to be sole director of the company. To protect him from people who would try to claim that he was the owner of the funds—that is, U.S. authorities—we could draft a contract between my investment company and him claiming that we requested him to assume that role. If anyone asked, he could refer them to us. We in turn would tell them—that is, the authorities—that our lawyers in Lichtenstein managing the Lichtenstein trust that owned the company had asked us to hire someone with his talents to manage the company's affairs.

Hell would freeze over before the U.S. could force answers out of attorneys in Lichtenstein. Our system would lead the government to a dead end. Guaranteed.

Armbrecht squinted and digested the suggestion. He liked what he heard. "Basically the whole purpose of this, Robert, is to establish a mechanism to have the monies in a very secure and very discreet way, okay? And not to expose the different persons that could be exposed, who are the owners of most of the money.... Obviously we will have you arrange more companies. We don't want to have one company with $100 million in it."

Armbrecht, the man with the power to direct a river of money from the cartel, planned to use us to hide *$100 million or more*. Astounding—but I had to play cool.

During the meeting, Howard called and left word that Chinoy was prepared to meet with Armbrecht, Uribe, and me in less than an hour. We adjourned our meeting, and agreed that Armbrecht and Uribe would meet me in the lobby of their hotel in forty-five minutes, during which I made a quick call to the Zürich lawyer.

As Armbrecht, Uribe, and I walked to the Champs-Elysées, I explained the background of the BCCI officers they were about to meet. And I told them the truth: I'd only recently met these gentlemen through longtime BCCI contacts in Florida and Panama. Our relationship grew from the urgency of finding an alternative to Panama. Embellishment at this stage could only backfire. Thanks to the call to the lawyer, by the time we arrived at BCCI Paris, I had also provided Armbrecht with answers to each of the questions he had raised at the hotel.

Ian Howard welcomed us at the bank but asked to meet with me privately. Chinoy joined us, so I was able to tell both of them that Armbrecht and Uribe were significant members of one of the Colombian groups that used my services. I requested they inform my clients why BCCI was a sound and reliable bank because I hoped these gentlemen would entrust me with substantial amounts of their group's money that could be placed with BCCI Paris. They wanted me to act as a buffer between them and the bank, and they wanted anonymity. Chinoy promised to put everyone at ease.

At the full meeting, Howard handed Armbrecht and Uribe packets of brochures, financial statements, and other promotional material. He and Chinoy made a polished presentation, stressing the bank's stability and global presence. When Armbrecht expressed concern about fees, Chinoy instantly reassured him. "We won't take a short-term view. We'll take a long-term view. We want a relation-ship. We want to make — we don't make on every deal, and we're quite happy to make smaller amounts and do larger numbers." It was music to the ears of a man who controlled tens of millions of dollars that needed placement in a safe bank.

Armbrecht agreed that BCCI was the right choice, but he wanted Chinoy and Howard to know how things would work. "We're going to have a more or less considerable amount of business with your bank. Bob will be in charge of everything, and he will make any contacts and do all the things and that kind of thing."

That was it — my promotion had just been announced. I was on my way to becoming CFO of the cartel's expansion into Europe, and Armbrecht gave me high marks for bringing him to BCCI, while signing documents giving him access to the million dollars of Don Chepe's money I'd placed in a CD. "We'll observe him from a distance in the future," Armbrecht said of Ospiña on the walk back. "If his behavior suggests that he may create problems, our group will eliminate the problem." Then Armbrecht stopped on the street cold: "Do you do business with a man named Fernando Galeano?"

"No, I don't," I said. "Why do you ask?"

"Galeano is one of *los duros*, but his business practices are reckless."

Ospiña worked with Galeano and had mentioned to Armbrecht that he intended to bring me Galeano's business. Armbrecht proposed not only that I turn down Galeano but that I also refrain from working with any other groups. Don Chepe's organization, he assured me, would bring more business than I could handle and on my terms.

"I'd have to see that your people are committed to channeling investments to us before I could consider turning everyone else away," I said. "I'm not saying it's not possible. First I'd have to see results."

We later learned that, like Moncada, Fernando Galeano reported directly to Pablo Escobar. The opportunities before us were unimaginable and unprecedented. When the bigwigs in Washington heard what we could accomplish, they would remove the arbitrary takedown date in October — surely.

The next day, Emir and I went to lunch solo, but as we wandered toward the George V we ran into Armbrecht, Uribe, and the three men from Medellín. Two of the men stepped back to avoid contact with us, but Armbrecht introduced the third as Gerardo Moncada. He looked amazingly young for a drug lord — his thirties, I guessed — and, other than a nod, he had nothing to say.

But it was time to visit Howard and Hassan to engage them in conversations confirming that they, too, knew where the money came from.

Howard confirmed that Chinoy had filled him in about my clients' business, which gave me the perfect opening to say, "Mr. Armbrecht is the type of person that I think ... You're dealing with me. I'm an investment adviser, and the things that can be said as to what it is that — a cover, so to speak, an air of legitimacy to me. That doesn't exist for Mr. Armbrecht. So therefore it's probably safest for everyone that a lot of—"

"That we would deal with you," Howard said.

"We cannot afford for drug investigators to be looking into things from your end of this."

"We both completely understood," Howard said, "and we organize things. Anyway, not to worry for that matter; it's in a bond we uphold.... We've recently, on behalf of heads of state in African nations, structured transactions through Monaco to enhance confidentiality. That's an area you should consider using."

No wonder Africa's poor never see a dime of the billions of dollars sent to their governments for relief.

Then Howard put me on the phone with Awan, who was visiting "a dear friend in London," Asif Baakza, my BCCI contact there.

"My friend is ready to greet you," Awan said, "when you arrive in London, and I look forward to seeing you back in Miami when you return."

Baakza and I spoke briefly and made plans to meet in London.

With Howard's confession on tape, and a similar confession from Hassan to Emir, BCCI Paris had cracked wide open. But we still had one more meeting in Paris with Armbrecht—a meeting that lasted for more than four hours.

Armbrecht rendered his verdict. "We are talking about the final layout of this.... We have approved the machinery up to this point, which I think is very acceptable. Now we have to give it the purpose of all the machinery. The purpose is to have the money over there [the U.S.] or to have a way to deposit money in different accounts over here that will be very secure."

Although he intended to direct a lot of the cartel's money to us, he wasn't offering a monopoly as their bankers. With the help of his uncle, a senior executive at the Commerzbank in Hanover, he was laundering tens of millions more for *los duros*. And he had other bank sources as well.

Armbrecht wanted to determine how much money to channel

through our system. Not good enough. I wanted a commitment, so he promised to start with between $2 million and $10 million per month. "You're gonna earn for what you know, not really for what you do," he said. "Your value, Robert, is the experience you have. That's like myself. I don't know a lot but I'm very fast in learning, and I got all my money because I'm very fast in learning, and they pay me for what I know.... I have a deep respect for your knowledge of this.... That's why I'm so worried if you miss—if you're absent."

"No problem, with friends like you I won't go anywhere," I joked.

"I think those workers are dealing in both places in two jobs for the organization," Emir said of the Giraldo brothers' distributing cocaine and delivering cash in Detroit. "This is risky for me."

"We will try in the future to differentiate that a little bit," Armbrecht conceded. "Obviously, the one who handles that shit, well, is of enough trust to handle the other one, too.... We're not interested in having the money there and the merchandise in the same place. Forget about that bullshit. Since we work more than fifty or a hundred little shits"—kilos of coke—"at the same time...We are distributors everywhere. We never have big falls, and we're always careful, and we don't put in [one spot] four tons or five because we think it's foolish."

Armbrecht now had no wiggle room about the source of the money. At his request I gave him phone numbers to three of my offices, my home, and my cell. He gave me four numbers at which I could reach him in Medellín, two of which he said were secure. Having the CIA or NSA intercept phone conversations on those lines would provide a road map to the cartel's fortune.

"I might simply surprise you," Armbrecht said before leaving the room, "and show up in Tampa next week."

Nothing would make me happier, I thought.

It wasn't more than a minute after Armbrecht left that Mora disclosed that Don Chepe and other cartel members maintained offices above the Marandua restaurant in Medellín. The joint was like the Chalmun's Cantina in *Star Wars:* drug lords, murderers, moneymen, and smugglers of all kinds gathered there. Hoards of machine gun–packing sentries guarded the fortress of a building. Mora grew pale and uncomfortable as he described it. Don Chepe had twice summoned him to Marandua, and he didn't want to return. But he would. Greed makes men do strange things.

Armbrecht called twice that night to see if I had done research he had requested that afternoon, which I had. Since it was our last night in Paris, I convinced him that we should all go to the local Regine's. The Moras and Armbrecht joined us for food, cocktails, and a social setting in which to see us as real people. We also floated the wedding possibility with the Moras. They wouldn't miss it for the world.

Morning saw us off to London on a train from Paris to Calais, then the ferry past the chalk cliffs to Dover. At a coffee shop we made contact with John Luksic, a Customs agent assigned to the U.S. embassy there. Our designated contact, Luksic appreciated our paranoia about going anywhere near the embassy and let us run around in circles until we were confident no one was tailing us. He knew why we were there, but we reconfirmed the plan and filled him in on the last two weeks in Europe.

After a few calls to targets — to check on paperwork or transactions or to have them return my calls at a five-star hotel abroad — it was time to meet Asif Baakza, manager of the Corporate Unit at BCCI London. Awan, a close friend and colleague, had handpicked Baakza for the inner team. I introduced him to Emir, Kathy, and Linda but arranged for Kathy and Linda to leave shortly after his arrival. Baakza needed to meet Kathy because, in the event of my demise, she would have power of attorney.

"What we need to accomplish," I said to him, "has to do with the placement and transfer of funds in a very, very confidential and secure fashion." He learned that I'd been banking with BCCI for years and knew the bank had the experience to help me reach my goal. Awan had sent me because I needed to avoid the instability of Panama.

"Good," he said, and he had a plan. To aid in the secrecy of my transactions, he planned to open a manager's ledger account, an account that has no name. The police had access to the information he had, provided they also had a search warrant—not issued easily. Foreigners often placed huge sums of money in manager's ledger accounts, which bolstered the bottom line of investments in the country. Other than Baakza and the assistant manager, no one would know the name linked to the numbered ledger account assigned to me.

Perfect.

Baakza whipped out all the forms needed to establish accounts. He pointed—I signed. I told him that many of my clients were Colombians who sold currency to buy large U.S. dollar checks in amounts of roughly $250,000 at a time. Baakza said his branch transported checks for clients to Panama. In turn, the Panama branch cleared each check and credited it to London. Money moved around the world, and the client didn't even have to leave Colombia.

"There's one or two little short things I need to mention to wrap it up," I said to Emir, using a code for him to leave the room. "While I'm doing that, will you be able to give John a call?"

"The thing I wanted to mention," I continued after Emir had gone. "As trusted as Emilio and I are, we recognize the importance of diversifying communications."

"Mmm-hmm," Baakza said.

"It's extremely important to me that I am in a position of knowing everything and that, for the security of the funds, not everything is known in other areas. When I'm dealing with the bank, I consider Amjad to be the major person. There may—there isn't anything that I think he could ask of that I wouldn't give him full authority to know about. With regard to other managers within the system, although I have an equal amount of confidence, sometimes it's best not to know what all the parts to the puzzle are."

"I agree," Baazka said. "I don't want to know anything that I have no need to know."

Then I played my necessary song about Lee Iacocca. If the president and CEO of Chrysler only knew.

"That's right! That's right!" Baakza said.

"Iacocca sells cars, and they sell coke, and that's the only difference. They're executives about this entire thing."

We'd done it. We'd finished two weeks of intense meetings, dozens of hours of recorded conversation, and collected a stack of paper that traced the boomeranging of drug money around the world. We had six BCCI officers on tape, selling their services to move dirty cash. We also had our first million-dollar investment from Moncada, and we had two new players in the cartel convinced that we offered some of the best money-laundering services on the planet.

But while I continued to build the trap for them, Armbrecht planned his own surprise for me.

15

REVELATIONS

Bayou Village Apartments, Tampa, Florida
May 31, 1988

THEY NEEDED TO KNOW every name, number, and fact we'd collected in Europe.

Tischler, Jackowski, Cook, Sherman, and half a dozen other agents were sitting in the living room of a safe house at the Bayou Village Apartments near Tampa International. Emir, Kathy, and I reviewed everything that had happened, submitted a report, turned over the dozen or so recordings, and presented a half-foot stack of bank records and corporate papers.

"You aren't getting a minute past the first week of October," Tischler said.

"October," I said numbly as she stared right through me. "Even though we're meeting new players every day who are at the top of the drug and money-laundering world, it has to be October?"

"You heard me, Mazur." She glared. "Don't give me any of your shit."

Anything more from me would only make matters worse. No one said a word.

Two days later, Armbrecht called. I'd grown used to Latin timing — one week often meant two or three — but Armbrecht was part German, and he obviously had his father's sense of punctuality when he called just days after I landed. He was in Miami, eager to meet, wanting documents, and anxious to see our operations.

"I've got almost everything ready for you," I lied, "but I still haven't received a few documents our lawyers in Zürich had to request from a law firm in Gibraltar. I should receive this stuff in a few days. By then I'll be in Miami. I'll call you when I'm there, and we can come back to Tampa together."

"My main business here is you," he said, disappointed.

Then Alcaíno called with a list of requests. He was promoting a rematch between Rojas and Roman in Medellín. He needed more phony loan documents to cover his financing of the fight, and he wanted me to join him and *los duros* to watch it. He also had completed his transportation line and was preparing to buy a big load of coke to ride the route. He needed investors and made an unbeatable offer. If I put up $250,000, he'd pay me back $375,000 in forty-five days.

I told him I'd think about it. I had to buy time to formulate an excuse. Seizing dope was one thing, but there was no way the U.S. government was going to invest in it.

When I called Alcaíno back a day or so later with the bad news, Casals answered and provided a clue to the puzzle of Alcaíno's transportation line. "Roberto's not here. He went to New York to take care of getting some anchovies through Customs."

Casals was talking openly — it wasn't code. He really meant anchovies, but I still needed more intel before we could pinpoint the operation.

In Miami, in Awan's unexpected absence, I brought an elated Bilgrami up to speed on the new companies and the $4 million in CDs deposited in the Paris branch, handing over an armful of documents on the new corporations formed in Liberia, Hong Kong, and Gibraltar. Bilgrami opened accounts for me at BCCI Luxembourg, London, Geneva, Montevideo, Nassau, and Miami. As he churned out forms, the conference room phone rang. Although he spoke mostly in Urdu, the phrase "U.S. Customs" peppered his conversation — and it occurred to me that I had never had a blatant conversation with Bilgrami about the source of my clients' funds. No time like the present.

"I heard you mention my clients' adversary there," I said, as he put the receiver down. "You do business with the U.S. government?"

"No, no," he blurted nervously. "Eastern Airlines have had a plane confiscated. They found some cocaine in this plane, so they've asked us to issue a guarantee in favor of U.S. Customs. Why should they be 'adversary'? They should be your friends."

Time to get blatant.

"You know, on that issue, we need to resolve it," I said impatiently. "We're alone, and I have gone through the painstakes of meeting those people within the bank who I know I can rely on. I have a tremendous amount of confidence in everyone I've met. I have to satisfy myself, and I have, that there is not a situation where I should have to fear that anyone within the system might otherwise alert authorities here."

"No, no." Bilgrami was fidgeting. "I was just, like, saying, uh…"

He explained how the bank posted bonds for clients whose assets had been seized, based on what was then Customs' zero-tolerance program: if an ounce of cocaine was found on a yacht, Customs seized the whole yacht. Good, but not good enough. He had to admit that he knew he was laundering drug money.

"You know," I continued, "if you were to—and you wouldn't ever—but if you were to meet my clients, you would—"

"No, no," he cut me off, squirming. "I'm not interested in meeting your clients. I'm only interested in their—"

"If they were in a room with Lee Iacocca," I persisted, "they would mix in quite well with him. He sells cars, and they sell cocaine, and that's the end of it. Never to be brought up again."

"I don't want to know what they sell," Bilgrami said laughing.

"Never to be discussed," I reassured. "I have a lot of responsibilities here in receiving cash, and I do what I need to do, and I have a situation with you where you deal with me and I'm an investment adviser, and I don't care to go into anything more than that."

"I'm not interested in what they do," he repeated. "In dealing with you, we know your business, and, uh, we keep all client relations confidential."

"Okay, Akbar, that's fine."

Gotcha.

Relaxing back into business, I told him that, in addition to the $4 million deposited in Paris, I was prepared to place another $2 million in Miami.

"We can do that right away!" he said, his head popping up like a cobra ready to strike. Slot-machine dials were spinning in his eyes.

"Akbar, you sure like to get your hands on my money," I joked, explaining that I had to leave.

"You just sign me here," he persisted, shoving another document under my nose. "Sign away."

But the pen he gave me went dry. He ran around the room like a newly headless chicken looking for a writing implement. If he had to barricade the boardroom to keep me there long enough to sign, he would have.

After I had signed and as I prepared to leave, I let him know that, because I was visiting clients in the Northeast, he might have a little difficulty reaching me in a few days, but I'd do my best to stay in touch. A lie of course. I'd promised Ev and the kids that I'd join them on a sorely needed two-week vacation. The case was heating up, Armbrecht was in town, and Alcaíno wanted to meet — but I absolutely couldn't let my family down again. Only four months of sand remained in the hourglass before the takedown.

As soon as I slipped from Bilgrami's grasp, I called Armbrecht and met him at Miami International. Happy to see me and full of questions, he eagerly awaited the paperwork I owed him, the last pieces of the puzzle needed to satisfy him that it was safe to reopen the floodgates of Don Chepe's dirty money. As we relaxed in the leather of our first-class seats to Tampa, I noticed that he seemed at ease to volunteer new information. But if I pushed, he grew wary. Best to play hard to get with him, then, instead of hardball.

He mentioned that he was going to be traveling to Nashville the following week to pick up another Rockwell Commander 1000, a twin-engine turboprop aircraft worth well over a million dollars. He was installing a new navigation system that was setting him back another $150,000. And he'd been buying as many of the Commander 1000s as he could find. A premier tool of the drug trade, the Commander 1000 can handle the short dirt and gravel airstrips common in the jungles of South America, and its turboprop power enables it to ascend quickly from short runways. Removing the seats would turn it into a cargo plane, able to carry a larger load, and auxiliary fuel tanks would give it more than excellent range. Armbrecht was building a flying armada — and tracking devices on those planes would provide a world of intelligence.

In Tampa, Dominic, playing the role of my driver and bodyguard, put on an Oscar-worthy performance as he drove us to a couple of his clubs still under construction, supposedly because he wanted me, the boss, to see how matters were coming along. I emptily begged Armbrecht's forgiveness for the slight detour — which of course was no problem.

Behind closed doors at Financial Consulting, Armbrecht graded our system. "It's like a merry-go-round. We get the money over here. We reroute it, we clean it, we do everything with it. Okay. Then we have it legally and totally in nice accounts with everything over here.... It's a good concept."

But I wanted to throw Armbrecht a curveball that would hook him into giving me new information. I had some concerns, I told him. It troubled me that he asked a lot of questions but did little business lately. I didn't mind if we did no business, but I didn't want to show him more until I was satisfied about his goal. Could he have a hidden motive? That is, was he working with the feds? Nothing like a little transference to cover my tracks.

"If you're not comfortable, then tell me," he said.

"It's not that I'm not comfortable," I replied. "It's just that it raised a little curiosity.... If we really build a strong relationship, there shouldn't be anything I shouldn't feel free to be able to say with you.... I mean, if they don't want to do business, they don't want to do business."

Armbrecht leaned back, took a deep breath, and exhaled loudly through his nose. "Now comes the part of establishing a more — a long-term relationship. It's not that we do little business and then, 'Bye-bye. Forget it.' No. Why I'm investigating everything and why I'm over here, this is because the interest is to establish a more long-term relationship. But, the fears that you have, they have."

Then he reviewed all the latest corporate documents from Zürich and the contracts covering for his role as managing director of the Gibraltar corporation that would hold tens of millions of dollars. With his strict German attention to detail, he ensured that each new piece of the puzzle fit perfectly into the overall scheme, throwing question after question at me.

Then he reviewed paperwork outlining the history of our front businesses, but I cautioned, "If you would, when you're done with it, if you decide that you're finished with it and you don't need it anymore, destroy it."

He picked Eric Wellman's brain about his banking career, and then he and I headed back to the undercover house where Kathy wined him, dined him, and plied him with long discussions about philosophy and faraway places I'd never seen. When they returned from an hour-and-a-half-long walk through the neighborhood's waterfront lots on the Gulf of Mexico, we three played a four-hour marathon chess tournament, in which neither Kathy nor I was much of a match for him. After I hit the sack, Kathy and he played on, which was great. I needed all the help I could get establishing rapport. After all, his opinion determined our fate with Don Chepe.

The next afternoon, after lunch on the beach, talking business, I should have played it cooler, but I got greedy. As I was promoting the upcoming New York tour, Armbrecht reacted badly. "Why do I feel, Robert, that you think it's very important for me to get that knowledge?"

"Because," I said calmly as my mind raced for an answer, "I

know that nothing has happened in the last couple of months, and I think we need to either move on—"

"Move on or move back," he said.

"That's right."

"Okay, good."

"I want a forecast, a reliable forecast," I nudged.

"You will have one when it's time"—he glared—"when I'm ready, and when I make a decision. Then I will tell you yes. I'll tell you yes," he said, promising a decision within ten days, and then adding that it was more or less a done deal.

Lesson learned. No more pushing his buttons. If I pressed any more, he would buck. Like it or not, we had to wait.

The next day I went home to my family. Our two-week trip included a family wedding in Connecticut, but, unlike Bob Musella, Bob Mazur didn't have the cash to fly everyone to Hartford. We had to drive in the family station wagon. By midmorning Ev, the kids, and I were heading north, but my mind remained on Armbrecht, Emir, and how everything was going in New York. I tortured my family with call after call on my cell phone to Alcaíno, Armbrecht, Bilgrami, Cook, Emir, Howard, Sherman, and others. Pickups continued, too, and so there were calls to move money around the world and back into the cartel's maw.

Ev crossed her arms and stared out the window, her body language screaming her unhappiness. The kids, almost teens and in their own world, knew they couldn't make a sound when I was on the phone.

As Armbrecht had promised, exactly ten days from our discussion in the undercover house, word came to Emir from Mora that Don Chepe's organization had made their decision. Emir called immediately.

"Gonzalo just called," he said. "He met with Don Chepe and was informed that their organization has given us their routes in New York and Houston. That is now our territory. We did it!"

"You deserve the credit, man. Without you, Gonzalo wouldn't be putting his neck on the line, and we wouldn't have a face in Medellín. That's the key. This is fantastic news. Now let's just hope we can convince New York and Houston that they need to play it cool. They can't get pushy and try to rip this money off or do a lot of surveillance. Armbrecht will let us put a lot of this money in accounts at BCCI. Everyone needs to sit back and let them fill the coffers."

I sat silently and soaked in the moment. It was almost too huge to imagine. A handful of agents, despite all odds, had become not only money movers but money managers for the biggest drug organization in the world. There was no telling where the next four months would take us.

Back in Tampa, after my much-needed vacation, in the comfort of the undercover house, I questioned Armbrecht on what had happened while I was away. Two days prior we received half a million in New York, and that day we were supposed to receive another half in Chicago.

"A little" — Armbrecht smiled — "just to keep you happy... You will eventually learn how to cope with the Latin American way of doing things, which is very effective. I can tell you that.... Very non-traceable."

I told him I thought our system, too, was non-traceable.

"Oh yes, I know," he agreed. "That's why I like it."

As he settled down and had a couple glasses of wine I couldn't resist asking him why he had so much influence in Don Chepe's organization. He pegged it to his intelligence, international experience, honesty, and lack of greed.

He seemed at ease, so I took a shot at learning just how close he was to Escobar. "Will you have your discussion [about our services] directly with the top person, or will you be dealing with others?"

Armbrecht stared at me with a slight smile, but my silence drew him out.

"They are people that are in the background, that very few people know about... and basically manage or control most of it or almost all of it.... And those persons will only have very few persons near them. Very intelligent guys."

He had endorsed us — not unconditionally, but to the point that he didn't want to risk losing me because of a lack of business. It was more important than ever, then, that everything go smoothly. We were hovering on the brink of total acceptance.

The trail of exhaust from the jet that took Armbrecht back to Miami had barely faded from the Tampa sky when the first catastrophe crashed in our laps.

At the Bayou Village safe house, Sherman and other Tampa agents forwarded important information from the Miami office. Miami had been watching the trailer that unloaded cocaine in Detroit earlier that year. Men had hooked the trailer to a tractor, and it looked like it would be leaving Miami soon. We couldn't let that semi out of Florida.

Tischler had the plan I wrote for the truck to be inspected at a weigh station where the dope would be found accidentally. Everyone agreed it was the best way to get the dope off the street without compromising our operation. Problem solved.

Sherman announced that Tischler wanted a plan to get as many of the dealers and bankers in Tampa at the time of the takedown, but no one had any ideas. Time to launch the plan Kathy and I had been discussing.

"Most of these people either truly like us or see me as an important business contact," I said. "In some instances, on their own, they've asked when we intend to get married, and some of the wives have offered to help in the planning. We both think most of them would come to Tampa to attend a wedding."

Everyone but Kathy chuckled and smirked. Sherman doubted the dopers and bankers would take the time to attend. No one else had the courage to explain his or her doubts.

"I think they'll show," Kathy added, "but with their families involved in the planning and the ceremony, the probability will be even greater. They'll feel obligated to show. I'd rather keep their families out of this, but they seem to want in."

A lukewarm reaction at best.

"Well," Sherman said, "if that's all you guys can come up with, then I guess that's the plan. I'll tell Bonni."

Before I left the apartment I gave the briefcase I had been using to one of the agents in our squad. "I've had a problem with this case that luckily happened when I was alone. The Velcro strips that hold the cover to the hidden compartment are starting to wear. When I opened the case, the compartment flopped open, exposing the recorder and wires. I'll use one of the other briefcases for a while, but I like this one because it has the Nagra recorder that produces the best possible audio of my meetings."

"No problem, Bob, we'll take care of it."

Fortune magazine's cover story on June 20, 1988, examined the Medellín cartel. I was reading it in the lobby of BCCI Miami as Awan approached. I threw down the magazine like a teenager caught reading his father's *Playboy*, and, as I hoped, Awan noticed.

At the couches, Bilgrami joined us. I'd brought them $1.4 million that needed bouncing, but I had ten days before the money had to be back in the cartel's hands. It was June 28, just two days from the witching hour for BCCI's inflated balance sheet. I threw Awan and Bilgrami a bone. I told them I would hold off borrowing against these funds and transferring the loan proceeds until after June 30, thereby bringing my total contribution of deposits to $7.4 million.

While Bilgrami worked out details, I noticed that Awan was preoccupied. "You seem intent. Are you ... ?"

"We have to do all sorts of window dressing for our books," Awan explained. "Our half-yearly balance sheet comes out on the thirtieth of June, so we have to pad our figures as much as we can with short-term business and deposits and stuff."

The pressure on him was showing.

When Bilgrami left the room I prodded Awan for more detail.

"We're sort of breathing down the necks of everybody out in the field," he said, "to improve their figures. They're not very happy with that. They're not returning calls. Since our balance sheet is audited every six months, we're always under a lot of pressure at the end of the period, you know, to...show window dressing."

Awan had no doubt about Musella, and Bilgrami wasn't far behind.

When Bilgrami suggested getting together the next day for drinks, it was time to play the *Fortune* article card. "I was reading the magazine in your lobby area there," I said. "Did you see that? Interesting cover story. It had a very interesting cover story about the trade, drug trade anyway. I was thumbing through the pictures and saw a client of mine."

Awan and Bilgrami laughed.

"Is that why you put it back so quickly?" Awan said.

More solid proof that they knew the source of the funds, so I poured it on. "Yes, I picked it up and said — I couldn't believe it. He's right on the cover. I always expected to have a client on the cover of *Fortune*, but not quite that way.... He must have seen the article by now, but I'll definitely need to pick up a copy of this recent issue. It's quite a detailed article about the drug trade."

When I came back to the bank the next day, Awan floored me.

"Akbar and I have been thinking over many things, and we want to talk to you about this," he said. "We'll probably be leaving the bank in due course and possibly setting up on our own. So maybe we can work together in that situation.... I have an old colleague in London who used to head our treasury department [at BCCI], very good in his line of work, and a few years ago he left and set up his own investment company in London, capitalized with about $25 million. He's had some pretty good backing, pretty good shareholders, and that was three years ago. He did quite well then. He's basically into all sorts of investment banking, currencies, stock market."

Ziauddin Akbar had opened a subsidiary of London-based Capcom Futures in Chicago, and Awan and Bilgrami had accepted an offer to open another subsidiary in Miami. They wouldn't completely cut ties with BCCI, hoping that BCCI would act as their correspondent bank and work with them. Either way, they would see to it that an officer who knew the "sensitivity" of my accounts handled my affairs at BCCI. All of this would happen in about six months.

It was the best of both worlds. I would continue with BCCI, but — another door opened — Awan and Bilgrami would take their most important clients to a smaller company. When our operation ended, we'd know exactly where to execute search warrants to find Noriega's fortune. I couldn't wait to hear more.

I explained that my number one problem was getting currency deposited into the banking system. What, I asked them, could Capcom do for me?

"I wouldn't deposit it in London," Awan said. "I'd send it out somewhere, deposit it, and wire transfer it . . . Middle East probably. You know, because we have huge sums of money coming in from there in cash. It's still rather primitive. A society where nobody believes in checks, let alone plastic. Everybody deals in cash."

Apparently depositing huge sums of cash in the Middle East was an everyday affair. This was news.

"What type of cash do they deal with there?"

Awan had all the answers. "U.S. currency wouldn't be unusual there. U.S., sterling, deutschmarks, Swiss francs, these are the four popular currencies. The most popular are the sterling and U.S. dollar."

When I asked him to name the best places to deposit, he quickly ran down the list: "Saudi Arabia is the biggest source of cash, but I wouldn't go to Saudi Arabia simply because it's so difficult to get in and out. . . . I would say Bahrain, Abu Dhabi, Dubai, these are the three main centers."

Awan estimated that he could arrange deposits there at a pace of $10 million to $20 million per month. All very interesting. I surely wasn't the first client to whom they made this proposal, and what Awan was suggesting lay totally outside traditional government thinking.

That night, at the Miami undercover house, Awan and Bilgrami indicated that the following day would be better for them to explain their new proposal. I countered with the October takedown bait.

"This will be a three-day event," I said. "Our families will be there on Friday, and you're welcome to join us, but if you'd prefer to wait until Saturday, that's fine. On Saturday, we'll party, and on Sunday the wedding will occur."

They wouldn't think of missing it, they said. More to do with dollar signs than friendship, but that didn't matter. Trap laid.

The next day back at BCCI, Bilgrami handled the paperwork and eventually delivered the real message, "You want to go somewhere? We can go to the Grand Bay...Café Royale."

I was all ears.

On the drive to the hotel, they couldn't resist coaching me on how to make the scam companies look real. They suggested I have stationery printed for each of the many paper companies our attorneys in Zürich had formed. Which would enable Awan and Bilgrami to prepare more formal documents.

At the Grand Bay Hotel, over caviar and cocktails, Bilgrami explained his new plan. "My idea was that we would receive your funds and then lend them out, in your case to three or four banks with whom we would tie up.... We'll give them the cash. There is a benefit there, that there's no linkage at all because there is not just one institution" — making the loan. "Four different institutions are involved. One could be a Japanese bank; one could be a Swiss bank; one could be an Arab bank; and then an English situation. The advantage in this is that, number one, investment houses are not scrutinized as banks. Paperwork would be a minimum."

In other words, they planned to confuse money movements by multiplying the number of loans against a deposit fourfold, making it that much harder for the government to follow the money. Pure genius.

"Well, how much of my clients' money do you think you can clean in a month, let's say?" I asked.

"There are so many ways of going about it," Bilgrami said. "You mentioned the currency situation, so, um, currencies can be changed for commodities. You can get a currency and change it for a cash delivery in gold, and you've done it, the whole transaction in two seconds."

The opportunities they were offering were unlimited—and we were on a roll. I wanted them to tell me which major players were marketing the dirtiest money of the underworld.

Citibank in Panama, they agreed. According to Awan, BCCI was "nowhere in the league of the big boys—Bank of Boston, Citibank, First Chicago, and London."

That same day I received a devastating call from Emir.

"I just got a call from Gonzalo," he said. "This shit is *bad*. He told me something bad had happened in Detroit and to stay away from those people. He warned me, 'Don't answer any calls from those people.' Then I called our office and just got word. Our office in Detroit took the Giraldo brothers down. Imagine this shit. I'm learning it first from the bad guys!"

"Please tell me you're kidding," I said. "Don't they know how deep we're into these people? How small-minded can they be?"

"Don't you get it? We are going to lose out to the theory of 'Me, Me, and I.' Other than Jim Glotfelty"—the case agent in Detroit—"who is an honorable man, these people don't give a shit about us or the big picture. If they can get more stripes on their shirt because they made the biggest cocaine seizure in Detroit, they'll sell out their mother. I just got word they got 106 kilos of cocaine. For that shit, the spotlight will be on us because they filed federal warrants to search the locations that only I and the Giraldo brothers know about, like the storage facility where they keep their dope. The affidavits filed by our own people tell the entire story about everything you and I have done for the past two years."

Shit.

"No!" I said, still in shock. "It can't be. How could they break their promise? What happened to the plan to stop the semi at the Georgia border? What happened to Detroit's promise not to do anything that would expose our undercover operation?"

"Bob, our own people in Tampa blessed this thing. This one was the second biggest load of coke that Detroit had ever seen. There were too many potential promotions in Detroit to let this seizure go to the locals, who knew nothing about our operation. That would have made sense, but the bottom line is they fucked us."

I couldn't believe it.

"A child would know that, if people in Detroit who know about the undercover operation write affidavits exposing us, it's only a matter of a month or two before those affidavits will probably have to be disclosed to the defense attorneys defending the Giraldo brothers."

I called Laura Sherman. "Emir just told me what happened in Detroit. *What the fuck is going on?*"

"Well, Bob, the decision was made to let the truck go on to Detroit. Our people there wrote affidavits to search the home and storage area of the Giraldo brothers, and they got a lot of coke. This was blessed by Bonni."

"How could this have been allowed to happen? Have you seen the affidavits for the search warrants? I understand they expose me and Emir."

"Don't worry. Detroit assures us they've been sealed."

"Sealed? *Sealed?* Are they fucking *crazy?* 'Sealed' means some minimum-wage clerk put that affidavit in an envelope with a note that it shouldn't be publicly filed. Moncada and Escobar control *presidents of countries* — a clerk is nothing!"

But it was worse than I thought. A Customs agent in Detroit not only had filed affidavits to get those 106 kilos of cocaine, violating their promise not to expose us, but the same agent had filed an affidavit four months earlier requesting authorization to tap the beeper of one of the Giraldo brothers. That affidavit had been under seal for the last four months — and no one ever told me, Emir, or anyone else whose ass was on the line.

Despite Customs' written obligation to coordinate busts like that with DEA — the agency with primary jurisdiction for domestic drug violations — Detroit Customs never told them about the hundreds of pounds of cocaine they let walk in January, nor did they call DEA about the 106 kilos that arrived in June until the very last minute.

It would take an act of Congress to keep those affidavits closed until October. Troubling enough, but knowing that the only barrier keeping Moncada from learning that Musella and Dominguez were federal agents was a low-paid clerk wore on me.

And time was against us. If we were going to take risks, now was the time. From this moment forward, more and more people were going to learn our secret.

I called a meeting with Emir and Kathy.

"Listen, this may sound crazy," I said to them, "but I'd like to make a pitch for authorization that we be allowed to travel undercover to Colombia. It will take time for Don Chepe to figure out that we had anything to do with the Detroit bust. If we make this trip soon, it will throw everyone off down there. If we show our faces in Medellín, they'll never suspect we're feds. Even if we're only down there for a twenty-four-hour surprise visit, that would go a long way. What do you think?"

Emir nodded. "I'm ready to go now."

"Count me in," Kathy agreed.

I submitted a request for authorization. The response came right back — REQUEST DENIED. DEA had ruled it too risky. But as bad as Detroit had been, it was nothing compared to what was about to go down in New York.

16

THE ENEMY WITHIN

Caliber Chase Apartments, Tampa, Florida
July 12, 1988

SECURITY ALARMS WERE BLARING. The Giraldo brothers weren't important — just mutts who knew next to nothing. The 106 kilos of cocaine didn't matter either: $500 per kilo for the cartel to produce, so a loss of $53,000 — chicken feed. But why? The feds knew too much. The Giraldos'.downfall was no accident. Don Chepe was looking for a leak, but we kept collecting cash in Miami, Houston, New York, and Chicago, so it was clear he didn't suspect us. In fact, we were on a roll — and then the phone rang.

"Gonzalo just called me," Emir said. "Don Chepe's people want us to collect $10 million in New York right away. *Coño*, brother, our people in New York are going to be salivating when they hear about this. We can't afford any slip-ups now, especially after Detroit. Our people in New York are going to want to either rip some of this money off or have surveillance all over the street trying to follow the people who drop the money. If they get burned, we're dead."

"We need our managers to work this out with the front office in New York," I said. "Call Steve to see what he can do, and I'm going to call Tommy Loreto" — the supervisor overseeing the New York part of the case. "Tommy and I go way back. He's an honest guy.... I think he'll try to help."

I called Loreto and explained Paris and how we were on the verge of setting up a $100 million nest egg for Medellín.

"I'll do what I can for you," he said, "but you've got to realize that people who run this office want to play this thing out so we develop as much as we can for New York. They're not used to how you're approaching this from outside the box. I'm not sure they'd understand it. They like to do things the way everyone does it around the country: follow the mopes away in hopes of finding their stash house, search the place, seize the money, and go home. End of story."

"I'm begging you," I said. "Please do whatever you can to be light on the surveillance. I know you need guys on the street to keep your undercover guy safe, but if your guys get burned trying to follow these mutts that drop off the money, our undercover operation may go down in flames. The Colombians will have countersurveillance, and they're going to be looking for guys who fit the profile of most federal agents: white guys in shape with beepers, cell phones, and probably fanny packs to hide their guns. Jeans, polo shirts, and high-end sneakers will be dead giveaways. They can't be gawking while they're parked in American-made sedans, and they've got to do something to cover up the radios, mikes, and red lights that hang from their dash. We've got to be sneaky."

A long silence.

"We know what we're doing here," Loreto said. "We're not going to fuck this up. I'll run as much interference for you as I can, but I can't promise you anything."

In too many cities I'd seen the same thing a hundred times over. All agents on the street — even those with the smallest roles — had to resist business as usual and stow their machismo. Loreto had a good heart and was trying to do the right thing, but he couldn't buck the system alone. Even with pressure from Tampa and Washington, New York would probably conduct business as usual.

It took a day to coordinate all the necessary approvals, and by then Mora had bad news for Emir. "Four of the $10 million has already been taken by someone else. There's only $6 million left."

"Mr. Bob asked how much of this money will go into an investment," Emir said.

"No one has said anything about that," Mora replied.

Time to call Armbrecht and lean on our friendship.

"Rudy, I need your help," I said. "We were offered ten big ones in the Towers, and when we called to get details four of the ten went to someone else. Now I'm being told that, of the remaining six, none of it is slated for investment. Can you call your people and get this resolved? If they won't budge on this, I'd rather cut my losses and move on."

Armbrecht would try to straighten things out in Medellín the following week. He didn't want to call Don Chepe immediately, for fear of looking biased and losing his ability to help.

The next day, Marta, a Colombian in New York City coordinating money movements for Don Chepe, arranged for some of her people to drop off half a million to an agent posing as one of Emir's workers in downtown Manhattan.

At the same time, Awan and Bilgrami were moving money around the world and into Don Chepe's accounts. During a break in the action, over drinks at the Hyatt Regency in Miami, our conversation turned to Ziauddin Akbar, founder of Capcom.

"I just said I had certain customers," Awan explained, "who might like to bring cash to be deposited in various banks.... He said he can't do it regularly, but he can do it on a, you know, once-a-month basis or something like that."

Good news. All we had to do was deliver the cash to Akbar in London. No problem, since Don Chepe and Alcaíno were selling tons of cocaine in Europe. When I asked how much Akbar could take a month, Awan glanced around the room to make sure no one was listening before he answered quietly, "Maybe ten."

Not only could Akbar take $10 million a month in cash, he could also arrange unlimited transfers disguised as loan proceeds. My mind raced. Awan was surely making this same pitch to his other "special" clients, including Noriega. I had to meet Akbar, establish a relationship, and get him on tape. We'd find Noriega's fortune at his doorstep.

When the conversation turned to Panama, Awan said, "Well,

put it this way. In Panama, I mean, we have no qualms about doing anything because the laws of the land allow us to do it. Anyone can walk in and deposit $10 million in cash—fine. We take it. That's the business we're in. The U.S. may call it laundering, they may call it whatever they may call it, but Citibank does it, Bank of America does it, they all do it. We do it in probably a smaller way, but every bank does it."

BCCI was ready, willing, and able—just like every other bank—to take as much dirty money in Panama as we could give them, and Awan would introduce me to the right people in those other banks who would take whatever BCCI couldn't handle.

The next day, Don Chepe's people passed another $1.5 million to us on the streets of Manhattan. Money was moving so quickly that Mora needed more checks in Medellín and Armbrecht wanted the balance of the documents to satisfy Don Chepe that the account in Paris was safe. That paperwork needed to get to Medellín, but mailing it was too risky. It might be intercepted and seized. Alcaíno offered to hand-carry everything on his next trip, but he was delayed and so suggested I hire Tuto Zabala to smuggle the documents down.

"Tuto," I said, coaching him, "give these four envelopes only to Gonzalo. They contain checks I've pre-signed on accounts and some other papers. Hide them as best you can, but if you're stopped give them my name, and tell them I asked you to drop this envelope off to a name we'll make up—let's say Rudolph Dominguez. Tell them you did this for me as a favor and you don't know what the envelope contains. I'll handle any fallout. Here's a first-class round-trip ticket and $500 for travel expenses. I'll take care of you when you get back."

Zabala obeyed like a puppy. "When I get back," he said, "I'd like to talk with you about doing some business."

Fine with me. Our new arrangement earned me the right to pick his brain later about the services he had to offer. One or two good conversations on tape would help prove his involvement with Alcaíno in moving thousands of kilos of cocaine.

The relationship among Armbrecht, BCCI, and Alcaíno was progressing quickly, but there was still Juan Tobón, the Santería devotee. We knew only that he frequently visited the home of his *santero* in Sweetwater, a lower-class suburb of Miami inhabited mostly by Nicaraguan immigrants. Kathy had dropped off a thank-you note for Tobón, but he hadn't responded. Emir cautioned me to stay away from the *santero*—too risky. If the priest got bad vibes, it would queer Tobón and therefore cause problems with Alcaíno. But we were running out of time, so we took the risk, and Kathy went first.

Antiburglary bars secured the doors and windows. A woman named Cookie welcomed her and explained that Tobón frequented her house in order to meet her godfather, Fonseca, whom everyone called Padrino. While Kathy spoke with Cookie in the kitchen, four men arrived, including Fonseca. Two of the men ran a florist's shop and were wedding coordinators, a lucky coincidence that allowed Kathy to discuss the October wedding.

By the time I got there, the Tobón family had also arrived, as well as some of Fonseca's other followers, who met with him separately in a private room. Always a pro, Kathy had everyone at ease.

"It is very important to me," Tobón said, taking me aside, "that Padrino meet you. When everyone is gone, I'd like to introduce you to him."

"No problem. It would be my pleasure," I said, noticing a library table by the front door littered with seashells, coconuts, nuts, vegetables, religious statues, and other gifts to the spirits.

Tobón escorted me down a dark hall toward a door that was slightly ajar. As it creaked open, a wall of heat from lit candles hit me in the face and pushed me back. Fonseca, an unassuming little man wearing a warm smile, beckoned me in. Behind him, a wall filled with shelves, configured like an altar, held a hoard of candles, dolls, snail shells, china filled with herbs, statues, and all sorts of secondhand knickknacks. The room oozed a strange odor—burnt herbs and dried blood from the sacrifice of countless chickens and other animals.

Tobón introduced me as Fonseca approached, extending his hand. We each looked straight into each other's eyes as I told him, "It is a great pleasure to meet you, Padrino. Juan has told me so many wonderful things about you. Thank you for accepting me into your home." After a few pleasantries, Fonseca turned back to the altar, and Tobón escorted me back to the living room before rejoining the *santero*.

Clara Tobón had invited Kathy to a dressmaker to pick out a wedding gown, and Cookie offered to have her friends print invitations and provide flowers. The Tobóns had already accepted Kathy's wedding invitation, and they offered to cover the tab for the flowers as part of their gift.

Tobón emerged from the hallway, smiling. "Padrino tells me that you are a good and honorable man who keeps his word. We will do business."

Tobón sat on the couch with me and opened up. He and Alcaíno had done a deal a few months earlier. The dope went to Europe from Argentina, but it had been seized. And there were other problems. DEA had also seized his Cessna Citation, and the owners of the cash he'd used to buy it — upset because he wasn't contesting the seizure — were threatening him and his family. Despite all that, he wanted very much to do business. There was no sense in complicating his life until his problems were resolved, I told him, but when he was ready I would be happy to listen to what he had to offer.

Tobón claimed to have well-placed friends in Medellín, including José Gonzalo Rodríguez Gacha, a sitting member of the cartel and Tobón's wife's uncle. Tobón also worked closely with John Nasser, a man he described as one of the most powerful people in the drug business, a notorious money launderer and drug dealer working with the cartel.

After warm goodbyes, we stepped into the stifling Miami night. The car's air conditioning blasted the putrid smell of Fonseca's altar from my nose.

"Well," I said to Kathy, putting the car into gear, "when this goes down, I'm afraid they're going to yank Padrino's *santero* license."

I had passed the *santero*'s test, but that was nothing compared to the challenge Mora soon threw at Emir.

"Marta in the Towers reported to Don Chepe's people," Mora said, "that there were strangers watching her people when they made the last deliveries in New York. She says your people are *los feos*. Here, they" — Don Chepe's people — "visited me at my office. They are very serious people. What is going on?"

"You have to understand," Emir said reassuringly, "that when people deal with this kind of money, everyone reading a newspaper or sleeping on the street looks to them like they're one of those bad people. This claim is bullshit. This is Chino's people in the Towers. There can't possibly be anything wrong there. I'll discuss this with him, but these people are seeing ghosts."

"Okay, but remember," Mora said, greed overriding logic, "this is my neck and my family's neck, too. Our lives are in your hands."

"You should have no concern," Emir said. "I have everything under control."

Emir immediately called and filled me in.

"I need to go back to the well with Armbrecht," I said. "He and Mora are the only voices in Medellín we have to combat this. You saw this coming before it happened. It's not Nelson's or Tommy's fault. I'm sure they did whatever they could to get their people to do the right thing. Regardless, our New York office did exactly what you feared. I'm not sure how I'm going to approach this with Armbrecht to get him on our side. I'll think about it, give it my best shot, and let you know what shakes out."

How would a calculating money launderer approach this? He would identify the most likely leaks, treat them well, give them a vacation so they had plenty of time on their hands, and monitor everything they said and did while they thought he wasn't watching. Which is exactly what I pitched to Armbrecht.

"The people are very worried about having your people there," he said tensely about New York. "We may not be able to do anything there. If the root of the tree is failing, that is the most important part of the whole operation."

"We need to just face facts that something needs to be determined before either side goes further," I reasoned. "We need to consider doing certain things. A plan needs to be put into motion that gets this thing flushed out."

I told him we had two people in New York who weren't longtime members of our group. I planned to treat them well, let them drop their guard, and watch them closely. I'd also suspend using our regulars in New York and bring in workers from Philadelphia. Armbrecht, approving of the plan, agreed to speak with Don Chepe's people to get back on track. I told him he could tell his people that, if I identified the problem, the problem would be eliminated because I was sending Emir to the Towers. He knew what I meant; it was exactly what he had done to Ospiña in Paris.

In the midst of the confusion in New York, the undercover house in Miami became a crossroads for meetings with the drug world. Tobón showed up and made a pitch to form a partnership. He had important friends who needed money laundered, so I explained the fees and capabilities of our organization and the role filled by Mora. Never cut a crook out of his fair share. After a quick call to Mora, he learned that Tobón might bring us new business, and Tobón learned that Mora was our face in Medellín.

No sooner had Tobón left the house than Alcaíno showed up fresh from Buenos Aires where he was organizing shipments of coke to the U.S.

"So what we're thinking with him," he said of his partner in Buenos Aires and the big plan, "is...to do something that we just be able to transport it and stay away from sales. Sell the transport to somebody else, bring the product here ourselves, and sell it outright to somebody at a discount. I'll make two thousand less or one thousand less" — per kilo — "but I don't have to sell and collect. I'd bring my own merchandise, and I will wholesale it to one customer or two customers.... That way it's less headaches."

Alcaíno ran through the math. He'd paid about $300,000 for

a factory in Buenos Aires that acted as a front for shipping goods to the U.S. and Europe. It cost him $2,000 per kilo to buy the coke from the cartel. He planned to bring a thousand or more kilos via his transportation route to New York and sell it in bulk at $14,500 per kilo. At that price, he'd gross $14.5 million on just one deal, and he planned on doing two more loads to Europe the same year: 2,000 kilos selling for $26,000 each in Spain and Italy, grossing $104 million.

Previously, Alcaíno had sold loads of fifty kilos or so at a time to many different customers, which exposed him not only to the feds but also to deadbeats. Various customers owed him a total of a million dollars, and he didn't like getting his hands dirty, especially with friends like Zabala. As Alcaíno saw it, it wasn't Zabala's fault that Zabala sold a shipment to five Cuban brothers in Chicago who owned a string of small grocery stores and they stiffed him. How could he put the squeeze on his longtime friend?

Then Alcaíno's eyebrows shot up, as a thought ran through his head. "Maybe you can, God, you can help me! Frank" — Serra, the undercover agent in Chicago — "can help us there. Some guys, they have a market there, and they don't even pay him a hundred thousand dollars. They just don't want to pay him. You guys have the people that can do that, right?"

I nodded silently.

"Yes," Alcaíno continued, "pick up one of the guys, and hold it, and the other ones will come with the money.... You have to force them. On their own, they won't pay. You have to force them. And forcing is hard. They will come with the money."

There was no way we were going through with this plan, but it gave me an opening to gather valuable information. I told Alcaíno he needed to get me all the details he had on each of his delinquent clients, especially the five brothers. Then I'd quote a collection price after we assessed the situation.

Not long after Alcaíno left, Mora called Emir to say that Don Chepe's people had decided to resume business in New York. I immediately called Laura Sherman and Steve Cook in Tampa,

Tommy Loreto and Nelson Chen in New York — anyone in Customs who would listen. We couldn't afford to get burned again in New York, and we had to use different people on the street, keeping the lowest profile possible. Marta's countersurveillance would be watching us closely, and the next drop had to go smoothly.

It did — half a million, no problems. Then word came that the next drop would be $2 million. That number might prompt New York agents to get overly aggressive, so Emir flew to New York to handle the deal personally.

While Emir was in transit, Tobón was knocking on my door in Miami. He wanted to bring us clients and had prospects. I had him translate for me while I called Mora, who had recently met with Santiago Uribe, Pablo Escobar's lawyer. Uribe was bringing us a new client who wanted the same services we were providing to Don Chepe. Not only did he want us to launder cash picked up in the States, he also wanted us to form offshore corporations and foreign accounts so he could hide the money in Europe. Uribe wanted copies of the documentation so this new client could better understand the system. We were getting closer.

In New York, Emir met our agents and they hatched a plan for him and Chen to meet Don Chepe's bagmen, who had the $2 million. Everyone knew the countersurveillance would be heavy, so all agreed to limit surveillance to ensuring the safety of the two undercover agents. Nothing more, and no tracking the mopes after they dropped the money.

Emir and Chen drove to a bodega near Canal Street in lower Manhattan. Inside, they met two young Colombian men in their early twenties, clean-cut, in casual clothes. One of them handed Emir a set of keys and said, "Eet's een da band."

Emir got it, but Chen didn't, turning to Emir with amazement and saying, "What the fuck is he talking about? Where's the band? Who's playing music?"

"This guy doesn't speak English very well," Emir said, laughing. "He meant *van!*'"

In the back of a van parked outside sat $2 million packed in boxes. One of the boxes contained $99,000 in one-dollar bills. That wasn't going to go over well — counting the ones would take forever — but with all the suspicions that we were cops, he couldn't make a scene, letting it slide.

The Colombian gave Emir instructions: drive the van wherever he wanted to make the drop, bring the van back, leave the keys in the ashtray, and take off. Then he added, "After you take that, if you're willing to wait an hour or so, I can come back with two million more."

It was a Friday afternoon, and Emir knew the surveillance team would rage if he made them stay out a few more hours. "Listen, man," he said to the Colombian. "We've been authorized to receive two tons. Your people down south will have to work that out with our bosses. We can only do what we've been told to do."

Emir jumped in the van, and Nelson led him to a rough part of the Lower East Side, near a public housing project. They parked amid passed-out bums and junkies playing dominoes and made the transfer. They returned to the bodega, completing the Colombian's instructions, then drove around for ten minutes, shaking any countersurveillance on their tail. And then the cover team caught up.

Normally, at this stage, an undercover car driven by a cover agent would lead them carefully back to the office by a circuitous route while a second surveillance agent cruised along a few cars behind. It gave undercover agents double protection in case bagmen tried to double-cross them and steal the money.

But now the surveillance supervisor pulled in front of Chen's Mercedes, put his red light on his roof, and waved for Nelson to follow him to the Customs office at the World Trade Center.

"What the hell is going on?" Emir shouted to Chen. It had only been ten minutes since they left the bodega — not enough time to ensure they weren't being tailed. But it was too late. They had no choice. They followed the lead car — red light flashing, siren blaring — as all of downtown Manhattan gawked at the speeding caravan.

When they arrived at the garage at the World Trade Center, Emir flew out of the Mercedes to the supervisor's car, screaming, "What the *hell* are you doing? Why did you throw your red light on your roof and draw all that attention?"

"Listen, pal," the supervisor said coldly. "It's Friday afternoon. I've got a summer home on the Jersey shore, and I've got a cement truck showing up early tomorrow morning to pour a new patio behind my house. I don't have time for this shit, and these dumb fucking Colombians were long gone before I led you to this garage. It's going to take us hours to count this money."

Emir explained that one of the boxes contained $99,000 in dollar bills, and then the supervisor hit the roof. "How could you accept that much in ones? Do you realize how long it's going to take us to count that?"

"You tell me what I'm supposed to do when these guys deliver $2 million to me undercover," Emir said, shaking his head. "Maybe I should say, 'Oh, I'm sorry, we can't take the ones, my bosses at Customs don't want me to take that. We'll only take twenty-dollar bills and above.'"

"I wanted to kick his ass," Emir told me later. "That bastard was more worried about pouring a cement *patio* than keeping us alive! He could have gotten us all killed the next time we went to pick up money. I'm pretty sure we got fried when those red lights came out."

Once again, the enemy within was proving more dangerous than the enemy we were attacking.

I called Armbrecht the next day in Colombia to feel him out. Noncommittal, he said only that he would be in Miami the day after. When the time was right, he'd contact me to discuss where things stood. As before when situations grew tense, someone smashed the window on my Mercedes and tossed the car. Nothing was stolen, but it was clear that someone was looking for something.

On a sweltering August night in Miami, Armbrecht called.

"I'm at the Airport La Quinta on Thirty-sixth Street. I'm ready. Come to my room, and we'll talk."

"No problem, Rudy," I said calmly. "Give me an hour or so, and I'll be there."

I called my contact agent in Miami, Matt Etre, and filled him in.

"Listen. Armbrecht just called and asked me to meet him at the La Quinta near the airport. His people are getting very concerned because they think they've spotted feds surveilling pickups. Their countersurveillance people claim they burned at least one of our surveillance teams in New York, and they may have burned us again a few days ago. They say they don't think I'm the problem, they just think the feds may be onto our pickup team. I can't afford for this guy to have any reason to suspect me, so I'm telling you right now: I don't want one agent anywhere near that hotel. I don't carry a gun or a badge when I'm working undercover, so I'm clean. If they toss me, I've got nothing that will compromise me. I'm going to leave my briefcase recorder in my car until I'm certain he's alone. When he asks me for some documents he needs, I'll tell him I forgot them in the car, and I'll get my briefcase. You've got my cell phone and beeper number. I should be at the hotel by no later than 11 P.M. I'll call you just before I go in. If you don't hear from me by 3 A.M., call me. If you don't get me, start looking for me. In the meantime, call anytime you'd like. If everything is okay, I'll tell you 'It's not a problem to meet tomorrow.' If I have a problem, I'll say 'I don't think I'll be able to make the meeting.' But please, don't let anyone try to cover me tonight. If you guys get close, the only thing you'll accomplish is that you'll be able to find my body quickly, 'cause you're going to get me whacked."

Etre exhaled slowly. He didn't like what he was hearing. "Okay, we'll play it on your terms," he said. "Let's stay in touch."

At 11 P.M., Armbrecht opened the door of the La Quinta room and welcomed me in, warm as ever. After ten minutes of small talk, he changed the subject to Mora, who he thought was doing me a disservice in Medellín. Aside from becoming too pushy with Don

Chepe's group, he'd made unrealistic promises, including a claim that my organization would make good on losses of $100 or $200 million. Armbrecht's people were losing faith in Mora's objectivity. He was trying too hard to impress.

When a natural break in the conversation occurred, I asked Armbrecht if he wanted the last of the documents from Switzerland, which he did. After a quick walk to my car, I came back to the room and tossed the Nagra-recorder briefcase on the bed. His eyes fixed on it — he looked like he was going to dive on the bed and tear it apart. As he talked, every few minutes his eyes flashed to it. He was clearly spooked.

When I pulled the case to my lap, the top of the lid facing Armbrecht, the false lid flopped down inside the case, exposing the recorder to me in a nest of wires. Once again, Joe Hinton's mantra rang in my head — *Don't count on someone else for something that could cost you your life.* I pushed the framing back into place, while trying not to let my eyes pop out of my head. Thankfully, the Velcro seals held before Armbrecht stood. He peered over the lid into the case as I handed him the documents. My heart was pounding so hard that, had I not been wearing a suit jacket, he surely would have seen it through my shirt.

When I asked how his people felt about me, he put it plain: "Nobody's questioning the honesty of nobody. It's simply a matter of the little things that were adding up...and there was a fault somewhere. That's what I know that they think. And then, for their good and your good, okay, they thought it was more judicious, more...It would be better for everybody to let things cool off a little."

He also mentioned that some of his people worried that because I was in the U.S. I could "change direction very easily."

I didn't understand.

"Somebody changes direction," he explained, "and if for some reason the government wants for its advantage to protect that person, they will..."

If I ever changed direction, he warned, "There's isn't a hole deep enough" in which I could hide. Message received.

Armbrecht continued, revealing that the problems started when Marta's people in New York saw a series of little things that caused them to report that the cops were surveilling our pickups in New York. After that, when Mora said I was offended that our group's integrity had been challenged, Armbrecht's bosses started to wonder why we were pushing so hard to resume the pickups.

As Armbrecht put it, "I personally don't think it's going to be cut off totally. My personal advice would be: Do your business, and have this on standby. You get or assume the same attitude they have. You respect.... We are able, but it's not so important for you. Just sit and wait. That's a powerful message...because when somebody pursues something very zealously, it has to be for another reason. He is very ambitious, and needs the money very badly—which I know it's not the case—or he is after something that nobody really knows about, and that's the thing we're not sure about. That's what makes trouble."

Damn, they were good. Time to play a little hardball.

I reminded Armbrecht of all the time, energy, and money I had invested quickly to accommodate his concerns about New York. I bore the cost of bringing in an entirely new crew, and my thanks for being so responsive was a reduction of business to a trickle? Very disappointing.

"There were plans to do business to a very big amount," he said, unfazed. "Put a lot of money in, like maybe $100 million.... The first things that were done...they were very, very eager. People were very eager. They wanted to do it because of you, because of the professionalism, and because of the things that you were showing. They were, okay, they liked it a lot. But, so here he comes, this little shit things. From that they go paranoid."

We had gone the extra mile to identify what upset his people in New York, I volleyed back. Emir took our main man in New York with him the last time we got money from Marta so they could meet her and her husband. Emir asked what they saw that upset everyone, and she said of the man in New York, "We don't have any problems with him. Everything is fine with us. We don't know what the problem is. We're monkeys." Marta had changed her tune, yet caused huge problems.

That argument scored points with Armbrecht, who said, "If we can get that worked out, I think that will be the only way. If that gets cleared, then I think it's a big step toward getting things in the right direction.... That tells me something. That's very important because they're coming this way with one story, and then when their guy does it they are saying something different, and that's very important."

I dropped another reason why Medellín should question Marta's claims. A competitor, Eduardo Martinez, had sabotaged previous work we had done for Armbrecht's group, providing Mora with inaccurate account information, which caused a transfer delay and displeased Armbrecht's bosses, worrying that our process was slow. It was probably a monkey wrench intentionally tossed in the gears of our system, designed to make us look bad. Marta probably had reasons for someone else to get our business. Maybe she wanted us to look bad to help a friend. More points scored.

Our conversation wandered off again — thankfully — and Armbrecht started ranting about America's arrogance. After all the saber rattling in Panama, nothing changed, and Noriega hadn't left the country. He didn't leave because he had received a quiet, much more effective message from Medellín: that coffin. His friends meant business. They knew the U.S. would replace him with a puppet who would give DEA access to account information leading to their pots of gold.

To put Armbrecht at ease I brought up the impending wedding, which he assured me he'd attend — and then I threw him a curveball, something that would reassure him I wasn't a narc. I reinforced his opinion of Mora by saying that I was frustrated trying to speak with important people in Medellín through him. Mora was a good man but prone to missing some of the finer points I was trying to convey. As a result, I was planning a trip to Medellín in late October, a few weeks after the wedding, and I wanted an audience with Armbrecht's bosses. He was willing to help, but he didn't want to look like he was pushing. Better for Mora to approach them while he encouraged from the sidelines.

Of course I had no intention of visiting Colombia. But the intention put him at ease, got him to lobby for me, and increased the probability he'd be in Tampa for the takedown.

It was nearly 3 A.M. when we shook hands and wrapped things up. He had every intention of letting his bosses know Marta was talking from both sides of her mouth, but he couldn't promise a positive outcome. We had hit a big bump in the road in New York, but all wasn't lost. The trouble was that there were now so many enemies in our midst that another crisis could emerge in no time.

And it did.

17

THE FIRST BIG CATCH

Key Biscayne, Florida
July 22, 1988

"CUSTOMS FUMBLED ON BIG DRUG CARGO, DEA SAYS," screamed the *Washington Times* headline just two days later.

A turf war had erupted between Customs and DEA over how Detroit had handled the Giraldo brothers. The article detailed how Florida Customs had traced the first shipment of 220 pounds of cocaine to Detroit, where they filmed sales of the dope to local dealers. No arrests were made, and DEA wasn't called in again until six months after the Giraldo brothers received another 106 kilos. Only then did authorities take the Giraldos and seven others into custody.

If Armbrecht read the article, he would know the leak came from Florida and would suspect anyone there dealing with the Giraldos, especially anyone involved in laundering — the only jurisdiction Customs had in domestic drug cases. Combine that with the bungled New York surveillance, and it was a wonder that he didn't have Emir and me whacked on the spot.

But we couldn't dwell on whether Armbrecht had read the article. Agonizing over that would take me off my game and broadcast fear. I had to deal just with what was before me, so when Alcaíno showed up at my doorstep, I smiled broadly.

As usual, he filled my ear with the latest cartel news, dropping details about who was doing what, including the latest about *La Mina*, one of my biggest money-laundering competitors, run by Argentineans in L.A. and New York. He gave me their names and the address of their office near Forty-seventh Street and Sixth Avenue in Manhattan — which helped New York Customs close in on them.

He mentioned, too, that his ton of coke was moving from Buenos Aires to New York and would arrive in two to four weeks. Our office had already sent out a bulletin to Customs inspectors, warning them to look for commercial shipments involving anchovies from Argentina or Brazil, but I needed more detail. Not the right time to press, though.

When I mentioned having problems with another competitor, he raised his brow and smiled. "You might have to go do some crazy thing, finish it, and then you take over the whole pie." He encouraged everyone else to pour blood in the streets, as long as the aftermath gave him more power.

His biggest new offer came to me in the form of Fabio Ochoa, his partner in the load on its way to New York. Ochoa's sales generated $10 million to $40 million per month in the U.S., and Alcaíno could land me the lion's share of that figure. Ochoa was having most of his money flown from the U.S. back to Colombia, but Alcaíno could get that rerouted to me if I was interested.

I was interested. "Count me in," I said.

Bilgrami came by the house early the next evening with new proposals. He had a client with $700,000 in a safe-deposit box and was offering a 6 percent fee if I'd work the cash through my system and provide a wire transfer. But what Bilgrami really wanted to discuss was bringing my dirty business to him, Awan, and Akbar at Capcom when they left BCCI. I pumped him for details, asking questions like a curious child. Bilgrami panicked when he realized how openly he was talking.

"I really get scared talking about this," he said, squirming.

"We don't have to do that," I assured him. "Whenever, okay? But it sounds interesting."

He calmed down and then dropped his pants.

"It's a very good system," he continued, "and it works out perfectly."

The plan: I'd give cash to Capcom, which would purchase and sell gold simultaneously through two separate gold dealers. The money from the gold dealer who bought from Capcom would go into whatever account I designated. No link, the flow of funds untraceable. I wanted details, but now wasn't the time. Bilgrami was tense. Better to wait him out.

When I asked for him at the bank the next day, Awan unexpectedly ushered me to the couches. Awan had been traveling in Panama, Colombia, London, and elsewhere for weeks—I hadn't seen him in more than a month. I told him I'd be flying to Europe in about three weeks and wondered if he thought I should contact Ziauddin Akbar at Capcom.

"It would be good if you would meet him and see his setup and all that," Awan said.

It was also a chance to get Akbar on tape. While in Europe, I could make separate stops at the BCCI Paris and London branches to shore up the cases against Chinoy, Baakza, and Howard.

"I don't know if Akbar [Bilgrami] mentioned to you," Awan said. "We're going through a bit of a problem these days. We think there's another investigation going on. I've been with the lawyers for the last couple of days, trying to sort out some things.... We're just anticipating it to come through. We should have our defenses ready."

"Why?" I asked, surprised. "Is there grumbling?"

He took a long drag from his Dunhill Blue and exhaled toward the ceiling. "Senate committee again."

The piercing ring of the boardroom phone interrupted the conversation. Awan reached for the receiver as anger swelled inside me. How the hell could Jack Blum and the subcommittee have resumed their investigation? Top-level Justice Department officials had given them written notice that resuming before October would endanger the operation and our lives. We needed two more months. *Dammit.*

"Hello?" Awan said, "Yeah, what's happening? Who? What do you mean? Who said? Who's saying that? Are you sure? Where did it happen? Who's telling you this? Yeah, in the embassy. Let me call. I'll call you back." He looked like he'd seen a ghost as he hung up. "Give me one moment," he said, dialing a number and confirming what he'd just heard.

"We just received some news," he said to me finally. "The president of my country was killed in a plane crash. We just got it — I mean, that's all I got, and they suspect that the Russians shot it down. The U.S. ambassador to Pakistan was killed, too" — as were other key Pakistani officials, including the director of intelligence and the chairman of the Joint Chiefs of Staff.

As Awan left the room, Bilgrami entered with documents needed to move money to Panama, which was still in play, and then addressed the Capcom plan. I'd have to place half a million in a portfolio account in London in the name of an offshore company I controlled. The only activity in that account would be the placement and management of that half million — seed money that entitled me to launder $1.5 million per month through Capcom's own massive operations account.

Our monthly delivery of $1.5 million looked like a cup of water poured into a fifty-gallon rain barrel with a hundred spigots. In the course of a day's business, Capcom might open a few or all of their spigots to pay different precious-metals dealers for gold. They might sell to fifty other precious-metals dealers, which lifted fifty more cups of water back into the barrel. But — and here was the trick — they could instruct the precious-metals dealers to whom they sold gold to send payment to any account in the world, rather than returning those funds to Capcom. Delivery of laundered money to the cartel went through unsuspecting gold dealers. Capcom didn't even have to risk wiring funds to cartel accounts. It was utterly perfect.

To cover their tracks and ensure they didn't lose money on the fluctuating gold market, Capcom would buy and sell $1.5 million worth of gold in their name simultaneously, charging me a fee of 1.5 percent. To launder the first installment, they'd take a $22,500 commission — and hoped, of course, that we'd occasionally increase the half-million balance in the portfolio account.

I offered to place the half million in seed money on deposit with Capcom immediately.

Bilgrami's eyes lit up. "Okay, why don't we do this? Why don't we do this? I have all the agreements here. Why don't you sign one, and we'll make the first run, and you meet him in September?"

Then he put the squeeze on and upped the ante, asking that I place a million dollars with Capcom, half on deposit and half as a test run for channeling funds to one of my clients. When I agreed, Bilgrami's pen darted from form to form, papers flying.

But before I left, he made a damning suggestion. He recommended I visit a spy shop on Brickell Avenue where he bought equipment for BCCI offices in Miami and Colombia. He had noticed equipment capable of detecting recording devices and thought I should invest in same for conversations with people I didn't trust. Yet more proof that BCCI was rotten to the root, and validation that the bank had probably monitored my conversation in the boardroom with Mora. Thankfully, Saul Mineroff's foresight and special alloy casing neutralized that threat.

Outside, I hit the pay phones and called Customs.

"I just left a meeting at BCCI. I guess you've heard that President Zia of Pakistan, the U.S. ambassador, and a bunch of senior officials were killed when their plane exploded in Pakistan?"

They hadn't.

"Never mind," I said. "I was just checking in to let you guys know everything was under control."

Later that day, news of President Zia's death hit the wire.

I learned consequential international news before the rest of the world and learned more from my dirty bank contacts and cartel clients in one day than anyone carrying a badge and a gun could by pounding the pavement for a month. It was turning me into an information junkie, wanting to run from target to target to learn as much as I could before our window of opportunity slammed shut forever.

Which reminded me...

Saad Shafi, head of BCCI Nassau, had asked me to visit him in the Bahamas to work out a more formal relationship. A quick call determined he still stood by his invitation. And there was Tuto Zabala, with whom I also had unfinished business. And he probably still needed help collecting the debt from the Cubans in Chicago.

"Yes, I would really appreciate your help," Zabala said. "Let's get together so I can give you the details. How much would that cost?"

Best if we talked in person, I said, promising to contact him in a few days. With less than two months left, I had just enough time to gather intel about his customers in Chicago. Time to turn to Dominic, who made a living prying money from the hands of dopers who'd stiffed his bosses. He could school me on everything I needed to know.

"First, you tell him your people charge fifty percent," Dominic said.

"Fifty sounds like a lot," I said.

"Well, it does to you 'cause you ain't done this before. Like I used to tell da guys I did this for: nothin' from nothin' is nothin', so for fifty percent you get a lot more than nothin'.... You'll need every piece of information he can give you, especially if he has any idea if dese guys are working with people who are connected. Tell him that if dese Cubans are working with someone connected there might be a peaceful way this can be resolved and you definitely don't want to fuck with somebody who you later find out is connected. It could start a war. You need to ask him how far he wants you to go, you know, to find out if you've got the green light to take these people out — just ask him if he wants your people to go all the way."

Zabala picked me up at Miami International from a quick trip to Tampa.

"I have the people in Chicago who can get this done," I told him. "It'll cost you fifty percent. How much do they owe you?"

"A hundred and ten thousand. The fee is okay," he said, briefing me about Pepe and José Hurtado, the Cubans in Chicago with ties to Miami who carried guns and ran two grocery stores on North Milwaukee Avenue and West Washington Boulevard. Zabala had sold fourteen kilos a month to them over the last three years, but he had no idea if they had mob connections. They did have a Chicago detective on their payroll, however. Zabala promised to provide their business addresses, home addresses, descriptions, and phone numbers.

When I requested photos, Zabala suggested that a member of his family, an employee of the Florida Department of Motor Vehicles, could help. He claimed that she routinely gave him information from state files.

"If we have to," I asked, making a gun gesture with my hand, "do you want my people to go all the way?"

He nodded.

When he dropped me off on Key Biscayne, I told him it would take two weeks to make sure the Hurtados didn't sell to the mob and another four to get everything in place to grab one of them.

"Thanks, Bob," he said, "and if you can use me to move money or merchandise anywhere in the States or foreign, keep me in mind."

The amphibious prop jet taxied past giant cruise ships in Miami harbor. We had six weeks before the world learned that Emilio Dominguez and Robert Musella were feds. So this had to be a quick trip: get Shafi on tape and get back to Miami as soon as possible.

Shafi offered typical BCCI hospitality, a chauffeured Mercedes and lavish meals. But I was there for business, and it was time to talk. Shafi met with me in the privacy of my hotel room. I asked if we could deposit large sums of currency so my clients in Colombia could receive wire transfers from his branch.

"Sure, sure," he said. "That's not — we are equipped here for everything.... You name a transaction, we know it, so we are fully equipped to handle any kind of thing."

"The biggest concern I have," I said, "is one that, if we do business, you and I would share, which is to maintain the absolute confidentiality and secrecy of every transaction that we have."

"Sure, sure."

I explained the services I provided to my Colombian clients, how we received boxes of cash, deposited them to accounts of cash-generating businesses, and disguised the transfer of funds to their accounts as loan proceeds.

Shafi didn't flinch. He was more than happy to take those funds, place them in secret CDs, and extend separate loans in like amounts unlinked to the deposits. He, too, had graduated with honors from BCCI's money-laundering 101 class.

Then I gave him my canned speech about the source of my Colombian clients' funds and Lee Iacocca. "What they do is their business. What I do is my business, and I'm a wall between them and yourself."

"Sure," he said. "We try to give the best quality of service in terms of good banking, plus confidentiality. Once you feel comfortable, you'll automatically give — that's our policy."

Shafi would happily launder as much as we could bring, but he wanted some funds to stay on deposit. If we had $20 million to clean, he wanted to hold $1 million while he pushed the other $19 million through, and he cited the importance of his end-of-year balance sheet. As long as I had big deposits with his branch on December thirty-first, I'd get first-class treatment.

"Now that you have taken me into confidence," Shafi said, "I can assure you that, if God forbid, if I have anything" — a problem — "I'll tell you up front. But that, of course, I'll do in confidence also. As of now, I don't feel any problem. I feel that everything should run perfectly."

To reassure me, Shafi claimed that, if the U.S. ever inquired about my banking in Nassau, he would know. He maintained a close friendship with the prime minister, Sir Lynden Pindling.

Back in Miami, Zabala was at my doorstep with a list of details about the Hurtados. In exchange, I invited him and his wife to my wedding, which he quickly accepted. Then, icing on the cake, I told him I needed him to pick up cash in Miami.

What he didn't know was that he would be receiving cash from undercover agents and, after holding the money for a day, delivering it right back to other undercover agents. This illusion of movement gave him the impression that he was a trusted member of our organization. Paying him to pick up, hold, and deliver the cash bought his loyalty, which I'd need as October drew closer.

Kathy and I resumed our social contact with Juan and Clara Tobón. We met them for lunch at the Rusty Pelican. Over stone-crab claws at a casual lunch, Tobón whispered in my ear. Alcaíno had at least $50 million hidden in European bank accounts, he believed. Tobón had worked closely with Alcaíno on a number of deals, and during the past year he'd given Alcaíno more than half a million to finance the purchase of an anchovy-packing plant in Buenos Aires—a front for his transportation line.

Bingo!

Tobón had just given me the last piece of the puzzle. How many anchovy-packing plants could there be in Buenos Aires with a container headed to a major city in the Northeast? Casals's earlier slip gave me a hunch that Alcaíno's route probably involved anchovies, but now I had the whole story.

Tobón explained that the factory commercially packed large tin cans of anchovies, some—but not all—of which contained cocaine. But they were having problems. They had recently lost a load headed to Europe. And the Colombians who financed Tobón's now seized Cessna Citation were hunting him and his family. Alcaíno and Nasser had offered to have them whacked, but Tobón preferred to resolve this issue without violence. To recoup his losses, Tobón was making arrangements for me to launder about $300,000 a week for Nasser, provided I shared my profits with him.

I couldn't wait to get to a pay phone.

"I just had another meeting with a close friend of Alcaíno," I said to Loreto in New York. "I've got some more information for you that you need to get out in a bulletin to the Customs inspectors.

Alcaíno's load of dope is hidden in a container full of large cans of commercially packed anchovies sent from a plant in Buenos Aires. Each can weighs about ten kilograms, and some of the cans contain bricks of cocaine. This load should be coming into New York or some port in that vicinity any day. You've got to get everybody hunting for that container. There's not much more time before it will clear Customs."

"We'll do everything we can to get the word out to every major port on the East Coast," he said, hanging up and instructing one of the agents in his group to get the bulletins out.

"I've got a bowling match tonight," the agent said. "Getting that notice out would take me hours. I'll do it tomorrow morning."

Tommy blew his New York cork, "If you *fucking* leave this office without getting that done, you're looking at thirty days without pay, and I'll make your life so miserable you won't have the strength to ever pick up another bowling ball!"

The updated bulletins went out that night.

While our office closed in on Alcaíno's anchovies, Gonzalo and Lucy Mora flew from Medellín to Miami. They had family in town, and Mora needed to give an updated accounting of the checks. To keep Lucy busy, Kathy and a new undercover agent, Millie Aviles, shopped and socialized with her.

Playing the role of one of Emir's girlfriends, Millie was a natural. A bright, dark-haired Spanish speaker from a small town near Mayagüez, Puerto Rico, she had only earned her agent's badge eighteen months earlier, but she was already taking on a seasoned agent's long-term undercover role. A dangerous situation, but many native Spanish speakers found themselves in this position. Because of their language skills, the front-office brass often threw them into big cases with no concern about the risks of deep-cover assignments. To make matters worse, she was also working undercover as a full-time employee at the Nevele Hotel in the Catskills in upstate New York on another case.

Along with an accounting of the checks and deals of the past few months, Mora also brought a lot of concern. He was wide-eyed and trembling when he talked about Don Chepe. "Mr. Bob, you have to understand. Our competition — his name is Eduardo" — Martinez. "He's the individual who handles all the interests for Don Chepe's organization. He is the one who has always created problems for us."

Martinez, Mora explained, had worked with Don Chepe for ten years and worked with his people in New York who claimed to have seen DEA agents watching the $2 million pickup last month. It was Martinez who ran to Don Chepe with this claim, and Mora thought Martinez had lied to undermine our business.

If he only knew.

"Don Chepe has six or seven secretaries" — money managers — "in his business," Mora continued, "and all of them fall under Eduardo. When we arrived to take away his piece of the pie, at first it was all right. But during the three months when they were continuously giving us money, I'm sure that he made a plot with the secretaries... like the problem in New York that they were following him."

Mora's trembling increased, and he started to sweat. "The day that man" — one of Don Chepe's workers — "leaves with the lentils [money] to deliver it to one of our employees... if the law catches them, I'm sure, I'm sure that they won't even ask me what happened. They'll just kill me.... Money doesn't mean anything to him. He's not interested in money. All that money is peanuts to him.... Five hundred, a million, two million — it's peanuts.... Mr. Bob, these Colombian drug traffickers are bad. It's just that the —"

"Gonzalo, my people are pretty bad here, too," I interrupted, trying to give him a little confidence.

"Correct, correct. It's Italian style. In Colombia, we're talking about a 1950s Italian style. We're talking about the same thing. We're talking about *The Godfather*."

Mora had come to a decision. He was too scared to continue doing business with Don Chepe, a madman whose power in the drug world played second fiddle only to Pablo Escobar and the Ochoas. Mora had many other contacts in the drug business who were much more reasonable. He wanted to continue — but not with Don Chepe. With Martinez in the middle whispering lies, it was only a matter of time before Mora was a dead man.

If I wanted to continue with Don Chepe, he said, I was free to do so through Armbrecht. Mora didn't want any of the profits or responsibility. I understood and supported his decision.

"My security, my family, my life, my business, my peace of mind are worth more than any more thousands of dollars that we may earn," he said, visibly relieved.

"Don't worry," I assured him. "That's more important to us, too."

Time to change the subject, so Emir wrung him like a paper towel for information on those other clients.

To put Mora further at ease, I called Bilgrami and explained that one of my clients from Medellín was in town. He and his wife invited us to join them, Awan's wife, and another BCCI officer at their home for drinks. Which led once again to a night at Regine's. Bilgrami, who at times also had doubts about me, was all over Mora with questions. Since Mora was loyal to a fault, his presence put Bilgrami at ease the same way Mora's confidence grew knowing that Bilgrami was on my team. They fed off each other.

After the Moras returned to Medellín, I headed back to Tampa for a few days, where, working late one night at Financial Consulting's office, I left a message for Alcaíno — uncharacteristically absent — to call, forwarded calls to my undercover phone at home, then drove like a madman to shake any tails.

Just before midnight, as I was barely through the door, the strobe light flashed. It had to be Alcaíno.

"How are you?" he asked, friendly as ever.

"Very good, Roberto."

"I thought you were far away," Alcaíno said, meaning Europe.

"No, not yet. I was calling about a friend of mine who seems to have been missing," I said, as he stiffened silently on the other end of the line, "in New York — Roberto is his name."

He laughed. "You know I got stuck here, and I'm...my girl-friend is ready to have the baby, so that is why we're hanging loose. So this is the thing. I've been going to Boston and going to Philadel-phia. I've been going all over the goddamn place. One day here and one day there, so hopefully soon she's going to have the baby, see.... So things are — thank God I have no problem. I've been working some, and so this is where I'm being very, very hectic."

"Does Gloria know about it?" I asked, thinking one of his girl-friends was in labor.

"No," he said, speaking to me like a father talking slowly to a child. "You know what I'm talking about?"

Oh!

How could I be so stupid? He was telling me the load was in and sitting on the dock. His main buyers were Italian organized-crime guys in Boston, I knew, so he had been in Boston working out logis-tics. Given what he'd just said, the load had to be at a dock near Philadelphia.

"How's the plans?" he said, changing the subject to the wed-ding. "They're still for October?"

"Oh yes, most definitely.... We're gonna do it Friday, Satur-day, and Sunday morning is the wedding. So there'll be a place there beginning Friday afternoon for you, if we can convince you to take out that much time."

"I won't miss that, wouldn't miss the opportunity," he said.

Good.

"I've got to tell you this," I said seconds later on the phone to Nelson Chen in New York. "I don't really want to say it because without your help, it could destroy all the hard work we've put in to coordinate the takedown that's set a month down the road. I got a call. Alcaíno said his girlfriend is pregnant. That was code to let me know the load is on the dock. It's definitely in. I gave you guys a heads-up on this more than a month ago, but you've got to look harder. Based on what he just told me, my guess is that it's some-where near Philadelphia. You guys should be looking for a shipping container full of anchovies that has arrived from a packing plant in

Buenos Aires. There can't be too many of those sitting on the docks near Philly.

"Here's my problem. The agents in Detroit fucked us and exposed our entire operation in their affidavits. It's an act of God that those affidavits are still sealed and won't be released until the takedown, but you know how that goes. The only thing between those affidavits and the street is a clerk that's supposed to safeguard them. We can't go through that again. You've got to cover my ass and keep any mention of the undercover operation out of any search warrants you decide to file. The best-case scenario is that you guys file an affidavit confirming that a routine Customs inspection stumbled on the load."

"Don't worry," Chen said. "We'll watch your back. You know you're doing the right thing, don't you?"

I had to think before I could answer. I knew I was doing the right thing, yes, but a single misstep by any one of a hundred officers who knew about the operation could get me, Emir, or somebody else killed. "Yeah, I know I'm doing the right thing. I just need you to look out for me, and I need time. If you guys find this load, please give me at least a day before you take him down. I don't want to be the last one he talked to about this when he gets popped. I'm going to call Tommy now and explain this all to him, but I called you first, Nelson, because you're the person I trust the most in New York. I'm counting on you."

"Okay, don't worry. I promise you the right thing will be done on this end."

I dialed Loreto and explained everything to him.

The next day he called back. "We've got it — congratulations."

The shipment contained 2,475 pounds of pure cocaine — at the time, the largest seizure in the Northeast, worth over $23 million.

It was odd, though. I felt happy for everyone who had worked so hard to make this happen, but I couldn't allow myself to exhibit any of that glee. It was out of character. I had to stay focused and deal with this as Bob Musella: a friend of Alcaíno and part of his organization. This news would devastate Alcaíno, Casals, Mora, Tobón,

Zabala, and dozens of others, and I was too tired to celebrate one minute and jump back into panic the next. Easier to remain stoic and deal with facts.

"How are you guys going to deal with this?" I asked Loreto.

"The agents in Philly are trying to muscle this case away from us and take the seizure on their turf," he said, confirming my fear, "but that's not going to happen. We put the bulletins out when you first gave us the leads on this load. This is our trophy. Alcaíno will be expecting the freight forwarder to have the trucking company deliver it to a warehouse on the Lower East Side. We'll make the delivery, and when he shows up we'll bag him. We're coordinating with DEA. After the arrest, we'll do a search warrant on his Thirty-fourth Street apartment. The Tampa office is coordinating with L.A. They'll hit his house in Pasadena, his jewelry store in L.A., and anything else they can find. We'll seize every asset we can lay our hands on."

"Arresting him is one thing," I said, "but the buyers of this load are big-time Italian mobsters in Boston. Isn't there any way you can try to sit on this for a while to see if you can nab him delivering to them?"

"Rudy Giuliani is our U.S. Attorney here in Manhattan. This guy likes publicity. I'm telling you right now: The front office isn't going to let this load leave New York. This is where they want the press conference."

"Let me know when you take him down. In the meantime, I'll call in any intelligence we get undercover."

"I've got an idea about how we can have eyes and ears on the ground in both Miami and L.A.," I said to Kathy after breaking the good news. "You don't have to do this. If they figure out who we really are, it wouldn't have a pretty ending, but I think we're in solid with these people.... Call Gloria Alcaíno. Tell her you're having second thoughts about the marriage because of what I do in the business. Tell her that you were wondering if she would be willing to allow you to come out to L.A. and spend a little time with her to get her counsel. That way, if Alcaíno smells a rat and sneaks out of

New York, you'll be in a position to hear and learn exactly what he's doing. I'll stay in Miami and keep my ear to the ground with Zabala and Tobón. What do you think?"

"I'm all for it," she said. "The Alcaínos don't suspect us in the least, and we'll have all our bases covered in case things go different than planned. After we get clearance from our people in Tampa, I'll call her and set it up."

It was crucial to be as close to Zabala and Tobón as possible when Alcaíno was arrested, so I called Zabala with news that my people in Chicago had taken pictures of the Hurtados that he needed to confirm before we grabbed them. I also told him he needed to pick up $150,000 and hold it for a day. Then I told Tobón I was ready to take the first shipment of money from him on behalf of John Nasser in Colombia.

The anchovy net was closing on Alcaíno, our first big catch. Kathy headed solo to Pasadena where Juan and Clara Tobón were staying with Gloria Alcaíno and her two daughters. She confessed her second thoughts while keeping one ear open for calls from Alcaíno. But Alcaíno was too busy to call.

On a balmy, clear September afternoon, Alcaíno was waiting in a suit and tie at a Chelsea warehouse when a truck arrived pulling a flatbed carrying the forty-foot container packed with tens of thousands of pounds of anchovies. Just as Tobón had said, each box contained several large tins, commercially packed; no one would otherwise suspect a thing. Anchovies in salt, under the brand name Dipez, manufactured by Mar del Mar, S.A., in Buenos Aires.

Customs and DEA agents posing as workers at the warehouse began unloading the truck. Alcaíno was already sweating the two extra days it took to get the freight forwarder to release the container for delivery. He had almost abandoned the deal, but he had invested too much in the load and transportation line.

As the boxes shifted from the truck to the warehouse, though, he noticed peculiarities about the warehouse men. These were new faces. Too many gringos. Tall, athletic, short hair, beepers. They were too well dressed; they didn't have laborers' hands. Men who offload trucks — mostly Hispanics or blacks'— wear dingy clothes, have weathered hands and faces and scraggly hair. These guys were educated — their vocabulary was too good, and they kept trying to engage him in conversation.

"You know," a nearby worker said to him, "I hear that a lot of times people will try to smuggle drugs into the U.S. by hiding it in shipments like this."

Alcaíno's face froze.

The cats were playing with the mouse, he realized, so he stepped to the side of the loading dock and immediately called his girlfriend at his midtown apartment. "Cecilia, listen to me closely. The package was delivered, but I think it has been spoiled due to the intense heat. You know that ugly guy wasn't supposed to get involved, but I think he's gotten right in the middle of everything. You need to make sure that the apartment is spotless, because I think they may visit there eventually. Also, since the air conditioner is broken there, and it is probably going to get very hot, why don't you take out the trash and find someplace comfortable to stay. I'll call you when I've figured these things out for sure."

Cecilia threw everything she could find in her suitcase — a triple-beam scale, lead ingots, a few kilos of coke, some cash, and records of prior drug sales. She ran down the stairs to the basement, walked from the garage, and entered the sea of millions of New Yorkers on the street. She found a cheap hotel and waited.

While agents struggled with the boxes, Alcaíno slowly walked around the corner, trying to act as cool as he could. Out of sight, he jumped in a cab, sped to his apartment, packed a bag, and quickly reappeared on the street. Agents watching the building saw him flag another cab and head to LaGuardia. At the terminal, he dashed into an elevator, went down to the ground floor, and got in another cab. The agents who followed him to the airport didn't see him leave, so they jumped on aircraft eyeballing passengers to see if he had snuck on a flight. Meanwhile, Alcaíno had returned to his apartment, where some of the agents who had stayed in case he returned took him down.

By the time Alcaíno was in cuffs, Kathy and Juan and Clara Tobón were getting ready to leave Alcaíno's house in Pasadena and head to the airport. She needed to get out before agents showed up to search the house. She thanked Gloria for her support and said it was time to come home. I picked them up at Miami International and we headed to Tobón's house, where he revealed his feeling that Alcaíno had problems. He'd spoken to Alcaíno on the phone and could feel the tension. In Pasadena, Gloria had noticed strangers in sedans near their home, possibly taking pictures.

I looked concerned but didn't say a word.

Not knowing what Zabala knew, I had him pick up $150,000 the next day from one of our undercover agents. Zabala called to confirm he had the money, and I instructed him to keep it secure until the following day when someone would pick it up from him. I threw him a grand for his loyalty, the most valuable insurance I could buy.

The same night at Tobón's home, a little old man showed up with a five-gallon bucket of PVC fittings and tools. Once inside, the top layer of fittings and tools came off to expose $63,000 in bundles of $20 and $50 bills — the first small delivery of Nasser's cash and a trivial amount, but the arrangement bought more credibility insurance with Tobón when the storm of Alcaíno's arrest hit.

"Roberto was arrested," Zabala said in person four days later, concerned. "He called me four nights ago and warned me not to have one of my workers meet him at LaGuardia. He'd seen people at the warehouse and knew he was being followed. Before I could talk to him, he hung up."

Zabala was supposed to send a guy to meet Alcaíno at LaGuardia with $25,000 from the sale of a couple of kilos of coke. Zabala aborted the plan and was still holding the $25,000. A few days later, Gloria called him asking for any money he was holding that belonged to Alcaíno. She needed it for a lawyer. Zabala tried to give me the $25,000 so I could transfer it to Alcaíno's attorney, but I declined.

"I think we should wait to see what instructions we get from Gloria," I said cautiously.

Zabala also disclosed that DEA was hunting Casals, who was hiding at his mother-in-law's house, and Alcaíno's girlfriend Cecilia, who had been hiding in a cheap hotel in midtown Manhattan, but Zabala had invited her to Miami, so she was on her way into our net.

After confirming the photos of the Hurtado brothers, Zabala left, thinking we were about to help recover his money in Chicago.

Everything seemed calm — until midnight when the phone rang.

"Hello?"

Nothing, and then a woman screaming and crying.

"Hello? . . ."

"It's me, Gloria. I'm sorry. I need to be strong. I'm not at home. I'm not going to call you from my home. I have a problem. I haven't heard from Tuto. Roberto's lawyer wants money on Monday. Would you please give Tuto a call and ask him to give me an answer in the morning."

"He has $25,000 for you," I said, "and will have somebody come out to deliver that to you. He's expecting more next week that someone can take to you."

"I could buy a cashier's check but we could be caught both ways," she said. "Tell Tuto to send checks made out to Roberto's attorney. Have him call so I can give him the name of the lawyer."

"Don't worry. I'll have my attorney find out as much as he can about what's been filed about this case, and I'll have Tuto call you. Please write down this number — that's a pay phone not far from my house. When you call me again, if I tell you to call me back at the other house, that's the number I want you to call."

"Okay. Please have Tuto send money to me soon."

"Don't worry; I'll take care of it."

No doubt Alcaíno was sitting in his jail cell rewinding every conversation he'd had over the past thirty days, looking for a flaw.

Would he point the finger toward me, or would I get a pass? I was alone on the streets of Miami, no cover team, no gun, no badge — just my gut feeling, feeling my way through. Which paradoxically increased our odds of success and my odds of survival.

Zabala had his man deliver $25,000 to Gloria the next day, and I stayed on top of him to keep the money flowing to her. He didn't mind talking with me, but he feared that talking to Gloria would bring the feds down on him.

That night, Gloria called. "It has been taken care of. Thank you. I'm going to call you at that other number in an hour."

The pay phone rang right on schedule. Between episodes of crying she explained the terror of the past few days. After agents searched her Pasadena home, she flew to New York to see Alcaíno. In whispers at a jail in downtown Manhattan, he told her to check a spot in his apartment he had once shown her. At his midtown flat, in total darkness, she unscrewed the kick plate under the dishwasher, where she found a passport he had in another name and $120,000 in cash. DEA agents had missed this hiding place. She shredded the passport and flushed it down the toilet, but she needed my help to convert the $120,000 into checks for the attorney.

"No problem," I said. "When you're ready, I'll send one of my workers to meet you. Once he has the cash, I'll send checks to the lawyer."

"I can't thank you enough," she said. "Everyone else is treating me like I have the plague. They're afraid to talk to me, afraid to help. When I met with Roberto he told me he knew you would be there for us. He said you're the only one he really trusts. He'd like you to take over some of his responsibilities. There are many people who owe him for merchandise, and there are some people who gave him merchandise that he owes. Tuto knows most of the details, and there is a woman, Cecilia, who is on her way to Miami, who also has details. Would you please help us?"

"I'll do everything in my power to help you and Roberto through this terrible time. I promise, you can count on me."

"Oh, thank God, I'll call you when I'm ready to meet your man and give him the hundred and twenty thousand. Good night, and God bless you."

It took a minute to filter out the guilt and to process the importance of staying on task. I had a job to do. It wasn't personal. I was the eyes and ears of the government, documenting what was occurring. I had to stay true. I had to override the emotion and assess my risks.

My verdict: Not only was I not suspected, Alcaíno was about to put me in his place to close the books on his outstanding business. I'd get names, numbers, details of distributors holding coke, and eventually the chance to lure his suppliers to the table with the bait of a claim that I was going to get them paid.

I just had to hope that Alcaíno hadn't double-crossed anyone — and that I wasn't walking into a trap.

18

THE CONFESSIONAL

Pasadena, California
September 15, 1988

AGENTS TOOK EVERY PIECE of their life they could grab. The $2 million home in Pasadena, the $400,000 inventory of the downtown jewelry store — seized. The entire fleet of Rolls-Royces, Porsches, and Mercedes was heading to the impound lot on flatbed trucks. The pay-phone business, the fight-promotion company, the downtown apartment complex — the government had taken control of it all. Or so they thought. Tobón whispered that Alcaíno had tens of millions more stashed in offshore accounts, too well hidden for the government to find.

At the same time, agents were moving in on Alcaíno's Argentina operation. He had purchased a plane through me that flew repeatedly from Fabio Ochoa's clandestine lab in the Bolivian jungle with thousands of pounds of cocaine to an airstrip on a ranch in northern Argentina. Workers then trucked it a few hundred miles to the anchovy packing plant in Buenos Aires, where it was hidden in commercial seafood shipments to Europe and the northeast U.S.

Before Alcaíno's arrest, DEA Special Agent Ernie Batista in Buenos Aires had already picked up the scent of the transportation line. A bulldog, Batista had seven hard years of narco-busting under his belt at the Palm Beach County sheriff's office before joining DEA. His rapport with an informant in Argentina landed him two truckloads—300 and 500 kilos each—along with machine guns and grenades, moving from a ranch in northern Argentina toward Buenos Aires. But he and the Argentinean federal police hadn't made the connection to the packing plant.

But when the forty-foot shipping container filled with anchovies and Alcaíno's dope spilled its secrets on the docks of Philadelphia, the boxes and shipping documents had Argentina all over them. The paperwork pointed to Carlos Díaz, a man from Medellín operating Mar del Mar in Buenos Aires. And the dope seized later in Chelsea—half-kilo bricks wrapped in foil embossed with a smiley face, then packed and sealed in clear plastic—matched the coke seized two months earlier by Batista and Argentinean narcs.

Traffickers emboss brands on their bricks of cocaine so whole-sale buyers know at sight the product's quality, just like cigarette packaging. When you buy, you know what you're getting. But it also offers prosecutors a handy road map to everyone involved in the pro-duction line.

Not long after Alcaíno ran from the Chelsea warehouse to LaGuardia, DEA agents and Argentinean federal police raided Díaz's home and arrested him. Díaz knew he couldn't beat the evi-dence, so he rolled on Alcaíno. Half a dozen of Alcaíno's Argen-tinean workers went down; agents searched several warehouses and homes, and Alcaíno's organization disintegrated.

It was only a matter of time before the transportation line pointed to a lab in the jungles of Bolivia—just as Alcaíno had told me. After squeezing an informant, DEA Special Agent Angel Perez, stationed in Santa Cruz, and Colonel Rogelio Vargas of the Bolivian national police led an air assault with four Huey helicopters and twenty Bolivian commandos.

They had been circling the jungles of eastern Bolivia for hours when Perez spotted a tiny green tarp peeking from the thick jungle canopy. It lay about two miles from a remote airstrip built next to a narrow, winding river. The canopy of the jungle didn't offer a single inch of opening for the choppers, so they touched down on the airstrip. To conserve fuel, half the team joined Perez and Vargas in one chopper that worked its way closer to the lab.

From the low-hovering chopper, the team deployed into the knee-deep water, grass, and muck of a heavily overgrown marsh. Vargas, a big man, fell clear through the grass cover and disappeared beneath the surface. One of his commandos crawled along the floating grass and pulled at the barrel of his rifle standing from the water like a straw. Vargas surfaced, gasped for air, and crawled to stable ground.

The entire team moved carefully toward the river where they found handmade wooden canoes they used to paddle south along the slow rolling waterway. As they glided along, insects, macaws, and monkeys screeched through the jungle above the sound of the pounding of their hearts. They came to a small trail leading into growth so thick Perez couldn't see more than five feet ahead of his fully automatic M-16. As they crept along, they passed dozens of fifty-gallon barrels of sulfuric acid and acetone, ingredients used to convert coca leaves to pure cocaine powder.

Suddenly Colonel Vargas raised his hand, halting the team in their tracks. A highly venomous eight-foot bushmaster viper slithered across the path in front of them. When the copper-colored monster with black markings finally slipped back into the jungle, Vargas dropped his hand, and the crouched commandos continued forward.

The camp bore clear signs of fresh abandonment. The food in the makeshift mess hall was still warm, and the fire in the outdoor kitchen was still burning. Less than an hour before, when the Hueys stopped circling and began to land, Ochoa's workers had scattered along three escape trails.

The camp contained dormitories, generators, drying tables, filtering stations—enough equipment and manpower to produce three tons of cocaine per week. In his sweaty, trembling palm Perez lifted a half-kilo brick, ready for shipment, wrapped in aluminum, embossed with a smiley face—exactly like the thousands of bricks at the Chelsea warehouse.

Vargas, Perez, and the commandos set fire to the camp and destroyed it.

Alcaíno's wasn't the only life crumbling. The Senate subcommittee was chasing Awan for answers about Noriega's fortune. He didn't want to meet me at the bank, but the solitude of a hideaway lounge in Coconut Grove appealed to him. At the Grand Bay Hotel, he had nestled in a corner among the comfort of plush cherrywood couches that offered the privacy of what looked like a private executive study.

He was nervously tapping his pack of Dunhills while sipping a tall, cold glass of Corona. He gazed at the wall as though it held answers to the problems weighing so heavily on his mind. He looked smaller and weaker than he had when we met to transform the fortunes of the underworld from boxes of cash to condominium complexes. Something troubled him deeply — and it was my job to coax that something from him into the recorder taped to the inside of my thigh.

When he noticed my approach, he smiled as though he had just seen his last true friend and then entered my confessional.

He took another deep drag on his cigarette, examining the ceiling as he exhaled a cloud of smoke. "Let me tell you what's happened, Bob. I'm in a bit of a poop right now." Another drag. "What I've learned has been not very pleasant. And I wanted to talk to you personally and tell you about it. What's happened is that we were served a subpoena last month. The bank was, and Mr. Shafi, our general manager, was. I was supposed to have been served also, but with their normal efficiency, they" — Senate investigators — "opened the phone book and there's some poor Amjad Awan who works for Rockwell International. He's an aerospace engineer, and they turned up at his house.... He didn't know what the hell was happening, poor man. This is why I've been going up and down to London ... with our attorneys in Washington, and we've had several meetings. I found that, although they're supposed to be among the topmost firms in Washington, they didn't come up with any sort of game plan of action."

Robert Altman, a bigwig in the Democratic Party and a partner in the firm headed by former secretary of defense Clark Clifford, chaired the meetings in London.

Awan instructed me to close my accounts at BCCI Panama as quickly as possible or run the risk of being compromised. He recommended I call Panama from a phone outside the U.S. because U.S. authorities were likely monitoring all calls between the branch and the States. After the accounts were closed, he'd have my bank records destroyed. "If there are no records," he said, "how do they get to the people? That's what I'll...I'm trying to work out."

Altman and the bank, they had decided, would lead the subcommittee to believe the bank was willing to turn over records from Panama. Before doing that, though, they needed Panamanian authorities to allow the disclosure, which otherwise would have violated Panamanian law. BCCI's lawyers knew authorities in Panama would never authorize the release of the records. If the ploy worked, no one would ever see my accounts, or the accounts of hundreds of others involved in the drug trade who moved money through BCCI.

At that point, Awan lowered an unexpected boom. To prevent the subcommittee from serving Awan with a subpoena, Altman advised the bank to transfer Awan to Paris immediately. Awan was fuming, confident that this move would accomplish nothing more than heating the subcommittee's interest in pursuing him for managing Noriega's accounts. Senior bank officials carried out Altman's recommendation anyway, which shifted Awan across the Atlantic to a desk with no title or responsibility, all to keep a subpoena out of his hands.

Then he hit me with an even bigger surprise. He had double-crossed them. He secretly hired a different lawyer to represent him independently. He returned to Washington and with his attorney met secretly with Jack Blum, counsel to the subcommittee. Awan was trying to extricate himself from BCCI's problems by obtaining assurances from subcommittee investigators that he could secretly provide information about Noriega in exchange for a pass. His plan: Tell Blum a little bit of the truth about Noriega's accounts behind closed doors. He felt the subcommittee had only circumstantial proof that wouldn't hold up—no smoking gun. He lied to them, denying that the bank was involved in money laundering. It looked to him as though he'd conned them; they were inclined to give him a pass. He and his lawyer had scheduled another meeting with Blum in Washington, but he was confident he could answer Blum's questions without implicating the bank or disclosing sensitive information.

As Awan unraveled, I asked how pressure could be applied on him and the bank from Washington when, based on his comments earlier in the year, it was clear that "there were some folks in Washington who were kind of, like, on your side."

Although the bank's attorneys included Clark Clifford, Awan believed, Altman and Clifford were intentionally giving BCCI bad advice in order to take control of the bank's hidden interest in First American, which of course BCCI secretly owned through nominee shareholders.

Then there was the problem of Noriega.

"I happen to be the only person in the bank," Awan said, "who knows all about Noriega's accounts and business. I've told them, 'I'm willing to tell you whatever you want to know,' because I think he can get away. But I said, 'I want to make a deal with you that whatever I say should be in executive session, and not in open session, so whatever I say is in camera,' the reason being that, if I say anything about Noriega and it's reported by the press, I'm dead. He's gonna kill me."

Awan planned to orchestrate a one-sided, ironclad deal with the subcommittee. "Otherwise I'll skip," he said, meaning he'd flee the country.

Then the conversation drifted painfully to small talk: what the future held, how much his wife enjoyed socializing with us. Painful because I had to act like a true friend. But Awan remained adamant that, regardless of his problems, he'd attend the wedding.

My bosses in D.C. would doubtless want to know the details of this conversation, which couldn't get back to a politically motivated subcommittee that Awan was playing like a fiddle — at least not for thirty days. By then the undercover operation would have ended, and anyone could use this information however he saw fit. Yet another reason that conditions on the ground should have determined the takedown date. Given more time, I could have pumped Awan easily for every last detail about the fraud behind the ownership of First American, but no one would have listened to my arguments. No matter what happened, October held strong.

As I left the Grand Bay Hotel, I marveled that the same international bankers orchestrating the laundering of drug fortunes were in bed with major political figures, not only helping them hide their crimes but also operating a multibillion-dollar U.S. bank chain secretly owned by powers in Saudi Arabia and Pakistan. Our allies, yes — but then why were they so deeply involved with the likes of Awan, chasing dirty money all over the world? It was more than just greed. It looked like a play for financial and political power across the globe.

Not long after, Awan made his clandestine trip to D.C. and met with subcommittee investigators, including Jack Blum. When asked if any of the bank's clients were involved in drug dealing or money laundering, Awan said stoically, "No."

The subcommittee thanked him for his honesty.

Now it was time to play charades with the Colombians, pretending to be on top of the fallout from Alcaíno's arrest.

I told Tobón about my system of communicating with Gloria Alcaíno from pay phones, which enabled me to act as her lifeline. Tobón couldn't wait to partake, so I took him and his brother-in-law, Diego Perez, to the Key Biscayne Winn-Dixie on a hot September night. Like clockwork, Gloria called. After she and I spoke, Tobón took the line. When they finished, Tobón informed me that he and Gloria had arranged future communication through one of

Alcaíno's lawyers. He'd cross the government's radar screen if he spoke directly to Gloria, he reasoned.

Little did he know.

Tobón, Perez, and I headed back to my town house. No cover team, no gun, no badge—and no other way to proceed. Any abnormal behavior would have raised flags of alarm. At my place, the audio-video system rolling, we spent an hour going over documents I claimed my lawyers had collected about Alcaíno's arrest.

Tobón pored over an article from the *Philadelphia Daily News* and a copy of the affidavit used to search Alcaíno's New York apartment. Just as Nelson Chen had promised, not one word threw suspicion in my direction. Everything pointed to an accidental find by Customs inspectors using dogs trained to sniff out cocaine. As far as the underworld knew, I had nothing to do with it.

After carefully reading each word, Tobón explained his role to me—and my confessional was open again. He had put up money to finance the anchovy packing plant, which, four or five times, had safely moved coke to the States and Europe. References to Carlos Díaz worried him. Díaz knew him, which could spell trouble.

From my place, we headed to Tobón's. During the drive, he confessed concerns about Alcaíno. Tobón theorized that Alcaíno was a very rich man because his partners had a habit of being mysteriously murdered. He worried that Alcaíno's hands were covered with blood. Which of course worried me. I'd just accepted responsibility to collect debts and pay suppliers for Alcaíno. I might find myself paying unexpectedly for his sins. But there was no turning back. There was still a lot of work to do and less than a month in the hourglass.

It had occurred to me that, after everyone went off in chains, I'd be a marked man. My testimony would determine the outcome of the majority of the resulting cases. Instinct was preparing me for the worst. One of these madmen—Don Chepe, for example—would put a price on my head and force me underground. So I found a cemetery in an Italian neighborhood, walking past hundreds of headstones, looking for the perfect fit: an Italian name, an infant death, someone born the year I was. There it was. I scribbled down details and, in my spare time, began building another identity — morbid insurance for me and my family.

Back in Tampa, I prepared for a ten-day trip to Europe, during which I would meet Ziauddin Akbar at Capcom in London and tie up loose ends with Chinoy and his staff at BCCI Paris, before everyone arrived at Innisbrook Resort near Tampa for the wedding.

Against objections from the front office, Kathy and I insisted that we handle the wedding plans at the country club straight up. No one there could know we were feds. If we made those disclosures, there was no way of knowing who might catch a whisper of the truth. Wealthy members of the community sat on the club's board, and any one of them could be one of BCCI's clients. We set dozens of rooms aside for the dopers and bankers who had agreed that they and their families would attend our lavish outdoor celebration.

Laura Sherman had learned that Rudy Armbrecht had come to the FBI's attention. An undercover Bureau agent in Tennessee had been posing as an airplane broker, confirming Colombian informant reports that Armbrecht had already bought twenty Rockwell Commanders for the cartel. But rather than strike, they let Armbrecht buy plane after plane, installing satellite tracking systems in each one. In time, D.C. could monitor the entire Medellín cartel fleet and identify every single secret airstrip the planes visited and each time any plane tried to return to the U.S. with its narcotic payload.

FBI Agent Brian Loader in Washington oversaw this sting, Operation Star Watch. A friend of mine, previously stationed in Tampa as a supervisor, he had tried to recruit me to join the FBI, but I turned him down in favor of Customs.

"I'm all for your operational plan," I told him, "but I'm the tail of the dog. You'll have to convince Customs that what you intend to do is so important that our operation shouldn't be taken down. Something unsaid is driving this beast to end in October, but if you can get them to prolong it, I think we can maintain credibility with the underworld and run it for another couple of months."

"Okay," he said. "We'll make that play from headquarters.

Being able to track the cartel's air force would be a coup. I can't imagine your people wouldn't understand that."

I couldn't imagine a lot of things my people did, I thought.

Just before Kathy and I left for Europe, we hit the Tampa office to review our itinerary with Steve Cook. As we were talking, a clerk interrupted with an intercom message, "Steve, Ira Silverman is on line two."

Cook picked up and started talking as Kathy's eyes grew big as saucers.

"Do you know Silverman?" she whispered to me.

I didn't.

"He's a lead producer with NBC News."

"*What?!* That can't be. What the hell are you saying?"

It was Steve's turn in the confessional. When he got off the phone, nothing could hold me back. "What the fuck is going on? Why the *hell* are you talking to the head of NBC News?"

"Kathy, let me talk to Bob for a minute," Cook said sheepishly.

"I didn't say anything," he said, looking beaten, after Kathy left, "because this isn't my plan, man. This is Tischler's thing. I've fought this every inch of the way, and I had no idea it was going on until a couple of weeks ago, when Tischler dragged me to D.C. All I knew was, we were supposed to give a briefing about the case. She sat my ass outside Bill Rosenblatt's office" — the assistant commissioner of enforcement for Customs — "in the morning, and I sat there waiting all day. Then she and Rosenblatt dragged me to the Four Seasons Hotel in Georgetown. When we got to the dining room, two guys from NBC News were at the table waiting for us to arrive, Ira Silverman, a producer, and Brian Ross, an investigative reporter.

"Tischler and Rosenblatt gave them a general idea about our undercover operation and then directed me to offer up details about everyone you've dealt with undercover for the past two years. They said I shouldn't be concerned about talking openly because they had dealt with Silverman for years, and he had given them great publicity. I told them to go to hell, and I wouldn't give them one name. It made for a very tense dinner. When it was over, Tischler told me my career was over. They're gunning for me now. It's only a matter of time. I didn't say anything to you because I didn't want you to explode. I'm sorry."

"We've got three more weeks of this undercover operation." I was seething. "Any of the assholes we're dealing with on the street would whack us in a heartbeat if they thought we were federal agents! How could our own people do this to us? I can't believe we've been putting our asses on the line while leaks to the press have been going on for weeks!"

"There's an agenda here," Cook said calmly. "I think Tischler, Rosenblatt, and von Raab see this as a stepping stone for their futures. The more publicity they get when this case goes down, the more likely von Raab will become the first drug czar. Tischler and Rosenblatt are on his coattails, and they'll be pulled along. Nobody told me that, but that's what I and Joe Ladow" — assistant special agent in charge — "read between the lines."

Customs officials later disclosed that Commissioner von Raab's rabbi was North Carolina Republican senator Jesse Helms. Helms had told von Raab almost a year prior that his days as commissioner were numbered. As soon as the election was over, Treasury secretary James Baker, who hated the commissioner, said that von Raab was out. But if von Raab wanted to move to another department and become the first drug czar, Helms already had twenty or so senators to support his appointment. If von Raab had a media splash demonstrating that he had the skill to lead the War on Drugs — well, that would make the appointment that much easier.

Mystery of the October cutoff solved.

"You have to do what you can to keep this under control," I told Cook, "while Kathy and I make this run to Europe. When we get back, there'll be about ten days before it's over. We all need to keep this thing together and make sure nobody gets hurt."

"Mazur, I'm doing everything I can to keep these idiots in check. They're out of control. But I promise you I'm doing everything I can." There wasn't time to get into details about what the front office was planning for the takedown. We'd talk about that later.

Then Steve dropped a bombshell. The front office wanted the $5 million flash roll back — the same $5 million I'd deposited with BCCI and Capcom — in their hands by the time of the takedown.

"You need to come up with something believable to get that done," Cook said.

"They've got to be kidding," I snorted. "Isn't it more important for us to lure these people back to Tampa so they can be arrested? Pulling all that money out of accounts at the same time we're trying to convince them to come to the States is asking too much. It could spook them. When this case goes down, there'll be plenty of time for prosecutors to recover the money from BCCI and Capcom."

"I'm just passing on the orders. That five million was borrowed from the U.S. Treasury, and it has to be returned by September thirtieth, the end of the fiscal year."

I couldn't believe it, but I'd get it done.

The Concorde to Heathrow was fast, but not fast enough to clear my mind of Cook's confession about disclosures to NBC. Not his fault, but the lives of undercover agents counted less than someone's obsession with political power. It was disgusting. I would have walked away from it all, but I, too, had my agenda. My unique placement in the underworld — a position I thought no one else would ever see again — obsessed me. It could have cost me my career, my family, or my life — it didn't matter. My own blind ambition was pushing me.

In a sense, the unmovable October wall saved me. I would have ridden the case longer and deeper than I should have — like a compulsive gambler not knowing when to walk away. But I had much more to lose than money.

When we landed in London, Kathy and I joined separate lines in Immigration. I handed my passport to an inspector who looked at each page, wrinkled his brow, then looked more closely. Time came to a screeching halt.

What's going on? Why is he staring so intently?

"Where'd you get the phony chops, mate?" he asked after what felt like a lifetime. I looked at him quizzically. "I said, Where'd you get the phony *stamps*, mate?"

"Excuse me, sir? I don't understand what you mean," I managed.

"What I mean, sir, is that one of these U.K. stamps is a phony. You see, every two years we change the emblem on our stamp, and the date in the middle of this stamp doesn't match the emblem."

"Sir, I don't know what to say," I said, breaking into a cold sweat. "Every time I come to someone like you, I hand them my passport, they stamp it, and I move on. I don't know who stamped that."

"Is that the best you can do, mate? Let me tell you something. Here's a consent form for a body-cavity search. You can either tell me how this phony stamp got in your passport, or you're off to the clink, and our people will have fun checking you inside and out, if you get what I mean."

My mind reeled. The FBI lab had promised the stamps were perfect. Joe Hinton's warning echoed in my head. *Don't let Washington make documents for you that you can otherwise get on your own. You never know if they'll make a mistake or compromise you.*

Joe was right.

"I don't know what to say, sir," I said quietly.

"Take this guy to secondary," he said smiling to another officer. "He needs a thorough search, inside *and* out."

19

LOOSE ENDS

Heathrow International Airport, London
September 18, 1988

THIS TIME MY ASS WAS REALLY ON THE LINE.

Her Majesty's Customs and Excise had escorted us to an investigation room. They held every piece of clothing in my bags up to bright lights to detect contraband sewn into the material. Then one of them escorted me to an enclosed examination room for a strip search. As I stood there, naked and mortified, an officer wearing surgical gloves told me to turn my back to him and bend over.

Oh God, I thought. *British Customs is about to give me a prostate exam.*

"Okay, mate," he said, scanning my rear end, "everything looks good here."

"Of course," I wisecracked. "I hear that a lot when people look at me that way."

Bad idea. The joke didn't land any laughs, just more determination to tear through my bags. After I put my clothes on and walked out of the examining room, one of the officers was inspecting my briefcase.

There's an $8,000 Nagra recorder hidden inside the lid, I thought frantically as my mind raced for a way out.

The officer's eyes popped as he felt a slight bulge along the top of the case. He started ripping at the lid like a bulldog — it was only a matter of time before the Velcro seals gave way and he spotted the recorder.

"Excuse me, sir," I said to the officer and his partner, the only other two in the room, "but I have something I'd like to share with you. I'm a U.S. Customs agent working undercover on a case with your office here in London, and I'd appreciate it if you'd let me show you how to access the hidden recorder in the lid of that briefcase. Otherwise I'm afraid you might damage it, and on my salary it would take me a year to pay for that."

They stopped, frozen, exchanging eye contact and smirks. "That's the best one I've ever heard," one said to the other. Then to me: "We're not buying your story. Just keep quiet."

"No, honestly," I protested, "I'm an undercover agent with the U.S. government. I can give you the name of my contact at the U.S. embassy, and you can call him to verify what I'm telling you. Please, you've got to believe me."

"I'll take the name and number you have to offer," said one of the men, budging. "If that name isn't on the list of employees at the U.S. embassy, don't open your mouth again."

"His name is John Luksic," I said, relieved, "and here's his number."

They delivered me to the cell holding Kathy and an Australian aborigine. Time crawled. Kathy and the aborigine started playing charades. He didn't know very many American TV shows or movies — she beat him hands down.

Eventually the lockup door opened and Luksic appeared.

"Come on," he said. "Let's get out of here. I've taken care of everything."

With my briefcase intact but my ego bruised, we left the airport as Luksic explained that all reports of our detention had been destroyed. Turned out that recent Korean espionage in the U.K. had led to a heightened alert about phony passports. Wrong place, wrong time, botched passport.

"Thanks for your help, John," I said, grateful that we weren't traveling with any targets, which would have blown the operation.

"No problem," Luksic said. "Let's plan on meeting for a late breakfast tomorrow morning to go over your schedule for the next few days. The lead officer in British Customs working on the London side of this case will be there. He'll have some questions. They've got a surveillance post set up across the street from Capcom, and they'll probably be on your tail most of the time you're here."

"We're in tight with these people," I said, "so it would be great if you could run interference with the Brits and ask them to take it easy on the surveillance. We can't afford any suspicion on the part of our targets at this stage. In two weeks, we want them to show up in Tampa."

Bruce Letheran, lead U.K. Customs officer on the case, understood and promised to keep all surveillance low-profile.

That night, Ziauddin Akbar met us at the Dorchester Hotel and whisked us to an upscale Japanese restaurant for dinner. We joined Sushma Puri, wife of the president of Capcom, who was representing her husband. No talk of drugs, Colombians, or anything sensitive, but Akbar couldn't wait to extol the advantages of business with Capcom. During the past six months, the company he had founded had conducted over $80 billion in precious metals and currency transactions, quite the camouflage for our needs. Before starting Capcom, he had spent thirteen years with BCCI, rising ultimately to treasurer of the bank.

The next day, Kathy and I visited Akbar at the London office of Financial Advisory Services, a Capcom affiliate. He treated us like royalty. While Sushma Puri had one of her assistants give Kathy a tour of the London diamond market, Akbar and I got down to business in the company conference room, where he started selling himself with the secrets of the big guns behind his operation.

He had spent the last two years of his tenure at BCCI in Oman. He had founded BCCI's treasury division and managed $5.5 billion of the bank's assets. His high position allowed him to meet many of the shareholders of the bank who had pumped money into Capcom. He rattled off the names of U.S.–based megamillionaires behind the bank and his company: Robert Magness, chairman of

Tele-Communications, Inc.; Larry Romrell, another executive with the same communications giant; Robert Powell, a senior executive of a U.S. company with contracts servicing U.S. military aircraft; and Kerry Fox of Rockwell International, which was involved in the manufacturing of missiles. All four had business ties to the Middle East.

Foreign investors included several Saudis who were close friends and Capcom shareholders. Kamal Adham, a brother-in-law of the late King Faisal, held several key government posts in Saudi Arabia, including the chief of intelligence. His net worth then exceeded $1 billion. A major shareholder of Capcom, Adham had also invested heavily in BCCI and First American. A. R. Khalil also worked for Saudi intelligence, and later research revealed that both Adham and Khalil liaised closely with the CIA. The third key Capcom shareholder, the vastly wealthy Gaith Rashad Pharaon, owned a big piece of BCCI, the U.S. banks that BCCI secretly controlled, and Capcom.

Akbar and Capcom had big plans. They had two offices in London, one in Chicago, and one in Cairo. They intended to open offices in New York, Miami, and Dubai. Longer-range plans included offices in Kuwait, Saudi Arabia, and Hong Kong.

"Our strength is in the Middle East and the Gulf," Akbar said. "Now we are trying to double up the relationship on our strength, our contacts in Latin America, in Miami, through Amjad.... We have doubled our relationship in the Middle East.... We are shifting from there through Amjad in Miami through your support, through your cooperation."

Ziauddin Akbar and his backers were targeting the Colombian drug cartels as sources of funds for a multibillion-dollar empire.

"We don't want to know how, what the customer is doing, what is his business," Akbar said of my clients. "I don't want to know. Our company doesn't want to know."

Then he confirmed Bilgrami's explanation of the system used to launder hundreds of millions through simultaneous purchases and sales of gold futures.

When Akbar heard I could provide him with $10 million per

month, he didn't blink. Instead, he agreed with Bilgrami: The cash was best washed through the heavy dollar markets in Saudi Arabia, Oman, and the United Arab Emirates. My clients' cash could be shipped there in safes to four different banks, each taking deposits ranging from $100,000 to $400,000 per day.

He knew my clients ran the Medellín cartel — I sensed it every time he assured me he didn't want to know anything about them. Awan and Bilgrami had surely filled him in. But that wouldn't hold up in front of a jury. I had to have an explicit conversation with him — but not now. I had pushed enough for one day.

In between reporting to the Tampa and London offices, my phone was burning up with calls. Emir continued to coordinate cash pickups, and Alcaíno's associates were using me as a clearinghouse either to report or learn about his arrest.

A little after 1 A.M. Greenwich time, I called Casals.

"Roberto is really sick," he said, meaning Alcaíno had been arrested.

"I know," I said. "I sent him the prescription" — money.

"I can't figure out what is wrong."

"Listen to me. It's probably best that you not visit him, but if you can get word to him through someone else, let him know he isn't alone. I'm going to be there for him. On my way back from Europe, I'll stop in New York, and we can talk."

Casals happily gave me his new numbers and agreed to meet when I returned.

The next afternoon, I gave Akbar the documents he needed to open accounts for me in the names of Hong Kong and Gibraltar corporations. As he did, I mentioned BCCI's annual fee of 1.5 percent to disguise the flow of funds, and I argued for no more than half that amount at Capcom. I also wanted him to halve the turnaround from ten days to five.

Given the numbers, the best he could offer was a 1 percent commission. Capcom would incur fees to buy and sell gold, after all, and those fees alone would eat up most of the 1 percent. "We don't want any dummy deals," he said. Everything had to look real. And he assured me he could beat the ten-day mark, but nothing less than six. "Mr. Musella...if you want to develop a long-term relationship, you have to feel comfortable with us, and we have to feel comfortable with you."

That was my opening. In order to close the deal, he had to convince me he was prepared to push the world's hottest money through his system.

"Why don't we take a walk," I said, leaning across the table, and mimed looking for bugs on the ceiling and underneath the table. "Let's just take a walk and talk about it for a minute, and I'd feel a little bit better if I could."

"I can assure you one thing," Akbar said as though I'd smacked him in the face with a cricket bat. "If you've got any suspicion of anything here, there's nothing, nothing tape-recording me. Don't worry about that, if you are worried about that, anything taping here. Nothing. But I can go out. I'm —"

"Let's go for a walk," I said, tilting my head toward the door and rising from the table.

He followed like a wolf after prey.

"Your clients are trusted," he said nervously on the noisy London street. "We are not the need to know. We don't want to know what purpose customers care about it. We tell you, because us, out of good customers, we can make them, um, they must trust us.... We are certain our contacts in the Miami, they have recommended you or any customer. So we are depending on them about the genuineness or about the respectability about the clients, everything."

Time to trot out Iacocca.

"I want you to know," I added to my canned speech, "that the only reason I asked you to come out here is because I don't ever want to have a conversation with you about these types of things again."

No problem. Akbar took what I had said in stride.

One last topic to broach, then: Noriega's hidden fortune. Awan had stashed his money for years within the maze of BCCI branches, but it was probably now wending its way to Capcom. I told Akbar to avoid him, explaining how my clients became so concerned when their Panamanian accounts froze that they had sent the general a coffin. Akbar nervously laughed, confirming my suspicion.

"I can assure you," Akbar said at the end of our meeting, "whatever we can, we'll help you to the possible extent. It is in our mutual interest, and you are interested in our interest.... We will do our best. I'm sure we will not let you down."

How would the Capcom revelations sit with Washington? Perhaps they'd reconsider terminating the operation. We had two multibillion-dollar financial institutions run by some of the wealthiest people in the U.S. and Saudi Arabia under our thumb. Both institutions had strong ties to government officials and intelligence communities in the States and the Middle East. Both were hunting drug profits from the underworld. They didn't care whether I was representing drug dealers, arms dealers, or terrorists. They only wanted the power they could glean from my money.

In Paris—before I firmed up Nazir Chinoy's knowledge of the money's source and pressured him to attend the wedding—I threw Akbar the only bone I could in the time remaining.

"Given what we discussed," I said on the phone, "I'd like to do a small one to test the system. This will give me something to discuss when I meet with my clients.... Should I route it from Panama to your Chicago office, the same way we routed the last money?"

"That's exactly the way to send it," he said.

Done.

The red carpet had rolled out for a hundred of Paris's rich and famous at Chinoy's home. Limos lined the street. BCCI bankers from around the world circled like vultures, pecking at businessmen, diplomats, and their wives. Tuxedoed waiters strolled the apartment with a symphony of champagne flutes and hors d'oeuvres while cello and violin players drowned out the low chant of BCCI's mantra: *Give me your deposits.*

Chinoy brought managers of BCCI branches from around the world to my side throughout the night. Each whispered that he'd oversee my affairs personally if I opened accounts at his branch, doing everything possible to serve me. Chinoy asked that Kathy and I stay behind when the party broke. As the night wore on, a chorus of people whom Chinoy had handpicked for the after party threw endless questions at us. A gracious offer on Chinoy's part, perhaps, but more likely an orchestrated test.

The next day, while discussing with Chinoy the purpose of my visit—attending to matters for my "family" and finalizing the mechanism for investing funds in Colombia—I brandished uncertainty about Awan. "It is troubling to see that he was leaving, and then I figured, *Well, if he's leaving, maybe there's some type of problem....* I got the impression that maybe there was some unhappiness in the BCCI family."

Chinoy assured me that Awan merely had a personality conflict with the head of the Latin American division stationed in Miami. The bank's president, Swaleh Naqvi, had smoothed everything, postponing Awan's transfer to Paris for as long as six months, at which point he would manage a new division within that branch to serve clients in Latin America. It looked like Awan had fed them a line so they wouldn't put him under a microscope while he was shuttling secretly back and forth to Washington, trying to con Blum into giving him a pass based on half-truths.

Customs still needed the $5 million flash roll back, so I told Chinoy that a close friend needed help pumping up his balance sheet. I needed to borrow against all of my deposits in Paris for three or four days. It was the only ploy that wouldn't raise alarm. I'd done it for them in the past, so they should understand doing it for me now. Still, I cringed inside as I fed him the story.

"Sure," he said. "We all depend on this area."

When asked how much money he could disguise and pass to Colombia, he said, "Twenty million a month.... Paris is large enough for ten million to go through without anybody noticing anything.... In my system, I would put a little bit through Monte Carlo."

When I told him that our Colombian clients had $15 million in U.S. currency each month in Europe they would like to deposit, he wanted in. He didn't have an immediate plan, but felt he could spin a cover.

Now it was Chinoy's turn to petition me. "Will you be — before December, you said there's some key dates — able to give me a little more funds?" He reminded me that December thirty-first was the date on which the bank's year-end balance sheet needed pumping up.

"You can rely on it," I said, forecasting that by the end of December we'd increase our deposits by another two million and place funds with corresponding loans to transfer another $30 million to Colombia.

"Thanks a lot," he said, grinning like the Cheshire Cat. "Thank you very much. That will help us a lot. Thank you."

Then I asked to see the records of my Paris accounts to confirm transactions since my last visit. Chinoy summoned Sibte Hassan, who led me to the files. I thumbed through the stack, and —

There it was. A letter from Armbrecht on July twenty-second, the day after he warned me that Don Chepe's people had detected the surveillance in New York. He directed BCCI to remove my name from the account and had the funds sent to BCCI Colón in Panama. My skin went cold as I stared at the paper, Armbrecht's unease — just one day before he'd written the letter — ringing in my ears: *We are concerned about friends present during the transaction, bad guys in the Towers where all the little beauties are delivered, all the little jewelry. They think foreign investors want to get their hands on the business, and they are worried.*

Everything Armbrecht and Don Chepe had to offer dissolved the day they spotted surveillance in Midtown. The cartel's plan to let me hide a $100 million nest egg for them in Europe had surely fallen off the table. They weren't certain I was a narc — if they had been,

Emir and I would already have died. But they knew that business with us came with too many problems.

A fog of dejection followed me down the Champs-Elysées. New York hadn't believed enough in our operation to think outside the box. Business as usual had killed part of our case. And there wasn't a damn thing I could do about it.

Before we left Paris, Chinoy and his family took me and Kathy to Le Chalet des Iles, a restaurant in a garden on an island in a lake in the Bois de Boulogne. Only a small ferry offered access to this restaurant originally built as a hunting lodge under Napoleon. At dinner, Chinoy informed me that, regretfully, he wouldn't be able to attend the wedding because he had an important BCCI board meeting in London that day.

After dinner, we strolled through the immaculate grounds. It was my last meeting with Chinoy, so I took advantage and played the only hand I had. I told him his change in plans had put me in a bind. Senior members of my family wanted to speak privately with him in Tampa. The wedding would have been the perfect setting because, with high security, they would be at ease to speak freely.

Chinoy promised to call the president of BCCI that afternoon to seek permission to join the board meeting late so he could meet my bosses at the wedding. Since that would never happen, I went a step further and advised that it was important to arrange a meeting between the senior members of my group and the bank's directors.

"This will be arranged to calm any uneasiness that might exist with your people," Chinoy said, agreeing completely. "This is only fair that you see with whom you deal."

A shame that meeting won't ever happen, I thought as we walked through the exquisite gardens. October stood fast. There could be no evidence more powerful than Swaleh Naqvi, president of BCCI, soliciting dirty money on tape. Hopefully, Chinoy — third in command — and eight other key officers would cut it.

I handed Chinoy an article from the *Times* of London, which underscored why he and other BCCI officials should prioritize a meeting with my bosses, all of whom had concerns. The article announced that a joint FBI and Scotland Yard undercover operation had exposed money-laundering activities by several banks, including one characterized as having Pakistani origins. The banks involved participated in the *hawala* system, an ancient Islamic method of moving money.

In *hawala*, a customer in one location gives money to a *hawaladar*, or broker, to transfer through a second *hawaladar* in another location to the intended recipient. In addition to taking commissions smaller than banks would charge, *hawaladar*s often circumvent market rates for currency exchange. There is no governmental regulation or paper trail of any kind — it all takes place by word of mouth — and the system also allows for the transfer of debt.

"That scared the hell out of me," I told Chinoy.

"It's not us," he said, staring at the article. "I think I know who it is. We don't use the *hawala* system. It's too risky." But he understood why I felt it was important to put my people at ease. "I will remind you that there's no problem here. On that side, we're really relaxed." He promised to do his best to make it to Tampa, but if that wasn't possible, I could count on a meeting between my people and the president and other directors of the bank soon thereafter.

If only.

Our first stop back took us to Manhattan's Omni Berkshire Place, a five-star hotel at Fifty-second and Madison. With Alcaíno behind bars, Casals didn't know where to turn, and he wanted to work for me. He was a good man, I told him, but I really didn't know much about him. Honesty and loyalty were what I needed, so he needed to tell me everything.

Casals rattled off every crime he'd ever committed. He'd worked for Alcaíno for about three years. Eight months earlier, Alcaíno had established his pipeline from the anchovy packing plant in Buenos Aires. They'd already run one successful load through Philadelphia — 1,200 pounds of pure cocaine. Zabala distributed some of the coke, along with Alvaro and Gladys Perez in

New Jersey. Casals gave me their numbers. Carlos Díaz fronted as the plant's owner in Buenos Aires, and then there were the New York men of Alcaíno's partner, Fabio Ochoa, pressuring Casals to give them any of Alcaíno's money he could find. Alcaíno had the freight forwarder in New York — who arranged the shipment of anchovies from Argentina to Philadelphia — on payroll, in order to get wind of any unusual interest the feds might have in imported anchovies.

Casals knew that Alcaíno had accounts in Switzerland in a fake name, along with a matching fake passport — the Jeweler's life-line if he had to flee the States. He also had safe-deposit boxes all over the U.S., filled with cash that only he and one of his girlfriends could access. Cecilia in New York distributed coke for him, as did Patricia in Ecuador and Sonja in Colombia.

"You have a lot of experience," I said. "My man who runs our operations in New York will be at my wedding in Tampa. I'd like to extend an invitation for you and a guest to join us there. That will be the perfect time for you to meet privately with him. I'll see that he puts you to work. Welcome to our family."

"Thanks, Bob. I can't thank you enough, and thank you for the invitation. My girlfriend and I will be there for sure."

Back in Miami, Tobón and Zabala needed to tell me about Alcaíno's money still on the street, which I could use as bait to lure one of his suppliers to Tampa just before the wedding.

With Tobón's help, Kathy made arrangements for flowers. The more she invested our targets and their friends in the ceremony, the more likely they were to show up. While I had Tobón on the phone confirming details about the flowers, I told him, "I have that stuff I told you about before. They got the stuff in from L.A." — copies of the indictments filed against Alcaíno in New York and Philly, which I had promised him. "I'll have both of those with me. Tuto says he knows the person mentioned in the document. We'll talk when you come by."

With BCCI back in the Senate's crosshairs, the lounge of the Grand Bay Hotel became the meeting place of choice with my banker friends. Over tumblers of Johnnie Walker Black and ice, Bilgrami buried his head in Capcom paperwork.

"How were your meetings at Capcom?" he mumbled, not looking up.

"Oh, he's a fine gentleman," I said. "Everything went well."

"I think you scared him a lot," Bilgrami said, then looked up. "I mean, we're talking frankly now. You tend to explain your business too much. People don't want to know sometimes what you're involved in, you know.... You went persistent later on, letting him, knowing what you do, which freaked him out, because he didn't understand why—"

"It was very minimal, very subtle," I interrupted, "and that was for a reason. I was curious about what his reaction of the little thing that I said, which I didn't think was that far."

"Bob, he got slightly, you know, slightly perturbed, to be very frank. Not with you. He found you very nice and very easy to deal with, but, you know, with what you elaborated. He didn't understand because confidentiality, I mean, it's usually best that people don't know what they deal in."

"Well, Akbar," I said, turning the tables, "it's usually best that, when a person has a conversation with someone privately, it stays that way."

"He was perturbed with certain details or whatever." Bilgrami backpedaled. "I don't know what you discussed with him. I mean I don't think we should go there.... I can imagine."

I told Bilgrami that I'd had a pleasant, formal meeting with Akbar in his office, and, when it was appropriate to mention a few sensitive words, we took a walk on the street so I was certain our conversation was completely confidential. "I just needed to make sure, you know, there're certain confidences you say. Maybe it's not more common in your area of the world...but if you're dealing on behalf of three or four people and you have the weight of the world on your shoulders, you wanna make sure that the person that you're talking to recognizes the importance of doing things."

"That's probably what freaked him out because he's not used

to taking a walk on the wild side," Bilgrami said curtly, laughing nervously, and the topic evaporated.

Without proof that a target knew the money we moved came from drug trafficking, there was no crime. Winks or nods wouldn't cut it. No matter how I tried, telling someone the obvious—that I was a money launderer for drug dealers—always raised red flags. But even cautious people let greed calm them and stifle their instincts.

Alcaíno had anointed me his heir, so the town house on Key Biscayne became a revolving door for Tobón, Zabala, and a new player, Alcaíno's girlfriend Marta Cecilia Carvajal Hoyos, a key member of his organization, who went by "Cecilia." Before Zabala brought her in, he told me everything he knew about her and the other members of Alcaíno's organization. I especially wanted the names and numbers of the coke distributors so we could collect the money they owed for the dope they were holding when Alcaíno went down. And then there were the suppliers expecting a payday.

Zabala fed me the cash he could collect from his buyers. Each time he handed me a bag of currency, he also gave me, at my request, a handwritten note detailing the source of the funds, ostensibly as an accounting for Alcaíno. "This $15,000 belongs to Roberto. He gave me five kilos a week ago. Those five kilos were part of the nineteen kilos he gave me from his last load. This didn't come through the anchovy plant. It was a separate deal. I agreed to pay $13,800 for each kilo. I got the dope from one of Roberto's men, Alvaro Perez, and sold it to my client in New Jersey, Alberto. Perez collected this money for me from Alberto. I just sent another $51,000 of what I owed on this to Gloria Alcaíno in L.A."

Zabala ran down the details of all his deals during the past year, including costs he and Alcaíno had shared to build a coke lab in New York City. He gave me every name and number he could offer, including Cecilia's. "She's Roberto's girlfriend. Her husband was caught in Tampa after one of his workers delivered five kilos there two years ago. The worker rolled, and the feds later grabbed her husband at a pay phone here in Miami."

Cecilia was hunting for money because she owed suppliers. She brokered the last deal for them with Alcaíno. Zabala suspected Cecilia had sent a woman to his home two nights ago to make a scene. At midnight, a woman had banged on his door and windows. When he wouldn't come out, she screamed to everyone in the neighborhood that Zabala sold cocaine for Alcaíno. Neighbors reported this to the cops, who came to his home, but he denied everything. If Cecilia didn't get money to the owners of the dope in Colombia, things were really going to get ugly.

Cecilia had known about me for quite some time. Alcaíno had spoken of me highly. Looking more like a secretary than a dope dealer, she filled me in about her role in the busted load. She was supposed to sell two hundred kilos, but she had other deals in progress that posed greater problems. A few weeks ago, after she received seventy kilos from Lucas, her source, she'd given half that shipment to Alcaíno. Alvaro Perez was still holding a lot of that coke and owed a few hundred thousand to Lucas, a twenty-nine-year-old Colombian who'd once lived in Tampa but was now living in Mexico on a ranch just across the border. Every month, Lucas's group moved loads of dope from the ranch into the U.S., and Cecilia sold part of each load to buyers in New York and Miami. She had to recover money from Perez to keep Lucas happy. If she didn't, Lucas might cut her supply off—or worse.

"I've been asked by Roberto to do some things he would normally handle," I told her. "He wants me to oversee the collection of any money he's owed. If you'll help me, I'm sure Roberto will authorize the release of as much as he can to Lucas, if it's rightfully owed."

She gave me every detail she could, including facts about new shipments coming from Cartagena and Mexico. Lucas was sending another load to the States, arriving in two weeks. Once I verified with Alcaíno, through Gloria, the amount to be paid to Lucas, I told Cecilia, I'd release that money directly to him.

"No problem," she said. "I'll bring him to New York."

There was our bonus, easy enough. A few days before the

takedown, Cecilia would bring Lucas to Tampa to get his money. I wouldn't have time to fly to New York because I was getting married, so I'd time the takedown of the delivery at the undercover house to parallel the takedown in Tampa.

Alcaíno had been a lot busier than he admitted, according to Cecilia. In addition to his transportation route through Buenos Aires, he was finalizing another route through the Dominican Republic, where he was paying off major politicians for protection. He'd arranged to have tons of coke flown there from Colombia to be shipped commercially to the States.

Less than a week left, and in L.A. I wanted to squeeze Gloria for every last bit of intel before the takedown; I also wanted to have a blatant conversation with Iqbal Ashraf, manager of BCCI L.A. We had danced around the issue of the source of my clients' funds six months earlier, but I had let it slide because I didn't want to unsettle Awan and Bilgrami in case Ashraf blabbed. Now it wouldn't matter. Awan and Bilgrami were about to fall anyway.

Gloria was paranoid and thought she was under constant surveillance. She probably was. She and Kathy had built a close friendship, so Kathy's presence at the meeting was critical. We rented a suite at the Buena Vista hotel downtown, and Gloria came to us. Pale and sleepless, she entered the room with the weight of the world on her back. She was doing everything she could to hold herself together.

"How are the girls?" I asked, trying to care.

"Not so good," she said, tears streaming down her face. "They're very confused. Paola talks too much, and Claudia doesn't talk.... It's very bad."

The girls had never suspected that their father was one of the biggest drug dealers in the U.S., of course, so his arrest came as a huge shock.

Gloria explained how her lawyer was passing information from Roberto about who still owed him money on the street. She gave me the names and numbers of those distributors and asked me to make the collections, which I promised to do. I was holding $115,000 in cash already collected for her — all she had to do was tell me where to send it.

Through a sea of tears, she explained a dream she had just before her husband's arrest. "I saw myself in a place, in a place so surrounded by people — nobody I knew. But in the middle of that place, I stood while it was raining so hard. But the rain came down in, like... I didn't feel it. And I looked at some corner there, and I saw some plastic bag with white powder. I saw many of them. I don't know how many, but there were many of them. And I fell, and the rain, it fell so hard, but I have... I lose all feelings. So, like, my mind was — I have no mind. Tears, it rained tears. I felt so lonely."

When Gloria recovered, she started to talk about how she intended to use her husband's connections to put another load together to make enough money to feed the lawyers.

"Gloria, let's step outside," I said.

Alcaíno was going to spend a decade or more in prison, and Gloria faced a stiff sentence for laundering the money passed to her husband's lawyers. But now she was talking about running a deal that could put her away for as long as her husband. Maybe I had been undercover too long, but I wanted her to be there for her daughters, despite the certain jail time ahead of her.

"Please listen to me," I said to her in the stairwell, beyond the reach of my briefcase. "If you want to put a deal together, let me front for you. I don't want you taking chances. If you tell me who to contact to bring in merchandise, I'll do that without taking a nickel. Everything will go to you and Roberto." If she bought my pitch, she'd put me in contact with yet more suppliers, and we could possibly take them down, too.

"I know your heart is with me," she said gratefully, "but this is something I may have to do on my own."

She didn't bite. I had tried. She was on her own to crash and burn.

The next day, she had about $10,000 in cash for us to take in exchange for a check for the lawyer. Kathy did the deal while I paid a visit to Iqbal Ashraf.

The meeting was a carbon copy of the dozens of meetings with other BCCI officers. When I told Ashraf I was looking for help selling a downtown L.A. apartment complex financed by a client recently arrested for possessing a few thousand pounds of cocaine, he didn't blink.

"Mr. Musella," he said, "how about your clients' placing any surplus funds that they have, say up to the thirty-first of December or fifth of January, some additional funds with us?"

It was always all about deposits.

Lee Iacocca did his duty, and Ashraf raised no objection. He only wanted more deposits. "I'd appreciate it, as far as surplus funds are concerned, if you'll have them placed over here."

But unlike every other BCCI officer I'd met, Ashraf was holding a get-out-of-jail-free card—and I didn't know about it. Before my meeting with him, Mark Jackowski had completed his presentation about our operation to the grand jury in Tampa, and they had already returned a true bill of indictment against dozens of people, including Ashraf. Which meant that my last recorded meeting with him in L.A. wouldn't hold up in court. It took place after he was charged. Without that, he'd walk—a very lucky man.

Our job was done. It was time to head back to Tampa, work out the details of the takedown, and end the operation. I'd done everything I could to get our people to see the opportunities of continuing for another month or so, but that wasn't in the cards. All I could do now was make the best of the last few days, which turned out to be the calm before the storm.

What was about to happen would send shock waves through the underworld so hard that they would shake the foundations of the cartel, the banking community, political parties, and the intelligence communities of the U.S. and its allies.

20

THE TAKEDOWN

U.S. Customs, Tampa, Florida
October 6, 1988

EVERYONE WAS THERE.

"Larry Mulkerns will be in charge of the takedown logistics," Tischler said of her right-hand man and one of the Tampa assistant special agents in charge. "Mazur and Ertz, you need to stay in communication with the targets. Find out when their flights will arrive, and we'll have agents posing as limo drivers take them to Innisbrook after they land in Tampa. People will be showing up at different times during Friday and Saturday. To keep them busy, we'll have some activities for them — a golf tournament, a go-fast boat ride in the gulf, and other things. Steve will coordinate social functions.

"Saturday there'll be an early evening poolside cocktail party, and on Sunday morning the wedding ceremony will start at 10 A.M. During the ceremony, everyone will be taken down. Since Monday is a federal holiday, there'll be a press conference on Tuesday that will be chaired by Commissioner von Raab. The Brits and French Customs people are here, and they'll participate in the press conference. The wedding gifts, gown, and other trinkets will be there on display."

No objections from the room.

"Okay, that's it," she snapped. "This meeting is over."

"Bonni, can I speak with you for a minute, please?" I said, after everyone had left the room.

"You've got thirty seconds. What's your problem?"

"Let me just say right now: if there's a ceremony, I won't be in it. Can you imagine the chaos that will ensue when innocent wives and children witness assault teams descend on the wedding, and these men are hauled away in chains? We have an obligation to do this without grandstanding. We can have arrest teams outside each guy's room on Saturday. Kathy and I can call each target, one at a time, and ask them to come to our rooms. They trust us; they'll go wherever we tell them to go. Their families don't have to see a thing. The plan you outlined makes this personal, and if you embarrass these people they'll take it out on the undercover agents.... If we needlessly punish their families, they're likely to want to respond in kind. I learned from Steve that NBC News has known about this case for a month, and *that* is criminal.... Beyond that, the intense media attention could cause us to lose venue in Tampa because of the undue publicity. This isn't right."

"You'll do what you're told to do," she said, smoke practically pouring from her ears. "This meeting is over. You get the hell out of my office, you manipulative little motherfucker.... *Get the hell out of here, you manipulative little motherfucker!*" She backed me out of her office, down the hall, and into the squad area, where a dozen agents looked on, wide-eyed. Then she stormed back into her office.

I'd had it. Trying to engage anyone above Joe Ladow, assistant special agent in charge, had proved futile. He was reasonable, but he spoke his mind, so Tischler had stripped his authority in this operation. I didn't have the energy to fight.

Minutes later, Tischler summoned Steve Cook and Joe Ladow. "I don't give a shit how you do it, but you two better find a way to fire Mazur's ass before the day is out, or I'll do the same to you!"

Cook and Ladow calmed her down, but that moment had marked me. It might take a month or five years, but she would make me pay for speaking my mind. And it had to do with nothing more than publicity.

Von Raab and Bill Rosenblatt, I later learned, had offered NBC News exclusive coverage of the wedding ceremony, with NBC cameramen posing as videographers. Tischler supported the plan fully and had announced it only a few nights earlier during a dinner party held for more than fifty top government officials at Bern's Steak House in Tampa, a world-renowned restaurant with one of the most impressive wine lists on the planet. In Lincoln Town Cars, five agents yanked off their cases chauffeured Commissioner von Raab, his Washington staff, and top officials from the Department of Justice, IRS, and Customs from the airport to this posh feast. Conservative estimates put the dinner bill alone at more than $5,000. It went down in the books as "investigative expenses for a conference" — paid for with profits from our undercover operation, of course.

But Cook and Ladow prevailed. The takedown scenario shifted. Near the end of the poolside cocktail party on Saturday night, limos would transport the targets to a club twenty-five miles away for a bachelor party, which enabled agents to lure the targets from their families without suspicion. No one would suspect anything for at least four hours — plenty of time to approach each family professionally and convey the solemn news that their loved one had been arrested.

Emir was tying up a big deal with Gonzalo for $10 million hidden on the Texas–Mexico border. But when he proposed the pickup, management killed the deal. Our bosses, he speculated, wanted it to look like we had been burned, which then forced them to shut us down. "That's bullshit," he said. "Gonzalo was developing new clients every day."

Kathy did yeoman work, getting as many of our guests to the wedding as possible. She worked the phones feverishly. People were arriving from Colombia, Panama, France, New York, and Miami. At the same time, I also worked the phones to squeeze every last bit of intel from Alcaíno's workers about his money on the street. Casals and Perez had both called me about their collections.

"Can you meet one of my guys at JFK to hand over whatever you have?" I asked Casals.

"I'll do that," he said. "Alvaro is with me; he wants to talk to you."

"Mr. Bob, I have $58,000 for you. I got $70,000 from Alberto in New Jersey, but $12,000 of that is mine. I'm doing the best I can."

"I'm sure you are," I assured him. "Since Joe will be visiting me here in Tampa for the wedding, I'd like you to deliver the money to my guy in New York on Saturday night. He'll page you to make the arrangements."

Then Chinoy called with bad news. "The president of our bank wants me to be at the board meeting in London. I'm afraid I won't be able to attend your wedding, but I'm sending Howard and Hassan along with my gift. It's a unique antique Persian rug, a one-of-a-kind. I hope you and Kathy will enjoy it for many years to come."

There was nothing to be done about Chinoy's conflict. He had no choice. The Brits would cuff him in London as soon as everyone went down in the States anyway.

I lured Cecilia to Tampa with a promise of $200,000 to give to Alcaíno's suppliers.

"Lucas and I can both meet you in Tampa on Saturday," she said.

"Fantastic. Call me with your flight information, and I'll meet you at the airport."

Then Armbrecht called. "I'm in Miami at the La Quinta Hotel. I'm not sure I'll be able to make it to the wedding because I have to pick up a few planes in Tennessee, but I wanted to wish you and Kathy a wonderful life."

Problem. We needed him.

"Please allow me to send my private plane to pick you up, bring you here for the wedding, and then take you wherever you need to be," I offered. "Kathy and I would be so disappointed if we couldn't share this moment with you."

Silence. Armbrecht was thinking.

"I would very much like to share your special moment. Let me see how things go. I'll let you know."

Good enough for the moment. Kathy could always call him. And then it was time.

Under the billowing white canopy of a tent assembled on Innisbrook's Harstan Lawn, a scarlet carpet, dividing 250 chairs, ran to an altar waiting for $20,000 worth of red Colombian roses en route from Miami — the Tobóns' gift. Dozens of Boston ferns sat atop white Greek columns along the perimeter of the tent between white latticework, offering privacy for the ceremony. Dozens of spotless two-bedroom condos lay in wait, each room fully stocked with wines, liquors, snacks — everything. All on the government's tab, but more than covered by operation profits.

Awan, Bilgrami, and their families arrived that Saturday morning. Undercover agents picked them up in limos and shuttled them to Innisbrook. Then the two bankers met at the bar for a drink.

"Until I saw the huge tent for the wedding and the placards announcing the marriage, I was still nervous," Bilgrami said to Awan. "Now that I see it's all for real, my concerns about Bob's openness are quelled. I was always a little nervous. You never know, but now I do. I'm fine with him."

"I sensed it all along," Awan replied paternally. "It was never an issue for me. You need to calm down, man."

They toasted to the good times to come.

Ian Howard and Sibte Hassan arrived from Paris lugging Chinoy's $40,000 antique Persian rug, while Aftab Hussain flew in from Panama. All three left their families at home, clearly on the hunt for fun. Agents posing as friends took Howard, Hassan, and Hussain to a gulf resort where they enjoyed the beach, a go-fast boat ride, and the local Hooters restaurant.

Joaquín Casals and his girlfriend flew in from New York, while Mora and family arrived from Colombia. Other guests were coming later, but it was time to host the poolside cocktail party. An enormous seafood buffet ran the full edge of the pool deck. Innisbrook staff decked out in white chef's toques and jackets served carved meats while waiters swarmed. Some guests sat at small round tables, while others pulled lounge chairs together for more intimate conversation. Faint music from a string quartet filled the air, while Mora's children played in the pool.

Some fifty agents attended the cocktail party, posing as family and friends. Each belonged to an arrest-and-interview team set to swing into action later that night. Most had never worked undercover before and bunched together, isolating the targets. Mixing and mingling the group, however, were Dominic and a girl from his escort service, Frankie and his wife, and Eric and Gail Wellman, who all played their parts perfectly.

Kathy and I worked the crowd and took advantage of the pockets of agents sitting alone, secretly identifying targets. "Over my shoulder, the gentleman at the table on the opposite side of the pool with the red pullover shirt is Joaquín Casals — he goes by Joe. He's an ex-marine, a bodyguard, and a distributor for Alcaíno. In New York, he carries a gun, although he flew here, so it's not likely he's packing. He's supposed to be pretty good with his hands."

At the same time, Kathy and I spent as much time as possible with the targets and their families, putting them at ease.

Armbrecht should have arrived already, I thought, scanning the crowd regularly.

"Armbrecht truly likes you," I said to Kathy while we were meeting with a pocket of agents. "See if you can reach him at the La Quinta Hotel in Miami. If you do, keep him on the phone for as long as you can. Steve will be with you when you make the call. If you make contact, Steve will direct an arrest team to the hotel, and Armbrecht will be the first one to go down. We're only an hour or so away from heading to the bachelor party."

"Kathy, how are you, you beautiful little rascal?" Armbrecht gushed on the phone.

"You rascal, you're somewhere you're not supposed to be!" she replied.

He was planning to arrive early the following morning—but that would be too late. Kathy kept him on the phone for almost a half hour. After he hung up, agents stormed his room at La Quinta, and he went down.

As the dinner wound down, Frankie circulated to each of the targets. "We're going to have a little bachelor party this evening for Bob. In about a half hour, he thinks he's going to the airport with me to help me pick up my mom. On the way, I'm going to get a call and then tell him I just learned the flight is delayed. To kill a little time, I'm going to take him to MacBeth's, a club on the top floor of the Exchange Bank building in downtown Tampa. By then I need you guys to be there. I've arranged a bunch of limos. You'll have to share the ride with a couple of other guys. In about ten minutes, the cars will line up over there."

Everyone swallowed the bait.

"I've got to leave, so I don't have time to do this myself," I said to Wellman before I left. "Here's the key to my condo. There are some gifts stacked in the closet. Would you please put those in your car, and, when you're ready to leave, call me. We'll meet somewhere south of here, and I'll throw them in my trunk."

"Sure, no problem," he said.

Then I called Cook. "You know how opposed I am to this circus of a press conference our bosses are planning. They want to make a big joke out of these people, and that's not right. I'd like your help to keep things from getting out of hand. I've rounded up half the wedding gifts. In a few days, I'll turn them in for processing as evidence. I couldn't find the rest of them or the wedding dress. Would you please hide those until the press conference is over?"

"I understand," Cook said. "This is making me sick too. Believe me, for the next few days, no one will be able to find any of that stuff."

Back at the pool, Casals led the charge toward the limos. Two or three agents got in with him, the other limos staggered a few minutes apart so the commotion of each arrest would fade before the next car arrived.

Half an hour later, Casals's limo pulled into the first-floor parking garage of the Exchange Bank building, near a bank of elevators. "Welcome to MacBeth's, gentlemen," said a maitre d' in a tux—Mike Powers, the agent in charge of the Tampa DEA office and a black belt in karate whose years of service in the military and intelligence community had enabled him to handle just about anything.

In the elevator, Powers shielded the destination panel with his body and pushed the third-floor button instead of the twenty-sixth. When the elevator doors opened, Casals walked forward into an ambush. Armed agents on both sides of the elevator forced him to the ground, shouting, "*Police!* Down on the ground. Put your hands out to the sides. You're under arrest."

"Would you guys do me a favor," Casals said, cuffed and standing in a daze. "Call my girlfriend, and tell her I won't be able to make the wedding, and give Bob my best."

Even then he didn't suspect me.

The limo carrying Hussain pulled up. When agents arrested him, he laughed.

"I've been to bachelor parties like this when women dress up like cops and act like they are arresting you. Where are the women?"

"This should be a blast," Mora said, rubbing his hands together in the limo carrying him, Emir, and another agent. "Tell me, Emilio, do you think I'll get laid tonight?"

"I can assure you, you're going to get fucked tonight like you've never been fucked before."

"Has Musella been arrested, too?" he asked after agents arrested him.

"Yes," he was told.

"I have nothing to say," he mumbled, staring at the ground.

And he had nowhere to hide.

Limo after limo came, each scene repeating itself. Agents took Awan, Bilgrami, Howard, and Hassan all into custody, putting each back in his separate Lincoln Town Car. Each car headed to the

Customs office parking lot where the arresting agents marched the men before the blinding lights of NBC News. Then off to processing.

Before I headed to the airport to meet Cecilia and Lucas, a dispute arose at the country club. Tischler wanted Kathy to gather the wives for a last-minute wedding shower, but Kathy refused. Kathy had heard that Customs had given NBC the green light to video the event secretly. Kathy wanted no part of embarrassing the wives, and she had even less interest in having her voice and likeness broadcast nationally.

Cook came up with an alternative plan. Because she knew Cecilia, Kathy would accompany me to the airport. Better her than a new face as backup. It was his best shot at orchestrating a plausible reason for the change, but he still took the heat for depriving Tischler of a precious publicity op.

Kathy and I met at a restaurant parking lot, where she jumped in my car. At the airport, she looked for Cecilia while I made one last call to Gloria Alcaíno.

"I have a friend of mine in California who has the checks for Roberto's attorney," I told Gloria. "Let me give you his number."

"I want you to know how disappointed I am," she stopped me before I hung up, "that I can't be with you and Kathy tomorrow when you're married. I love you both and can't thank you enough for your help."

I took a deep breath. "I understand completely. Thank you very, very much."

This wasn't her world. Hopefully they had family who could take in their two girls — Roberto and Gloria Alcaíno were going to sit behind bars for quite a while. Within an hour, she'd discover the setup as an agent hauled her off in cuffs.

Kathy found Cecilia, and, while we were waiting for Lucas, he called to say he wasn't able to come to Tampa, but he had sent his right-hand man, his brother-in-law, Mono, who would arrive on a flight in the next thirty minutes. Not ideal, but two members of a supply group were better than none. When Mono arrived, we all got in my car and drove to the undercover house.

"This is $175,000," I said, pulling out a duffel bag packed with cash bundled in $5,000 stacks. "The first installment of the $420,000 owed for the thirty-five kilos you gave Roberto." I pulled out my fake driver's license. "I wanna see something like mine, so I know who you are, 'cause I don't need you to only say, 'I'm Pedro.'"

Mono pulled out his license, wrote out a receipt, and signed for the $175,000, as did Cecilia. An undercover agent posing as one of my workers arrived to drive them to a hotel. Two blocks away, a heavily armed arrest team took them both down.

By now, early morning in Europe, raid teams were descending on BCCI London and Paris and Capcom, about to haul away truckloads of financial records, including the road map to Noriega's fortune.

The next day, trucks would haul away crates of records from BCCI Tampa and Miami that traced yet more drug-money movement around the world.

It was over.

My last undercover incarnation as Bob Musella had finally passed. A strange mixture of relief, concern, and remorse filled me. We'd reached the end in one piece, unharmed. We'd gathered powerful proof that the financial community was sleeping with the underworld. But there was no telling what they'd do, and years of grueling legal battles lay before us. And we'd created a lifetime of pain for innocent wives and children in the orbit of the criminals we'd taken down — to say nothing of the pain we'd inflicted on our own spouses and children.

I felt no joy.

"It's done," I said to Ev on my way home. "I just wanted you to know that I'm safe, and as soon as I can I'll be on my way home. It's late, and I didn't want you staying up worrying."

Then to Steve Cook: "I'm done, man. I've got a splitting headache, and I'm exhausted. I'm headed home."

"Congratulations," he said. "Great job. It looks like some of these guys may start talking."

"Great," I said, completely worn down. "I'll check in with you tomorrow."

I drove home and collapsed into bed.

At about eight o'clock in the morning, while I was still fast asleep, Eric and Gail Wellman met the employees of Financial Consulting and Tammey Jewels, many with their spouses. Many had beautifully wrapped gifts tucked under their arms. Outside their office building, they all boarded a bus headed to the wedding. Or so they thought.

Just before the bus pulled away, Wellman stood up. "I'd like to make an announcement. I have something to share with everyone, something that I've kept secret for two years."

He played a cassette I had given him a few days earlier.

"By now, Eric has told you that I'm not really Bob Musella, the investment adviser, and that I have another name. I'm a special agent with the U.S. Customs Service, Investigations Division. I have to admit I'm rather embarrassed for having had to be less than honest with you about who I really was and what I really do. Hopefully you will find it in your hearts to forgive me for that deception and will understand why it was necessary to maintain the secrecy of this operation and to maintain the safety of the undercover agents. I am so grateful for having met you all, and I hope someday to come back into the community to thank you each personally again. Your brave support and that of the Wellmans and many other dedicated citizens helped make the operation a success."

Wellman then announced that the bus was heading to a special breakfast at a restaurant where he would answer questions. The announcement shocked everyone. They supposed I was a nice guy involved in shady business deals — but not a cop. When reality sank in, time passed, and national broadcasts hyped the case all over the world, the husbands of only two employees expressed their anger that their wives had been exposed to dangerous people. It was a fear we faced every day of our lives.

I slept for sixteen hours straight. When I awoke — as if from a two-year-long dream — Cook gave me a rundown of what had happened during the night. Agents at the Innisbrook guard shack took down Tobón at 2 A.M., when he arrived. Alvaro Perez went down in New York as Nazir Chinoy, Ziauddin Akbar, and Asif Baakza did in London. Agents caught Pedro Charria, Don Chepe's number-one man in New York, while attempting to burn records that later confirmed the importation of tens of thousands of kilos of cocaine and the laundering of untold sums of cash.

Of the eighty-five people indicted, we had most in custody, but Miami agents couldn't find Zabala.

"What happened?" I asked Matt Etre.

"We can't find him," he said. "We went to his house last night, but he wasn't there."

I had a thought.

"Bob, congratulations," Zabala said on the phone minutes after I had paged him.

Is he being sarcastic?

"Congratulations for what?"

"For your marriage, of course! I'm sorry we couldn't make it. I have some problems. The feds came to my house last night looking for me."

Just when I thought Bob Musella had died, he sprang back to life.

"Tuto, didn't you hear?" I said, jumping back into character. "The ugly ones came to the country club last night. They arrested Joe. As soon as I heard about it, I got the hell out of there. I don't know if they're even looking for me, but I'm not taking any chances. I left Kathy in Tampa, and I'm going out of the country until I know what's happening. Can you help me? I'm just now getting to the Tampa airport. I'll be on the next flight to Miami. Can you pick me up in an hour and a half at the American Airlines baggage claim?"

"Sure," he said, taking the bait, "I'll be there for you."

"If you have a team of agents in plain clothes at the American Airlines baggage claim in Miami in an hour and a half," I told Etre, "you'll find Zabala there waiting for me."

"Can you give me a description?"

"If you miss this guy, you need to go back to the academy. He's a fifty-year-old Cuban, about five-ten, heavy-set, salt-and-pepper hair. He wears a huge gold necklace that spells TUTO, and his right eye is permanently skewed to the right."

"We've got him," Etre said an hour and a half later.

Late afternoon found me exhausted again as Ev and I convened a family meeting. We had always preached security with the kids, and they knew my job necessitated special caution, but it was time to talk details. We all needed to keep an eye out for anything out of place. Teenagers often gossip, but mine never breathed a word to anyone outside the family.

After dinner, I fell asleep again.

I woke up the next day alone, Ev at work and the kids at school. In the kitchen, Ev had left a detailed list of all repairs needed to the house, yard, and cars, many unaddressed for nearly two years. I couldn't blame her for it; she'd done everything herself for far too long—and she'd done it well.

Unfortunately prosecution of the case was just starting. The world's most powerful drug cartel and a $20 billion bank weren't going to take this sitting down. They'd come at us with all barrels blazing. Twelve hundred tapes needed transcribing, and endless motions from defense counsel would keep us busy for years. I didn't have the heart to tell her. She'd realize soon enough.

First order of business was a total makeover. In order to shed the skin of Robert Musella, I had my hair cut short, shaved off my beard, and—even though I still had perfect eyesight—bought a pair of clear glasses. Ev came home before the kids. As we sat on the couch and talked, they came in, looked at us, said, "Hi, Mom," and went straight to their rooms. They ignored me completely, cold punishment for my absence from their lives over the past two years. Ev checked on them, and they said they thought she'd prefer that they stayed in their room until the man who was visiting left.

They hadn't recognized their own father.

· · ·

The next day, Commissioner von Raab summoned all Tampa personnel to his hotel suite shortly before appearing at an international press conference. NBC, CBS, ABC, and foreign news companies were buzzing everywhere. One of a few people I've met who is shorter than me, von Raab had an ego that filled the room and sat in a dining chair with his feet propped up on the table.

He thanked us for a job well done and then asked me, "What new things did you learn from dealing with these people undercover?"

"Well, sir, I can tell you that Europe better brace itself for a massive influx of cocaine. The cartel enjoys twice the profit selling their merchandise there, and they are gearing up to take advantage of that."

Before the meeting broke, someone asked if I knew where the wedding gifts were.

"I don't know," I lied. "I've been sleeping for the past two days. I haven't been in the office."

At the press conference, von Raab revealed that the Medellín cartel had targeted Europe as its new frontier.

At the start of my undercover assignment, eighteen agents worked the Tampa office, but that number had swelled to more than sixty. There were many I didn't know, and those I did all had trouble recognizing me. A little light investigation revealed that most of the evidence I had passed to my handlers during the operation was sitting idly in file-cabinet drawers. Tapes lay uncopied and untranscribed. The handful of agents in the Tampa office assigned to the case had worked endless hours, sometimes around the clock. But there was just too much to do.

First on my list of office duties was tracking down Dominic's cross. It hadn't surfaced on any of the paperwork I had seen, which worried me. Who was going to approve a $25,000 payment to cover that loss? I called L.A. for an inventory of items seized from Alcaíno's Pasadena home. No cross. But there was an entry for a small paisley-patterned jewelry box found in a nightstand beside his bed. That had to be it.

"I hate to bother you," I said to the L.A. seizure clerk, "but can you pull an item from the Alcaíno seizure? It's listed as a small jewelry box with a paisley pattern. Would you please look inside that box and tell me what's in it?"

"Okay, pal, hold on.... That's strange. There's a diamond-studded cross in that box. Somebody screwed up. It should have been listed on the inventory. We should be able to get a pretty penny for this. It looks like the real deal."

I explained the story, faxed him a copy of the agreement with Dominic, and got the cross back.

"Here it is," I said, handing it back to him at his club early one night. "Thanks for everything. I hate to bug you with formalities, but here's a receipt. The office would like signed proof that you got the cross back."

"No problem," he said, signing. "I'm glad I could help. I told you, I know you went to bat for me. I'll never forget that. Thanks to you, I get to play with my kids instead of having my ass rot in jail. From what I see on TV, you really knocked down some big pins. I'm sure your star must be rising."

"I doubt my star will go anywhere. That's not what makes my clock tick; you know that. We're going to be in for the fight of our lives. These guys and this bank have all the money in the world. They'll roll out the highest-priced lawyers money can buy. I'm going to be tied up for a while on this thing, but if you ever need anything, call. What you and Frankie did for us in this operation made the difference. I really appreciate it."

A few days later, I pulled up to the high-rise that shared the Tampa Customs office along with other private companies. Fire trucks and squad cars had blocked the street.

"What the hell is going on?" I asked a few guys from the office.

"They found a bomb in the stairwell on our floor. The Tampa P.D. bomb squad is working on it now."

They were coming. Whether it was a prank or a warning

didn't matter. I could feel it. Escobar was bombing the hell out of his competition. Cops and innocent people were dropping like flies in Colombia. And he was exporting terror just as he had been exporting narcotics.

I slept fitfully that night. The next morning, my daughter was riding her bike in the front yard when a white-paneled van rolled down our block. The panel door slowly rolled open to reveal the muzzle of a gun. I ran out of the house screaming *"No! No!"* A hooded gunman opened fire as I dived on her and —

I jolted bolt upright in bed in a pool of sweat. It was only a dream. My heart was pounding. It had seemed so real. It was only a dream.

Come on, Mazur, pull yourself together.

Even with the help of a dozen transcribers, it would take more than a year to transcribe the tapes and proof the transcripts. While I was struggling with that Herculean task, dozens of news trucks and investigative reporters thronged the city, attending every hearing and digging for clues about the global effects of our operation. Their number one question: Who was Robert Musella? — a secret we intended to keep for months.

Then my phone rang.

"Bob, something strange just happened that you need to know," said IRS Special Agent Dave Burris, who was coordinating his office with ours. "One of the guys in our office just did something stupid. He was on the phone with a defense attorney in town who asked him who played the Musella undercover role. This idiot told him it was you. We're stunned. He's been sent home; our bosses want him fired. I can't apologize enough. I know you and Ev are already under a ton of pressure. I can't undo what this jerk did. If there's anything I can do to help you deal with this, just tell me. I'll do it."

"This is terrible," I said as my mind reeled. "This coming on the heels of the bomb threat is not good, and the last thing my wife and kids need is a street full of news trucks and reporters. That will lead to a story that will let the cartel and the bank know exactly where they can find the government's primary witness.... I've got to get ahead of this curve fast and relocate my family. I'm going to come up with a plan and see if I can get my office to support it. Thanks for calling me right away."

"This is what I'd like to do," I told Tony Weda, head of the Customs undercover unit in D.C. "You gave me the green light months ago to start building another fake ID, just in case there were threats after the operation went down. I've put that whole ID in place. I have a driver's license, birth certificate, bank accounts, credit cards, everything I need. I want to put all our belongings in storage, put the house up for sale, and get my family into a rental. I wanted to discuss this with you first because I'm going to need support here in Tampa. I'm not very popular in the front office."

"I'm with you," he said. "After you speak with Steve Cook, have him call me."

Time for another family meeting. Ev was so pissed, the IRS should have put a security detail on the agent who revealed my identity. When the anger subsided, we all agreed that we had no choice.

In three days, we packed up and put everything in storage. We gave power of attorney to a lawyer and put the house up for sale. We moved into a hotel for two days before flying to Eleuthera in the Bahamas — no phones, no TV, just sorely needed family time.

A week later we moved in with a relative for two weeks while the other pieces of the security plan fell into place. The superintendent of schools sealed the kids' records and briefed the deputy sheriffs assigned to each school. At the school where Ev taught, custodians locked all perimeter doors every day after students arrived, and the administration sealed all her personnel records.

With the new identity, I rented a house with a good security system in another county. We slashed back contact with family and friends, and used only a cell phone when we did. A friend in the auto business gave us a dealer tag for our car. That was about all we could do.

We couldn't totally uproot and hide. I wanted to increase my family's security, not terrify them. In the course of cutting the paper trail to us, I discovered another Robert Mazur in our town listed in the phone book. The office informed him of the problems that unfortunate coincidence might bring to his doorstep.

It took almost a month to arrange everything comfortably. Just when the situation had finally calmed down, a familiar face came my way. It was Al Henley, a Tampa DEA agent working with us on the operation. But Al wasn't wearing his usual smile. He looked concerned.

"I don't know how to tell you this," he said. "I just finished debriefing Joaquín Casals. Last night, he overheard Armbrecht and a few other defendants talking. They claim there's a hit squad that's been dispatched from Colombia, through Mexico, with the sole purpose of coming here to take you out. It was said that these guys are being paid $500,000 to get the job done. Now this may be a coincidence and unrelated, but an intercept by NSA recently picked up some chatter out of Medellín from the phone of a very high-ranking cartel member. NSA's intercept suggests there's a hit squad being sent from Colombia, through Mexico, to take out unknown government officials. I don't know what to say, but I wanted to come to you immediately so you could do whatever you think you should to deal with this."

"I know this is going to sound strange, but I was almost expecting this," I said. But I never expected what came next.

21

BATTLES

U.S. Customs, Tampa, Florida
November 18, 1988

HENLEY GAVE TISCHLER THE NEWS.

An hour later, she called me. "Mazur, I just spoke with Al Henley. I understand he already told you about the threat. We're going to assign some agents to guard you until we can assess it. Steve Cook will get with you on the details. I just want you to know that we're going to treat this very seriously, and we'll do whatever is necessary to ensure your safety and the safety of the other undercover agents."

I agreed. The less said to Tischler the better.

"Tischler is on the warpath with DEA," Cook said when he saw me. "She's upset that they told you about the threat before going to her. She decided that we're going to put a heavily armed four-man protection detail on you around the clock. We'll use two four-man teams; each will pull a twelve-hour shift."

"Are you serious?" I said, astonished.

"This is what she wants. On top of that, she's ordering a protection detail for herself."

Of course she was.

"Don't I have any say in this?" I said. "This doesn't make any sense. You and I both know that we don't have the resources to do this for very long. So the only thing this protection team is going to accomplish is scaring the shit out of my family by having guys lugging machine guns around, in, and outside our home. Then, four weeks from now, when some idiot says they've assessed the threat and can't confirm or refute it, the detail will be dropped. There's no way in hell that I'm going along with this. I've spent half a year putting a new phony ID in place that enabled us to make it very hard for anyone to find us. On paper, Robert Mazur stopped existing in commercial databases. I'm responsible for my and my family's security, and I'm telling you right now I've got that covered as well as it can be addressed. I'm not going to allow my children to be emotionally scarred. I refuse the protection detail."

"Mazur, I don't think you have a choice," Cook said, eyebrows raised.

"Oh, really, Steve? I know a way that I have a choice." I pulled off the ankle holster holding my Smith & Wesson .38 Special and laid it on the desk along with my badge. "If you're telling me that I have no choice in this matter because I'm a federal agent employed by this office, then I quit. Now I'm a civilian, and this office can't make me do shit."

"Come on, you know you don't want to do that. Take your stuff back. If you feel that strongly about it, write up a memo making your points, and I'll take it to her to see what we can work out."

"I don't want to screw this case up by quitting before these trials are over," I said. "You'll have the memo in an hour."

Ev agreed completely — a protection detail was the last thing we needed. But that didn't stop Tischler from trying to convince her otherwise.

"Hi, Evelyn, this is Bonni Tischler, the special agent in charge in Tampa. How are you?"

"Fine, Bonni. What can I do for you?"

"I assume Bob has told you about the threat we identified against him. In light of that, I think it's important for you and him to accept the protection detail we've arranged. I suggest you talk to him and have him reconsider his position. We have to take this very seriously."

"Bob and I have already discussed this, and there is no way Customs is going to continue to traumatize my children. Throughout

Bob's career and especially during the past two years, I have worked really hard to give my kids as normal a life as possible. This is the first call I've received from anyone at Customs since this case started. The kids and I have been treated like nonentities for the past two years, and now you want to help. Where were you six months ago, a month ago? Not here, not calling to see how we were or if we needed anything. No one called. So neither you nor anyone else is going to tell me how to manage the lives of my children."

"Well, if Bob is not going to follow my orders," Tischler persisted, "he may not be able to continue to work in this office. For his safety, I will have to transfer him to Washington or maybe Pembina, North Dakota."

"Oh, please." Ev laughed furiously. "You don't care about his safety. You can threaten a transfer all you want, but you can't do anything to harm us. We've been through hell and back. We don't need this Customs job. We'll be just fine without it. Our mission at this point is to put our family back together. We won't move to Washington, Pembina, or anywhere else. It's not going to happen. We'll decide what's best for us. Customs will have no role in any decisions we make about our family. There's no need to discuss this any further. Good-bye."

Assistant Regional Commissioner Leon Guinn — who had supported our undercover operation since the beginning — approved my memo declining the protection detail. But that didn't resolve the underlying issue. I had a lawyer draw up a last will and testament.

The slightest irregularities automatically triggered my defense mechanisms. Late one night, while I was working on transcripts in the dining room, the phone rang.

"Hello?"

"Hi," said a strange male voice. "How are you?"

"Okay."

"Are you a compromising kind of guy?"

"Who is this?"

"Oh, you don't know?" and then he hung up, sending my mind spiraling into what-ifs. But the voice never called back.

Another night, after picking up my son from a sporting event, I noticed a truck parked 150 yards away from our front door, on the other side of a wooded pond, pointed in our direction. Someone was sitting in the driver's seat.

Ev killed all the lights in the house while I pulled out my binoculars, which, through the blinds, revealed a man with his own pair of binoculars trained on our house.

"I'm going out the back," I said. "You guys lock the door behind me, and don't open any door for anyone. I have a key. Just stay in the kitchen with the lights out."

Ev and the kids understandably freaked out as I told them not to worry and grabbed my badge and my Colt .357 Magnum.

I worked my way down the street, out of sight, staying low, through the woods behind the truck. Its windows were down, the engine off, and a burly guy was sitting in the driver's seat staring at our house.

He jumped as I popped up on the passenger side holding my badge out in one hand and my .357 in the other, shouting, "I'm a police officer. Put your hands on the wheel so I can see them. Who are you and what are you doing here?"

He grabbed the wheel, stuttering, "I-I-I'm just w-watching w-wildlife. There's three alligators that l-live in that pond. I swear — I'm just studying what they do at night. I live close by, just across the county line, five miles from here."

"We've had some burglaries in this area, and you got me and some other folks in this neighborhood nervous."

I wrote his tag number down and walked back to the house, where I reassured my family. "It was nothing. That was just a nice guy watching alligators in the pond. I'm sorry I overreacted. Let's have dinner. Everything is fine. We've got nothing to worry about."

The next day, the tags checked out — and I'd been one second away from blowing away an innocent man. If he had made a stupid move, I wouldn't have hesitated.

What the hell was I thinking?

. . . .

Meanwhile, at the office, while my fellow agents and I put in long days transcribing tapes, I constantly had to submit lengthy affidavits to be filed in London to extradite Chinoy and to prosecute Akbar and Baakza. And I was preparing to testify in the Detroit trial of the Giraldo brothers and the New York trial of Pedro Charria.

As if that wasn't enough, internal audits were questioning the expenditure of every last dollar on C-Chase. Putting in fourteen-hour workdays seven days a week left me averaging four or five hours of sleep a night. And agents on the case kept getting reassigned to other duties at a time when we needed a dozen more agents to work with us. We lobbied for more people to comb through the truckloads of records seized from BCCI and Capcom. We needed to uncover the banks' relationships with other drug dealers. Instead, we dwindled to a skeleton crew, despite repeated pleas from Cook, me, and every over-worked agent on the operation. Recurring memos to the front office detailing tasks still undone and resources needed changed nothing.

I was starting to come unglued. At a self-serve, automatic car wash before a meeting, I rolled down my window and plopped coins into the machine. I pulled forward and put the car in park as the equipment made its way toward the car. My mind was a thousand miles away, contemplating the trial in Tampa, when a wave of water and soap deluged me. I'd forgotten to roll up the window, and now there was a two-inch puddle of water in my lap and on the seat. I was a mess.

One Sunday, four months after the takedown, the phone rang.

"Hi, Bob," said Bill Rosenblatt in D.C. "I'd like to pick your brain and discuss something with you. You've done a great job. Infiltrating the cartel and the bank really put our agency on the map. We're going to gear up our initiatives in international money-laundering cases, and I'd like you to join me here in Washington by taking a position in the currency branch. I promise you that, after six months, I'll promote you to a GS-14, and in two years I'll send you back out of Washington as a GS-15 running your own office in a major city. I'd like a commitment from you, even if you have to stay in Tampa for another six months to finish up on the trials that are pending. I didn't call sooner because I wanted you to have some quality time with your family before I made this proposal."

Either he had no idea what we were facing, or he was trying to get me out of town.

"Sir, I'm scheduled to testify in five trials," I said, "one of which is scheduled to last six months. I've got more than eight hundred transcripts that aren't finished, and it's my guess that these trials won't conclude until about two years from now. I suspect that Mark Jackowski, the prosecutor in Tampa, will object to my reassignment until the trials conclude. Would it be possible for me to have a little time to think this out? Maybe things aren't as dire as I think they are."

"Sure, why don't you take a week to assess the situation and then call me back?"

It was absurd. There was no way I could testify unless I spent every waking minute in the next two years preparing. If I didn't, the two dozen law firms with tens of millions in legal fees on the other side of the table would chew me up and spit me out. "Are the people who run your organization idiots?" Jackowski laughed when I told him what Rosenblatt had offered. "This is the most important case Customs has ever brought, and they're going to ship my key witness to Washington—for what? Unless they want to lose these cases, they better abandon that idea. If I have to, I'll get the attorney general to explain reality to them."

I relayed to Rosenblatt that the U.S. Attorney's office intended to make a formal complaint, and I agreed that the transfer would seriously jeopardize the cases.

He didn't like what he was hearing. "At some stage, Mr. Mazur, you may have no choice. For now we'll table this discussion, but don't be surprised when it comes up again at a time when you'll have no other option."

Why did my own people want me out of Tampa and away from the case? Something was going on. What had Tischler said to me a year ago? *Stick to the bank's dealings in drug money, and keep your nose out of whatever else they're doing.* And Awan had told me how deeply BCCI's ties and shareholders ran with the Bush family, half a dozen other major politicians, and the world's intelligence community. Was Washington nervous about this investigation going any further? If they weren't, based solely on what happened with the first portion of Noriega's bank records, they should have been.

British Customs had raided BCCI London and netted a trove of records detailing the movement of tens of millions in dirty money, including $50 million in accounts secretly controlled by General Noriega. Just as he had told me, Awan was the principal manager, and just as he had done for me, much of Noriega's cash moved through London to Luxembourg.

A British court released the records to our office solely to be used as evidence in a U.S. court of law. Before the engines of the plane carrying the records to Tampa had cooled, a copy of the records went to Rosenblatt in D.C. A day or so later, NBC producer Ira Silverman met privately with Rosenblatt at his home. Less than twenty-four hours later, NBC investigative reporter Brian Ross delivered a news special about the Noriega records, displaying copies of them to TV cameras.

When irate Department of Justice officials demanded an investigation to identify the leak, Customs posited that defense attorneys, who also received the records, must have made the disclosure. In case that wasn't enough, Customs also suggested that someone in the IRS might have given them to NBC. Not surprisingly, a Customs internal affairs investigation found no leak.

With each major news story, the defendants felt a little more heat, and many of the traffickers, including Alcaíno, were testing the waters for deals with the government. Alcaíno wasn't giving up everything he could, and agents debriefing him were actually buying his bullshit. Jackowski endorsed my idea to meet Alcaíno to hear what he had to say firsthand.

Three agents checked the Jeweler out of jail and brought him under guard and in chains to a nearby hotel.

"Excuse me," Alcaíno said before I arrived, "but do you have a comb? I like to look my best."

When I walked in, his first stare was so bitter that I returned it in kind.

"Please, please," he said, "you know we're friends. You know you can trust me. Can I please have these handcuffs off?"

"Business is business. I'm going to do everything I can to help you, just as I would anybody else who is in this predicament. There are things you can do to help the government. You'll get fair benefit for fair help. But you have to realize now, this is reality. That other stuff was just me doing my job, and hopefully you can accept that. But let's sit down. There seem to be some differences between what I think is the truth and what I hear you've said. That's why I'm here. If what I hear isn't the truth, I'm walking out of here, and you're on your own."

"You can't leave me now," he said, "please."

"I'm gone if you lie," I repeated.

But it was time to eat lunch — a few cheap sandwiches.

"Well," I said, "it's not *palafitta*, but —"

His eyes lit up. "Oh, you remember?" I said, "I'll never forget."

"I didn't really know there was coke in the shipment until after I was arrested," he said, claiming Díaz had been so concerned about earlier seizures that he had been reluctant to put the coke in the anchovy shipment.

A bald-faced lie. Alcaíno was there when it was packed, and he had called me the night before the delivery and blathered in code about his pregnant girlfriend.

He did roll on a lot of people in Colombia, but they couldn't be extradited. Nine months had passed since his arrest, and the cartel had no doubt told him through his lawyers what he could and couldn't say. He had two teenage daughters, so he wasn't going to stray from his script.

Although he clearly was lying, preparing for his trial would drain precious resources, and we didn't have many. He was prepared to accept a fifteen-year prison sentence and forfeit several million dollars' worth of seized assets. If that's how the prosecutors wanted to proceed, I had no objection. Other agents could loosen his tongue over the next decade. Besides, if he took the deal, Gloria would receive time served. She'd already been languishing in prison for nearly nine months. It was probably fair to give her a chance to go home to her girls.

Then we lost Steve Cook as our supervisor. He stood up for me one time too many. Thankfully, the brass allowed him to finish working with us on all pending cases related to the operation.

Dan Dunn, a consummate professional, came in to supervise the five of us left, but he had another five agents working on other cases. It wasn't perfect, but Dunn fought to get us as much support as he could. He listened and, unlike those above him, welcomed what he affectionately termed "Mazurgrams," my biweekly memos noting what had been done, what needed to be done, and what resources we needed to do it. He didn't win every battle for us, but he always tried.

By the time of my first public court appearance — to testify against Don Chepe's right hand, Pedro Charria — defendants were taking deals and pleading guilty or getting in line to do the same. The Alcaínos folded first; then Casals, Cecilia, Mora, Mono Rendon, Tobón, and Zabala followed.

But it was time to face Charria in New York. Don Chepe would have his spies in the courtroom hunting for information — and me.

22

THE TRIALS

U.S. District Court, New York City
July 18, 1989

THE PRICE ON MY HEAD called for a security plan. Targets now knew my real name, so using that was out. Nor could I put the new identity at risk, so for trial travel I created yet another, bringing the total in active use, including my real identity, to three.

The trial travel identity first came into play to get me to New York for the trial of Pedro Charria, who had counted every kilo of cocaine that came into the Towers for the part of Pablo Escobar's empire managed by Don Chepe.

A rotund man in his late twenties, Charria lived with his wife and young children in a 3,500-square-foot house outfitted with every amenity imaginable, on an acre of land in an exclusive neighborhood in Dix Hills, on Long Island. Trained as an electrical engineer, he also counted the tens of millions collected from the sale of Don Chepe's cocaine—and owned a Jennings .357 Magnum handgun with four barrels. It was small enough to fit in the palm of your hand, but in seconds it could blast all four rounds at its target.

Speeding through the streets of New York in his flashy BMW, Charria regularly met Nelson Chen in the parking lot of the Forest Hills Mall in Queens, where he handed Chen a duffel bag of cash. On the day of the wedding, he sniffed out the cops in his neighborhood and started a fire in a fifty-gallon drum outside his house, tossing page after page of records into the flames. When agents arrived and doused the fire, he claimed he was cold. What he hadn't yet destroyed proved every detail of the movement of 6,900 kilos of cocaine and $90 million in drug profits during just five months.

Charria was screwed.

Not only did the records nail down the details of his dealings with me, it linked him also to *La Mina*, which proved that *La Mina* was receiving the same kind of money I did. Charria received a twenty-five-year prison sentence.

During the trial, though, his lawyer asked a hundred questions of interest to the cartel. What did I know about Don Chepe? Who was he? What did others know about him? On and on for two days. Clearly Don Chepe was concerned — and footing the lawyer's bill.

After the Charria trial, the *Tampa Tribune* published on its front page an article by Bentley Orrick, a talented investigative reporter with unmatched integrity and a nose for news. It was the first front-page story in the country exposing my identity, and Bentley had known my name for almost a year. Ten months prior, when I got wind he was about to file, I begged him to hold off. He honorably agreed, but asked in exchange for a heads-up when I first appeared at a trial. The mask had shattered, but it had bought me time.

In London, magistrates presided over committal hearings, at which I testified and which would determine whether evidence against Ziauddin Akbar and Asif Baakza was strong enough to warrant trying them in a higher court.

Four heavily armed City of London police officers assigned to their anti-terrorism squad met me at Heathrow. With the U.S. Customs attaché assigned to the embassy, I jumped in the first of two cars, as did two of the police officers, the other two following in the chase car. Double alternating sirens blared and blue lights flashed as we raced northeast to the heart of London and arrived at what became my home for weeks, the City of London Police headquarters then at 26 Old Jewry. Built in 1842 as the residence and offices for the commissioner of the department at the time, its Victorian exterior stood unchanged, despite a renovation between the wars in the 1930s. My bedroom lay directly across the hall from the surveillance post for my guards, a bathroom, and two other quarters, one of which contained a kitchen. It was dreary but perfect. All I intended to do there was study the facts and prepare to testify.

A secret tunnel to the Magistrates Court a few blocks away eliminated any security risks in getting me from the station to the courthouse. Each day, after I dressed for court, I carried my bundle of notes and reports to the basement, surrounded by the protection detail. Through a creaking bulkhead door that gave access to a metal ladder bolted to the building's foundation, we descended into what looked like a dry sewer, lined with steaming pipes and decades of dust. At the base of the ladder, over our clothes, we donned lightweight white zip-up overalls that made us look like astronauts preparing for a space walk. The one-size-fits-all suits fit my 6' 4" guards just fine, but on me the crotch dipped practically to my knees, forcing me to walk like a prisoner in leg irons.

The tunnel, through which they walked and I waddled, narrowed our convoy to single file, at which point we had to hop a three-foot wall to access the next tunnel. Finally emerging in the Magistrates Court basement, we shed the overalls and walked up a flight of stairs to a small office outside one of the four courtrooms in the triangular house of justice built under King George IV that also housed ten cells, which, for more than two hundred years, have held hordes of prisoners.

Under British law, the barrister presenting the case for the committal hearing is a hired attorney, sometimes for the prosecution and sometimes for the defense — a little unsettling — and the presiding magistrate, who is not a lawyer, relies on assistants for legal interpretations.

The first week of hearings concerned Asif Baakza. As I climbed into the witness box, his eyes looked sunken in his skull and lined in black hatred. Our conversations had changed his life. And then in the gallery I spotted Ziauddin Akbar, who shuddered in the corner and, according to one of the officers guarding me, prayed constantly while feverishly fingering prayer beads. During a break, he struggled to the hallway and vomited.

At the end of the day, we retraced our space walk to the police station, where I worked out, ate, studied, and fell asleep with transcripts in my hands. The protection detail rotated every twelve hours, and the night crew proved a little more adventuresome. On rare occasions, they treated me to trips to the U.S. embassy cafeteria, where I could feast on steak and a couple of pints of beer. Both shifts of the detail took our trips outside the station with deadly seriousness. They bolted from the parking garage and sped through London on constant lookout for an attack. What at first seemed like erratic driving proved to be adroit precision. While pedestrians gawked, we turned on a dime — so much so that we once nearly ran down a drunk bum in the street and then a motorcycle courier.

It paid off. The magistrate committed the cases against Akbar and Baakza to trial. But I had to return to the States for the showdown in Tampa.

The solitude of the station house in London had given me an immense advantage. No commute time, no downtime in the office, just total focus. In three months, I was scheduled to take the stand again, but I needed six to prep properly. The only way to accomplish that goal was to eliminate the two and a half hours of commute time each day and the distractions of the office.

From undercover profits, Customs agreed to pay for a hotel room, five minutes from the office, where I could work around the clock during the week. I'd come home Friday night and return Sunday evening. With that arrangement, I *might* be ready. Ev wasn't happy about it, but she has supported me since we met in high school. We've had our bumps in the road, like most couples, but she's remarkable, my best friend, and I will love her forever. Neither of us liked the situation, but she understood why I had to do what I had to do. Anything else would invalidate the last three years of sacrifices we had both made.

In the solitude of the hotel, I devised a way to go head to head with the defense attorneys being paid tens of millions of dollars by the Saudi power brokers who owned the bank. First, I identified the top forty facts we needed to prove at trial, assigning a number to each. Then I dictated summaries of every ten pages of each transcript, after which I stated which of the forty facts appeared in those ten pages. A cross-referenced database would sort the data by category, and every morsel of information on each key issue came out chronologically by transcript number, page, and line. It took me almost the entire three months to dictate the necessary information and for a pool of data processors to dump it all into a program — but at the end it provided not only detailed summaries of each meeting, but chronological reports of each key trial issue. If a defense attorney asked me when, if ever, I had told his client that my clients were drug dealers, I immediately had a full and devastating answer.

As I was preparing, Operation Just Cause sent U.S. troops into Panama under President Bush's authorization to hunt Noriega down like a dog. Roughly two thousand Panamanians died in the assault, and I couldn't help think that the meetings Awan had offered me in Panama might have permitted a more peaceful plan for overthrowing Noriega. Others in Panama might have been more likely to offer him up if the case was airtight. We'll never know.

Not long before I took the stand, BCCI agreed to plead guilty. The deal, which I vehemently opposed, gave them little more than a slap on the wrist. They paid a $15 million fine and agreed to a five-year period of probation. Some counted it a victory that the bank's every move during the next five years would come under the U.S. government's watchful eye, but the bank was still operating in Panama, Luxembourg, Switzerland, and sixty-nine other countries, taking in hundreds of millions of dollars in drug money under the guise of legitimate business. How would we know what was happening in every corner of the world?

It was a farce, but it was also time to enter the lion's den to testify against Armbrecht, Awan, Bilgrami, Hassan, Howard, and Hussain. If convicted, they faced stiff sentences — and then they would spill the bank's secrets.

"They're ready for you now," said a deputy U.S. marshal, breaking my reverie as he opened the door of the waiting room and led me into the courtroom, jammed with hundreds of reporters and spectators.

I climbed into the witness stand on March twenty-sixth and testified every day the court was in session until June twelfth — eleven consecutive weeks of questioning, each defense attorney with his own shot at me for days or a week at a time.

At first the glares of the defendants and their families were distracting. Trying to predict what the defense attorneys would ask about the last three and a half years overwhelmed me. Each night after court, I dragged my three boxes of notes back to the hotel and studied until I fell asleep with a transcript in my hands. But as the weeks wore on, the jury seemed to be growing sympathetic to my plight, and the mental anguish grew familiar. I saw nothing other than the lawyer at the podium and heard nothing but his question. Time seemed to slow as my mind raced through every synapse, searching for the words each defense attorney least wanted to hear.

Washington lawyer John Hume tried to convince the jury that these transactions were nothing but normal business. As he leaned into my face, close to the witness box, he said, "Would it be more accurate to say that the bank served a banking function?"

"No," I said. "They laundered money. That's what they did."

Hume's eyes grew huge; he reddened with rage; and he screamed to the judge, "Your honor, I move to strike that! That is unresponsive. It's argumentative. I think it's improper, and I move for a mistrial!"

"Well, I'll deny that motion, Mr. Hume," said Judge Terrell Hodges, one of the most respected District Court judges in the nation, taking Hume's theatrics in stride. "He gave a direct response, followed by that explanation, which is obviously his interpretation.... Put another question."

"Agent Mazur," Hume said, "I would like you to stick to fact and not opinion, if you will, please, sir."

"I thought I had," I snarked.

Renowned Miami criminal defense attorney James Hogan tried subtly to suggest I had suffered role reversal during my two years undercover. Throughout my three months on the stand, he frequently addressed me as "Agent Musella." Each and every time, I politely reminded him that my name was Mazur, not Musella. He always apologized and claimed he'd made an innocent mistake —but I knew better. He was trying to lure me into answering questions under my assumed name so he could later claim I didn't know who I was. His little game lasted months, but I never once failed to correct him.

During the third month, when he addressed me as Musella for what seemed like the hundredth time, the jurors all rolled their eyes. His little game was backfiring, and I sensed an opportunity. After I politely corrected him, I offered to bring a name tag I could wear to aid him. The jurors smiled, while Hogan paid little attention to my comment. But he did it again the next day.

"Now, Mr. Musella, can you tell us if you talked with anybody from the Bank of Credit and Commerce after December twenty-ninth, either in Boca Raton, Tampa, anyplace, before the new year?" he said as the jurors shook their heads and pressed their lips together.

"Sir, my name is Mazur," I said, "and you know that."

The jury laughed.

"Yes, I do—"

"And I promised you I'd bring you a gift, which was a name tag."

From the notepad on my lap, I pulled a large yellow Post-it on which I had written my name in bold black letters. The entire courtroom erupted in laughter as I put it on my lapel.

"You may have to put it on the front of the witness stand," Hogan said sheepishly.

"I brought you one for the podium, too," I said, brandishing a second yellow Post-it featuring my name. Hogan took it and was halfway back to the podium when I added, "because I know you really know my name."

"Well, now, don't take it too far!" he yelled, pointing at me.

You could hear a pin drop in the courtroom. The jurors shook their heads. Hogan never called me Musella again.

I testified for a full half of the six-month trial. It left me mentally and physically exhausted. When I was done on the stand, I helped behind the scenes for about a week, but then made good on a family promise to rent a motor home and head north for a month. I thought less about the case in that month than I had in years.

Until Steve Cook called.

"Every defendant in the Tampa trial was convicted," he said. "The jury returned guilty verdicts on seventy-six of the eighty charges. After the verdicts were read, the place erupted. Dozens of family members were screaming and crying. One woman wailed, 'Where did God go? I don't know where God went!' Another one fainted, and then Bilgrami's mother-in-law turned to me and said, 'Your children will pay for this!' One of the deputy marshals took her into custody, and Jackowski is going to draw up a complaint to have her charged for threatening me. All of the defendants were taken out in chains. I wish you were here because we're all going out to celebrate!"

"That's great," I said, relieved but not happy. "I hope you guys have a great time. I'm where I want to be. We really needed this. I'll see you in a week or so when we get back."

Regret lingered in my stomach after I hung up, regret for the bankers' families. Awan, Bilgrami, and their colleagues shouldn't have been moving dope money, and surely never saw this coming because so many international banks did just that. And no one else had been nailed like this before. But it was my job. I didn't make them do anything new or anything they didn't want to do. They cleaned the dirtiest money they could find. That's what they did.

There would be more trials, but, when I returned to Tampa, we needed to comb through the warehouse of records seized from BCCI branches, Capcom, and the defendants' homes while we pressured them to talk.

It became clear, as I prepared to fly back to London to testify in the criminal trials of Asif Baakza and Ziauddin Akbar, that I needed to leave Customs. The front office would be training its sights on me soon enough, and I couldn't fight the system anymore.

"I've come to the conclusion," I said to Mike Powers, DEA's top man in town, "that one agency should handle all investigations related to drug trafficking, including the money-laundering side. I'd like to be a part of helping DEA establish themselves in that position within the law-enforcement community. If DEA is interested, I'd be happy to resign from Customs and join your agency. I can't afford to take a cut in pay, and I need to stay in Tampa for five years, until my kids are out of high school. After that, you can send me anywhere you want in the world."

"Let me make a few calls," he said, "but I think we'd be willing to make those concessions. We want to become more active on the money-laundering side of the drug world, and you're obviously one of the best in the country at that. You'd have to go through our academy at Quantico with all the new hires. I'm sure you'll have no problem with the physical training, firearms, and classwork, but if you wash out you'll have to take the risk that you'll be out of a job."

"I'm ready for the challenge. If DEA wants me, I'm ready to serve."

In London, I testified for two days at the trial of Asif Baakza at the Old Bailey, London's superior criminal court, erected in 1673 and rebuilt several times over the succeeding centuries. Lawyers and judges still wore wigs and the black robes donned to mourn the death of Queen Mary II in 1694. Sicilian marble covered the interior lobbies and monumental staircases, and ornate paintings adorned every hall. High-gloss oak paneled the courtroom, which had special sections for barristers, court reporters, and press. A second-floor gallery for family and friends overlooked the proceedings. An amazingly spacious dock, enclosed by low partitions, held Baakza throughout the trial, and stairs led directly from it down to the dingy jail cells below.

Judge Parker presided. In his nineties and no friend to undercover cases, he wore the obligatory white wig and a crossed white collar over his black robe. His ruddy complexion and upper-crusty disposition, as well as a belly that protruded from his frail frame as though he had swallowed a bowling ball, turned him into a full-fledged caricature. As is the practice in the U.K., Judge Parker enjoyed the courthouse bar during the lunch recess and consequently had difficulty staying awake in the afternoon sessions.

In the end, though, the jury found Baakza guilty, and after a brief recess the judge sentenced him to a year in prison. The sentence was short, but there was something gratifying in watching Baakza descend immediately to the basement of the Old Bailey and his cell.

A few weeks later, Ziauddin Akbar took his turn in the dock, with the same result: guilty on all counts, a sentence of a year and a half.

Records seized from Capcom confirmed that more than $23 million of Noriega's fortune was moved from BCCI at around the same time Awan did the same for me. Noriega's money also landed in accounts controlled by Ziauddin Akbar in the name of Liberian front companies like Finley International at Middle East Bank. To untangle the mess, we needed to sit down with Awan and Bilgrami and give them their options: rot in jail or cough up details. But first they had to be sentenced.

Judge Terrell Hodges gave us just the leverage we needed: twelve years in prison and a $100,000 fine for Awan, twelve years for Bilgrami, seven for Hussain, five for Howard, and the lightest, three, for Hassan. Armbrecht received the longest sentence: twelve years, nine months.

Awan had already lied to the Senate subcommittee, claiming BCCI never laundered drug money. He had a history of backdating bank records, and he claimed during pretrial hearings that government agents had lied about him. Which, of course, they hadn't. Bilgrami on the other hand was less of a salesman, too flappable to lie convincingly.

Prison guards walked him into the interview room, dressed in an orange standard-issue prison uniform. Hatred burned in his eyes and on his face. He grunted faintly under his breath as he sat down next to his attorney, across from me, IRS Special Agent Orin Oakes, and prosecutor Andreas Rivera.

"I'm glad I'm going to have an opportunity to help you," I told him before we started. "I can promise you this: if you're completely truthful, I guarantee you I will vigorously request that the prosecutors in Tampa and Miami file motions for a reduction of sentence. But I'm also promising you that, if you attempt to mislead us, I'll do the exact opposite. I recognize this is a little awkward because I dealt with you for so long undercover, but I assure you none of what I've done or will do is personal. I'm just doing my job, and if you'll give me the opportunity, I'll do the right thing and make sure the court knows you've provided substantial assistance."

"Mr. Mazur, I have every intention of truthfully answering questions," he said formally. "Given what has occurred, I have no allegiance to the bank or anyone other than my family."

Oakes and I interviewed Bilgrami for seventeen days, spacing interviews out and using the days between sessions to pull records and corroborate what he had to say—and he said a lot.

Not long after Bilgrami started at the bank, the president, Agha Hasan Abedi, selected him to manage the investments of BCCI's major shareholder, Sheikh Zayed bin Sultan Al Nahyan, ruler of Abu Dhabi and founder of the United Arab Emirates. On the sheikh's behalf, Bilgrami and another BCCI officer managed billions hidden in Lichtenstein trusts that controlled Zayed's fortune around the globe.

After BCCI exploited all of the underground money they could find in the Middle and Far East, Abedi chose Bilgrami to head up a fact-finding group to explore the potential for BCCI's expansion into the western hemisphere.

"Identify the underground sectors from which we can grab deposits," Abedi had instructed him.

Bilgrami traveled through South America with Dr. Alberto Calvo, an Argentinean with decades of experience at the World Bank, hired as a consultant. They identified and spoke with bankers throughout the region and determined what BCCI needed to do to establish a bank and build a branch structure that capitalized on the needs of the underground economy in South America.

Bilgrami came to see South America as a reservoir holding at least $100 billion in flight capital—that is, money seeking secrecy. Whether for evading taxes, bypassing currency control laws, or avoiding inflationary losses in local currencies or funds tied to other crimes, a huge pool of South Americans wanted help hiding their wealth, and Bilgrami quickly learned that drug dealers and money launderers comprised the largest percentage of that group. He also learned that Miami was the best place to center an initiative to help South Americans, and that a bank centered there needed a supporting branch system in key areas like Grand Cayman, Luxembourg, Nassau, Panama, and Switzerland, countries with strict banking-secrecy laws.

After reviewing Bilgrami's findings, Abedi and BCCI's board sent him back to South America, with orders to establish BCCI's presence in several countries, including Colombia. To make this happen, BCCI hired as a consultant a former finance minister of Colombia. He submitted BCCI's application for a banking license to an immediate family member of Colombia's then president Julio César Turbay Ayala. When the process stalled, BCCI learned that this family member needed to be paid for his help. So BCCI began making $3,000-per-month "consulting" payments to one of the family member's close business associates. Two weeks after the first payment, BCCI's application for a banking license in Colombia received approval. Monthly payments to this business associate continued for another two years.

Then Bilgrami and the BCCI board turned their sights on the large but floundering Banco Mercantil in Colombia. Again, with the former finance minister's help, BCCI applied to Colombian authorities for purchase approval. When challenges arose, Abedi took action. With Bilgrami's help, he arranged a meeting with the Colombian president who succeeded Turbay, Belisario Betancur. As Abedi and Bilgrami were about to meet Betancur, Abedi told

Bilgrami to wait outside. An hour and a half later, Abedi emerged, announcing to Bilgrami that he had struck a deal. Once BCCI's purchase of Banco Mercantil was approved, the BCCI board would loan $100 million to Colombia for a coal project. But not one dime until Banco Mercantil was his.

The last hurdle in the Banco Mercantil acquisition was Colombia's requirement that BCCI own no more than 49 percent of the bank's stock. To circumvent this condition, BCCI funneled a "loan" from their Grand Cayman branch to the former finance minister, who then bought shares of Banco Mercantil on behalf of BCCI — problem solved.

BCCI knew how much they needed Colombian branches in order to find dirty deposits. They had spent hundreds of thousands of dollars to finance a study of the region and interviewed dozens of top bank executives from major banks, after which Abedi made a Zen pronouncement: "Colombia has a greater potential for dollar deposits than pesos. You must have a vision for the Americas. You must allow your imagination to expand and bring more deposits." And on the heels of that proclamation came the position of BCCI's board: "It is okay to take drug money because all banks do that." When BCCI officers asked Dildar Rizvi — BCCI's man in charge of their Colombian branches — about accepting deposits from dangerous sources, he said, "Just cover your ass."

The acquisition of Banco Mercantil instantly gave them 112 branches, including many throughout Medellín. BCCI also began greasing political and military powers in Panama, which allowed them to establish branches in Panama City and Colón. Panama readily used the U.S. dollar as local currency and put little or no restriction on the depositing of U.S. cash. And Colombian traffickers favored Panama as the place of choice for their deposits. BCCI eventually set up offices in Argentina, Brazil, Paraguay, Uruguay, and Venezuela, building a laundering machine that matched those of the best international banks.

Bilgrami rationalized this machine in the Americas by comparing it to what Brazilian, Colombian, German, Swiss, and U.S.

banks were already doing in the same region. He named each bank and explained their techniques. One Swiss bank routinely flew large shipments of gold bars into Colombia on a private jet, then sold the gold to Colombian traffickers for 15 percent above market price by exchanging it for trunkloads of U.S. dollars that the cartel had smuggled back to Colombia. To cover their trail, the Swiss flew the cash out of Colombia, quietly depositing it in accounts in branches in Panama and Switzerland.

BCCI quickly developed its Dollar Deposit Mobilization Program, a fancy term for getting deposits from any possible client, even drug dealers. They enlisted more than a hundred bank officers to participate — the inner team — and as the program matured they renamed it the External Marketplace Program (EMP). The initiative strove to educate South American customers of high net worth about the perks BCCI offered if they coughed up their money. Deposits could be used as hidden collateral for like-amount loans. Forms normally required by authorities would be withheld. Customers could open accounts in seventy-two countries by completing forms at their local branch. Bank officers could smuggle cash or checks to other parts of the world for deposit. Customers could establish manager's ledger accounts in Gibraltar, Grand Cayman, London, Nassau, and Panama. Customers could open numbered accounts in Switzerland and Luxembourg. The bank helped customers establish offshore shell corporations to front as the owners of accounts. The perks went on and on — and no one would know.

When agents raided BCCI Miami and Bilgrami's home, they found incriminating records documenting his long and close relationship with Daniel Manrique, a Bogotá-based trafficker who sold thousands of pounds of cocaine supplied by Juan Luís Castaño of the Medellín cartel. Manrique had a currency-exchange business in Bogotá as well as a thoroughbred horse farm and an investment company in Florida — all fronts for his drug empire, and Bilgrami knew it. With Bilgrami's help, Manrique opened BCCI accounts in Bogotá, Panama, Nassau, and Miami.

Bilgrami had also made many marketing trips to Colombia,

developing account relationships with cartel contacts like Paulyna de Quintero in Barranquilla, a rotund, blond launderer for Escobar and Ochoa who controlled hundreds of millions of dollars for her bosses. Taken by jeep to Quintero's home, Bilgrami and another bank officer passed several guards holding Uzi machine guns and found that she had converted one of the bedrooms into an office, where, at her desk and a bank of phones, she fielded calls from dozens of underlings collecting the cartel's fortune each day. In a corner of the office, a dispatcher operated a shortwave radio, communicating to workers around the world.

After Bilgrami introduced himself, Quintero shrugged. "What special services can you offer? We have so many bankers visiting us, trying to get us to deposit with their bank."

Bilgrami offered her a 1.5 percent under-the-table commission on all deposits with any branch in the world. She thought for a second and suggested he return the next day. When he did, Quintero explained that most of the money she sent to BCCI would have to be moved quickly through their system to other banks, but in time her bosses would allow as much as $50 million to be left on deposit.

"Fifty million is no big deal," she said, "because they deal in hundreds of millions all the time."

When Bilgrami reported on his meeting with Quintero and her job with Pablo Escobar, his bosses were thrilled. They repeatedly asked him to forge a stronger relationship. He dutifully called her time and again, as he and the rest of the BCCI marketing team aggressively did with dozens of other drug dealers and money launderers.

According to Bilgrami, Carlos A. Gaviria V. managed money for *los duros* at BCCI. Later, when an article published in the Colombian paper *El Tiempo* linked Gaviria to Pablo Escobar, it was like throwing blood to sharks, sending BCCI bankers into an even greater frenzy to do business with him. Using a front Panamanian company named Nolexand, Bilgrami and his team helped Gaviria place millions of dollars with BCCI in Boca Raton, London, Switzerland, New York, and Medellín.

Not only did José Gonzalo Rodríguez Gacha —*El Mexicano*— have nearly $40 million at BCCI Luxembourg, one of his key money launderers, Mauricio Vives Carrillo, had another $20 million at BCCI branches in places like Hong Kong, London, and Panama. Not to mention the $60 million deposited in accounts at Merrill Lynch, Lehman Brothers, and the London branch of Nomura Securities. Like me, Vives established a sophisticated front offering plausible deniability to any banker caught dealing with him. But there was no denying it. Any seasoned international banker would know exactly what Vives really did for a living.

Another marketer, Wilfredo Glasse in BCCI Colón, feverishly sought deposits from cartel members, including Don Chepe. Unbeknownst to me, Glasse had signed up Moncada and his underlings as BCCI account holders more than two years before I met my first BCCI officer.

The executive board at BCCI fueled the EMP program with perks to bank employees who brought in big accounts, often in the form of six-figure loans that never had to be repaid. The men at the top did everything they could to catch up to the other international banks already on the scene, and their zeal brought on their demise.

Awan, unlike Bilgrami, had something the government needed: the complete story of Noriega's banking activities with BCCI. Only he knew those details, and interviewing him was like wrestling a snake. Questioned into a corner, he tried to slip away from the truth. After grappling for the better part of eight days, we got as much as he was willing to give.

He had managed Noriega's accounts since the day they were opened. Tens of millions arrived at the Panama City branch in suitcases. Either Awan picked up the cases directly from Noriega, or loyal officers in the Panamanian Defense Forces delivered as much as $3.4 million at a time. Those details proved devastating not only for Noriega, but they also implicated senior BCCI officials and Ziauddin Akbar.

After they learned of Noriega's indictment in a massive drug-trafficking conspiracy, bank senior management helped him dig a deeper hole to hide his money by transferring it from London to Luxembourg. Later, when Noriega grew concerned the U.S. would find his fortune there, Awan moved the funds to Capcom, where Akbar laundered it, trying to prevent its seizure. Awan's testimony offered a cornerstone for a second indictment of Ziauddin and a first-time indictment of his former bosses at BCCI, including bank president Swaleh Naqvi.

In the midst of wrapping up the debriefing of Awan, my phone rang.

"Headquarters has approved your application," Mike Powers said, "and they're prepared to meet the two requests you made. You'll remain in Tampa for five years, and you won't have to take a cut in pay. I don't have a reporting date for you yet, but I should have that soon."

Time to move on.

I submitted a resignation letter to von Raab's replacement, Commissioner Carol Hallett, which railed against the unethical and illegal disclosures to the media repeatedly made by Customs leadership. I urged an impartial review of the inadequate resources applied to the case and offered to provide details prior to my departure. No one ever responded.

Before I left, Nazir Chinoy flew from London to Tampa in chains. He wanted no part of a trial and quickly agreed to cooperate. He really had no choice — Awan, Bilgrami, Hassan, and Howard had already been convicted and looked likely to testify against him for the prosecution. And then, of course, there were those damning tape recordings of conversations with me in Paris.

When Chinoy finally sang, it condemned his fellow board members. The bank's mission was to gain power in the financial community by gathering deposits from every corner of the underworld. They laundered money, bribed regulators, corrupted politicians, financed arms dealers, and even provided prostitutes for favored customers.

Awan, Bilgrami, Chinoy, and other bankers offered enough evidence to justify new cases against the entire BCCI board. Our operation had caused a fatal crack in the foundation of the bank. Tongues were wagging, and other agencies began to reap benefits from our five years of work. Investigators from the Federal Reserve, the New York District Attorney's office, and John Kerry's subcommittee all gained access to the convicted bankers, who provided road maps for prosecutions. Despite all that heat, though, we lost a lot of valuable time and leads because we never had enough experienced people to comb through the warehouse of records.

After reporting to DEA Tampa, I was out on the street a night or two later with the entire office, helping with raids and arrests in Tampa's biggest cocaine seizure to date. A few weeks later, they shipped me to the DEA academy in Quantico where I joined about forty other recruits. Despite my twenty-year lead on most of them, my classmates welcomed me with open arms and even voted me class representative—their voice to the instructors who tortured us every day.

Basic training for the Army had prepared me. We wore fatigues and spent our days training physically, handling firearms, and doing classwork. For the first month, instructors screamed at us just like recruits in any boot camp, and I took every moment seriously. If I washed out, I'd have no more options in the government, and I'd lose my pension. Everything was going fine until an old friend called.

"I want to give you a heads-up about something brewing in Washington," said Lynn Cole, a former federal prosecutor. "I just got off the phone with our mutual buddy Eleanor Hill. Since Eleanor left the U.S. Attorney's office in Tampa she has become the chief counsel to the Senate's permanent subcommittee on investigations. She has contact with other subcommittees and is close to people on John Kerry's staff. She got wind that Customs is in the process of doing a hatchet job on you. They're being pressed by Kerry's people to explain why they ended your undercover operation when they did, why they didn't put more resources on the case after it broke, and why you resigned. Kerry's people have a copy of your resignation letter. I hate to be the one to tell you this, but Customs is blaming you."

I almost fell over.

"*Me?* That's the biggest bunch of bullshit I've ever heard, and they know it!"

"They're going to claim that they had no choice but to end the undercover operation and then pull back resources because you had lost it mentally. They're accusing you of being the leak that led to the recent exposé about Capcom done by the national network news, and they claim that your going to the media is further proof that you've gone off the deep end."

"I've been here at the academy for more than a month, and I haven't had time to even think about Customs or BCCI. For them to claim that I'd lost it is absurd. Protocol required me to undergo psychological evaluations, and those showed no indication of any issues. They've given me the highest evaluations possible for the past five years, plus awards and bonuses for outstanding performance. They know damn well why they ended that operation when they did — it was all political. *They* fed this case to the media, and *they* got pissed when I called them on it. As far as the lack of resources is concerned, I wrote more than a dozen memos explaining the crisis they were creating by cutting resources for the operation, and most of those were ignored. Plus, there are internal memos in the Department of Justice confirming all of this."

"I can tell you now," Cole said, "that they've thought this out. How much do you want to bet they did a file review recently, and your memos no longer exist?"

"That's fine; I'm not an idiot. There are copies of each of those memos in a safe place. If I'm called to testify, I'll have them with me."

"I'm getting pressure to dump on you," Dan Dunn told me when I called him, "but I promise you I'm not lying for anyone. If it wasn't for what you and a handful of other agents did on these cases, this whole thing would have been a disaster. You can count on me to tell the truth, and Steve Cook will do the same. No one is going to bully us."

"You don't know how proud I am to call you my friend," I said. "I suspect I'll be contacted here at Quantico by investigators for Kerry's subcommittee. When they come, I'll be ready."

Not long after, Tony Wilson, assistant special agent in charge at the academy, yanked me out of class. "We've had a formal request from a Senate subcommittee asking to have access to you to answer questions about a Customs matter. We're working it out through headquarters, but I suspect they'll be here in a few days to interview you. What the hell is going on?"

I explained everything.

"Okay, just don't do anything to embarrass our agency, and, as long as you carried yourself honorably, everything will be fine."

"I assure you, sir, there'll be no surprises. I just did my job."

For the next couple of weeks, Wilson pulled me out of class every few days so investigators could interview me. First came Rosenblatt's replacement, John Hensley, the new assistant commissioner of enforcement, and his staff, the new blood leading Customs. When it came to the issue of credible resources being withheld from our operation, I told them about my more than a dozen memos.

They looked surprised.

"I have copies of each memo," I continued, "as well as memos from the U.S. Attorney's office acknowledging my attempt to get help. Here's a copy of them. It doesn't surprise me that you've never seen them before."

Their predecessors, I explained, had put the lives of the undercover agents at risk, making repeated disclosures to national media. I gave them dates, names, and details no one could walk away from.

Next came the counsel and investigators from Senator Kerry's subcommittee on terrorism, narcotics, and international operations, along with a phalanx of lawyers and staffers representing Customs. Our discussion mirrored my session with Hensley and his staff. They, too, took the discussion seriously and made it clear that they wanted me to appear before the subcommittee in open session.

Then representatives from Congressman Charles Schumer's office at the subcommittee on crime and criminal justice took their turn.

The fruits of our labor after the Tampa trial paid off before I graduated from the academy. Prosecutors were charging six more BCCI executives with laundering for Medellín and Noriega. Ziauddin Akbar got wind of another indictment, so he fled from London to Pakistan. Authorities caught him in France. That indictment also charged Swaleh Naqvi, president of BCCI, four other bank executives, and five high-ranking members of the Medellín cartel, including Gerardo Moncada — aka Don Chepe.

And then it was time to graduate.

As class representative, I had the honor of giving a commencement speech. I'd been in the game for almost twenty years; I knew exactly what these kids were facing.

"It's not an easy life we have chosen," I said. "There will be substantial sacrifices we will have to endure together in the future. There will be many missed birthday parties, many lonely nights away from home, many long phone calls in the middle of the night to the people we love the most, many cups of coffee while on twenty-four-hour surveillances, and many potential threats to our lives, which we will overcome. But despite these sacrifices, we know that we will prevail because we have each other and your relentless support."

Senator Kerry wanted me to know the bottom line. He saw me as a hero, and he didn't want to pull any punches or surprises. He gave me a full copy of the exhibits he would ask me to comment about the following day. He didn't have time to get into details, but he could easily have spent days talking with me about the issues that drove his passion.

The next day, I testified from behind a screen with a distortion microphone. For hours, Kerry and other senators put questions to me.

In the end, Kerry made some very pointed observations. "Customs management placed at potential risk a critically important investigation and possibly the lives of the agents involved, for the purpose of obtaining favorable publicity.... Mazur's willingness to press on in the face of threats to his life gave the U.S. government the evidence necessary to begin the prosecution of BCCI, highly placed Colombian drug lords, and money launderers.... I wish to express my personal admiration for Robert Mazur, who not only took the lead undercover role, but fought valiantly against the bureaucratic difficulties which he found were undermining his ability to make the kind of case against BCCI he wanted to make, and wish him good luck in further endeavors."

The biggest bomb of all dropped a month to the day after my testimony before Kerry's subcommittee. BCCI entered into a joint agreement with the Department of Justice and the New York District Attorney's Office, pleading guilty both to federal racketeering charges and a New York State indictment. It agreed to forfeit its $550 million in U.S. assets, to pay a $200 million fine to the Federal Reserve, and to dismantle its corporate presence throughout the world. The government officially and permanently banned it from operating in the U.S. Not long after, the bank collapsed entirely, and account holders around the world lost hundreds of millions of dollars.

"Bob, come in here for a minute," Mike Powers said as I walked back into the DEA office, wondering where my new career would take me. "Some informants will be coming to Tampa next week. They have very detailed information about some lawyers and bankers in Panama that are servicing the Cali cartel in Colombia. I've talked this over with our people in Miami and Washington. We'd like you to develop a new identity and go back undercover for a couple of years. We'll give you all the resources you need to do this right. You'll need to spend a good amount of time in Panama, and you'll need a sophisticated front in the States. What do you say?"

"It's tempting," I said. "There are a lot of things that could have been done better in the BCCI operation, and I'd love a second chance."

As we talked, I considered the risks. Cali and Medellín lie a few hundred miles apart. The cartels were fighting each other, and the odds of running into anyone from my BCCI days were slim. Plus, I'd changed my appearance considerably — even my own kids hadn't recognized me.

"Well, what do you think?" he said.

"Count me in."

Back to the cemetery to find my next undercover life.

Less than a year later, I was ready to infiltrate once more. It was starting again.

What happened next almost got me killed — but that's another story.

Epilogue

THE AFTERMATH

Regine's nightclub, Miami
2:00 A.M., September 3, 1988

As our night on the town was coming to a close and Scotch had loosened Bilgrami's tongue, he said, "Bob, do you know who the biggest money launderer is in the U.S.?"

"Who?" I shrugged, smiling.

"The Federal Reserve Bank. They are such hypocrites! They know that the Bank of the Republic in Bogotá has a teller window known as 'the sinister window.' Under Colombian rule, any citizen who has huge piles of cash can come to that window and anonymously exchange their U.S. dollars for Colombian pesos — no questions asked. This causes the central bank to accumulate palletloads of U.S. dollars that are shipped to the Federal Reserve and credited to the account of the Bank of the Republic — again, no questions asked. The people at the Federal Reserve aren't idiots. They see this river of hundreds of millions in U.S. dollars being shipped to them from Colombia. They know what generates that cash. That's drug money that has been smuggled from the U.S. and Europe to Colombia. The Federal Reserve takes that because it's good economics for this country's banking system. The Americans' so-called War on Drugs is a sham."

I was floored. If this was true, why were we risking our lives?

Later research confirmed Bilgrami's claim, and I had never felt more betrayed. For the first time, I questioned whether we'd been naive to think we could make a difference.

BCCI got caught. Only that detail separates them from the rest of the international banking community. They've been out of the game for twenty years. The drug trade has produced about $500 billion per year since then, but no one has been prosecuted for laundering those $10 trillion.

Operation C-Chase took a different approach from the normal one. C-Chase worked because we did the unexpected. No one before had simultaneously established a sophisticated, verifiable front within the financial community and the drug world, becoming a middleman for both. No other undercover operation before had offered a well-designed money-laundering scheme to the cartel with the unwitting assistance of international bankers, a plan that drew important men from the underworld out of the shadows. A litmus test for the private-client divisions of international banks, C-Chase enabled us to hear voices in boardrooms and behind closed doors speaking candidly about the acceptability of drug money — not leaving us to rely on duplicitous policy statements or deceitful public speeches. It proved twenty years ago that the banking community is incapable of monitoring itself — and unwilling; the lure of money is just too strong. Regulations and forms can't measure character, and the private-client divisions of international banks will always find a way through or around them.

No one in our government or any other country's government wants to test the integrity of the financial community anymore. I continue to interact with and train thousands of law-enforcement officers throughout the U.S. Their hands are tied. Bureaucrats have established regulations obstructing anyone from doing what we did. When hearing this story, most agents say, "If I did that today, they'd put me in jail. We'll never get the chance to do that — but we should."

The greatest weakness the drug trade has is banking relationships. Each dirty banker serves dozens of big-time traffickers, but those bankers don't have the stomach to sit in prison for life. That's the best weakness we can exploit and attack. I only hope that someone someday will think about that.

Life has changed for the players in this story, but little has changed in the world of international drug trafficking. It's like men's ties. Some years they're wider, some years they're thinner, but they're all still ties. As long as a demand exists, the underworld will make adjustments to maximize its profits. Colombian cartels less frequently bring cocaine to your neighborhood. Instead, they've become mass producers, feeding hundreds of tons of it to Mexican cartels that have taken on a bigger role moving it across the border and distributing it to the never-ending glut of consumers in the U.S. The men in Medellín and Cali know that Mexican corruption will always ensure safe transport. What happens after that isn't their problem. But billions of dirty dollars still flow back and forth, and the same banks are still washing untold wealth.

Intelligence sources in Colombia and Pakistan have revealed the following reliable (though unverified) information:

Ziauddin Akbar served only six months of his eighteen-month sentence for laundering drug money I passed to him because he was granted a bond while his case was on appeal. During the pendency of that appeal, he was indicted again in the U.S., this time for laundering Noriega's money. Hearing of the new charges, he attempted to flee to Pakistan but was arrested in France and imprisoned for two years in Europe, while he fought extradition. He was indicted a third time, in the U.K., for masterminding the pilfering of BCCI's treasury of £512 million, then the biggest fraud case ever brought before a British court. He pled guilty to the charges and served another two years in prison. On completion of his sentence, American authorities attempted to extradite him. But there was speculation that his contacts in the intelligence community exerted their influence. U.K. authorities released him, and he fled back to Pakistan. He has never returned to the States to face either of the two federal money laundering indictments brought against him in Tampa. Those cases were dismissed in 1999 and 2006, preventing Akbar from ever being tried here for those offenses. In Pakistan, he became a member of that country's stock exchange.

Roberto Alcaíno, while serving his fifteen-year prison sentence, met other federal inmates who were international drug traffickers and money launderers, including Boris Nayfeld, a longtime associate of Ricardo Fanchini, one of the highest-ranking members of Russian organized crime in Europe. In June 2003, Nayfeld and Alcaíno began planning the movement of tons of cocaine and tens of millions in drug proceeds around the globe for the Russian mob. Their alliance spanned South America, the U.K., Belgium, Poland, Russia, and the Far East. DEA agents arrested Alcaíno and his mafia associates in October 2007.

Rudolf Armbrecht served his sentence and was deported to Colombia. He relocated to Germany — where authorities had seized millions of dollars from accounts maintained on his and Moncada's behalf by Armbrecht's uncle Jürgen Moeller, an officer at Commerzbank. Armbrecht travels often to South America, and German authorities suspect that he may have resumed a role in international drug trafficking.

Amjad Awan was deported to Pakistan after serving his prison sentence. He is said to be living in Dubai at the posh Marina Jumeirah Beach Towers. He travels frequently to Africa, Pakistan, and East Asia on unknown business.

Akbar Bilgrami was also deported to Pakistan after prison. He is believed to live in the affluent Clifton / Defence Housing Authority area of Karachi, Pakistan. He dabbles in the stock market and provides consulting work to the financial sector.

Nazir Chinoy, after serving his sentence, was also deported to Pakistan, where he is believed to live in Bath Island, Karachi. He sat on the boards of directors of several publicly traded companies, but in recent years his health has deteriorated. His businesses and wealth are said to be managed by his children.

Fernando Galeano managed half of Pablo Escobar's cocaine routes and in July 1992 Escobar had him hung from his feet and tortured to death with a blowtorch.

Sibte Hassan served his sentence and was deported to Pakistan by the time the court of appeals heard a motion filed by his counsel to overturn his jury conviction on the basis that the evidence presented by the government was insufficient to sustain the jury's guilty verdict. The court of appeals closely examined the evidence—the recorded conversation he had with Emir—and ruled in Hassan's favor.

Khairi Kalashol, one of Moncada's primary buyers in Detroit, found new suppliers after authorities arrested the Giraldo brothers. He continued to flood the streets of the Motor City with drugs and to reign as the boss of Detroit's Chaldean mafia until February 3, 1989, when he was gunned down in retribution for murders he had committed.

Don Chepe turned out to be Gerardo Moncada, a university graduate and industrial engineer managing half of Pablo Escobar's cocaine shipping routes. Despite his 1991 C-Chase indictment, Moncada continued to pump more than four tons of cocaine per month into New York, while operating simultaneously in almost every major American city. In 1992—after Escobar learned that Moncada had hidden a mountain of money in a Medellín home to evade Escobar's efforts to finance a war against the Colombian government and its efforts to establish an extradition treaty with the U.S.—Escobar summoned Moncada and his brother to "the Cathedral," the plush, self-built prison where Escobar was being held. According to Moncada's wife, Escobar and his bodyguards hanged the Moncadas from their feet and tortured them both to death with a blowtorch.

Gonzalo Mora, after serving his prison sentence, was deported to Colombia and returned to Medellín. He is believed to be back in the business.

Swaleh Naqvi fled to Abu Dhabi prior to his indictment and avoided prosecution for several years. As a result of a deal struck in 1994 between the U.S. and Sheik Zayed bin Sultan al-Nahyan, Naqvi was extradited to the U.S., where he pled guilty and served five years in prison and paid a $255.4 million restitution.

Javier Ospiña escaped arrest by staying in Colombia, but he faced other perils there. Escobar's declaration of war against the families and associates of Galeano and Moncada put Ospiña's life in jeopardy. Thinking he could never be extradited, the government dismissed the indictment. His fate is unknown.

Saad Shafi was at his home in Coral Gables, Florida, at the time of the takedown. Agents never looked for him there, thinking he was in his office at BCCI Nassau. When he learned of his indictment, he fled to Pakistan. Because prosecutors couldn't extradite him, they dismissed his indictment in September 1999. Shafi promptly returned to the U.S. and resumed his banking career. He established residence in Anaheim, California, and was employed as the manager of the Los Angeles branch of Habib American Bank, an affiliate of Habib Bank, Pakistan's largest bank, which claims to offer "the highest levels of honesty and integrity." Due to the publication of this book, ABC News learned that Shafi was a bank manager in LA and confronted him with cameras and a reporter as he left his office. After ABC's exposé about Shafi's past, Senator Charles Schumer, a member of the U.S. Senate Banking Committee, called for U.S. regulators to prevent Shafi from participating in banking. He is no longer employed by Habib American Bank.

Juan Tobón served a portion of his prison sentence but escaped before completing his sentence. He fled to Colombia, but was arrested on a fugitive warrant in 2013 as he attempted to cross the border from Peru to Colombia.

Santiago Uribe Ortiz escaped arrest by staying in Colombia, which then had a nonextradition arrangement with the U.S. In 1992, Colombian authorities raided a farm owned by Uribe in Llano Grande, where they found letters from Escobar and other evidence linking him to drug trafficking, bribery, and murder. Because they didn't want to maintain the paperwork on Uribe's open indictment, the Department of Justice dismissed all charges against him in November 2006, which automatically precludes the government from ever bringing those same charges against him again. Uribe now maintains a low profile in El Retiro, a small town near Medellín, where he practices law representing private companies and local government institutions.

Emir Abreu continued to work as an undercover agent for Customs for more than ten years after C-Chase. An adjunct professor at a Florida college, he has trained thousands of law-enforcement officers, primarily in Puerto Rico.

Steve Cook was transferred to the U.S. embassy in Bonn, West Germany, shortly after the conclusion of the BCCI trials, continuing to focus on international money-laundering cases. He is now employed by a defense contractor in Iraq.

Kathy Ertz continued as a special agent for another fifteen years, focusing on international money-laundering investigations. Since her retirement, she has provided anti–money laundering compliance services to financial institutions.

Mark Jackowski in 1995 was appointed a prosecutor with the Office of the Independent Counsel investigating former Housing and Urban Development secretary Henry Cisneros. Retired from government service, he practices law with a firm in Cleveland, Ohio.

William Rosenblatt retired as assistant commissioner of Customs, Office of Investigations, and became a card dealer at a Seminole Hard Rock Casino in Florida.

Bonni Tischler's career stagnated after a scathing finding about her conduct in the BCCI affair by Senator Kerry's subcommittee, but it revived quickly when she became assistant commissioner of Customs, Office of Investigations, overseeing all Customs special agents here and abroad. She later assumed a similar position supervising Customs inspectors worldwide. On retirement, she was named vice president for global transportation and supply-chain security at Pinkerton. In August 2005, she lost a long battle wth breast cancer.

William von Raab's supporters in Congress, including Senator Jesse Helms, led a delegation in August 1989 to President George H. W. Bush, urging that he name von Raab drug czar — or at least reward him with an ambassadorship. Their request was declined. Instead, Treasury secretary Nicholas Brady forced von Raab out of office. As he left, von Raab claimed the administration's War on Drugs was "a war on words," adding that it wasn't a priority for Congress or the White House. A 1991 *National Journal* article reported that von Raab registered as a foreign agent on behalf of a Swiss export-inspection firm. The prior foreign government agent for this Swiss firm was Robert Gray from Hill & Knowlton, the same public relations firm that represented BCCI.

GLOSSARY OF NAMES

Agha Hasan Abedi: founder and first president of the Bank of Credit and Commerce International (BCCI).

Emir Abreu: U.S. Customs undercover agent. AKA Emilio Dominguez.

Kamal Adham: BCCI shareholder, former chief of Saudi Arabia's General Intelligence Directorate, and brother-in-law of King Faisal of Saudi Arabia.

Ziauddin Akbar: treasurer of BCCI, who, later, with backing from Saudi investors, established Capcom, a group of financial service and brokerage companies, that laundered drug money for Manuel Noriega and others.

Gloria Alcaíno: wife of Roberto Alcaíno.

Roberto Alcaíno: cocaine transporter for Fabio Ochoa and other members of the Medellín cartel.

Robert Altman: attorney and partner, with former secretary of Defense Clark Clifford, Clifford and Warnke law firm. Altman represented BCCI and sat on the board of BCCI's U.S. affiliate, First American Bank.

Rick Argudo: officer at BCCI Tampa.

Rudolf Armbrecht: operative of the Medellín cartel entrusted to evaluate money-laundering plans and other major projects.

Iqbal Ashraf: officer at BCCI Los Angeles.

Rosanna Aspitre: paramour of Amjad Awan.

Adella Asqui: Customs undercover agent who played the role of one of Emir Abreu's girlfriends.

Millie Aviles: Customs undercover agent who played the role of one of Emir Abreu's girlfriends.

Amjad Awan: BCCI Miami officer assigned to the bank's Latin American division who personally handled the bank's relationship with Manuel Noriega.

Ayub Awan: former head of the Pakistan Police Force, former director of Pakistan's Inter-Services Intelligence, and father of Amjad Awan.

Asif Baakza: officer at BCCI London.

Banco de Occidente: Colombian bank with branches in Panama.

Bank of Credit and Commerce International (BCCI): seventh-largest privately owned bank in the late 1980s.

Banque de Commerce et de Placements (BCP): Swiss bank partially owned by BCCI.

George Barbar: multimillionaire Lebanese businessman based in Boca Raton and a client of BCCI, affiliated with Jeb Bush.

Jim Barrow: FBI agent stationed in Tampa.

Ernie Batista: DEA agent assigned to Buenos Aires.

Akbar Bilgrami: BCCI Miami officer assigned to the bank's Latin American division.

Jack Blum: chief counsel to Senator John Kerry and the U.S. Senate subcommittee on terrorism, narcotics, and international relations.

Charlie Broun: convicted drug-money launderer with ties to Las Vegas casinos.

Bruno Securities: Manhattan brokerage firm used as a fake front.

Dave Burris: special agent with IRS Criminal Investigation Division stationed in Tampa.

George H. W. Bush: forty-first president of the U.S.

George W. Bush: forty-third president of the U.S.

Jeb Bush: son of President George H. W. Bush and later governor of Florida.

Alberto Calvo: Argentinean banker employed by BCCI as a consultant to evaluate the South American money market.

Enrique Camarena: DEA agent murdered in Mexico by drug traffickers.

Capcom: a group of financial service and brokerage companies established by Ziauddin Akbar that laundered drug money for Manuel Noriega and others.

Tony Carpinello: IRS group supervisor stationed in Manhattan.

Jimmy Carter: thirty-ninth president of the U.S.

Joaquín Casals: Roberto Alcaíno's right-hand man.

William Casey: director of the CIA during the Reagan administration.

Juan Luís Castaño: drug trafficker aligned with the Medellín cartel.

Joseph Cefaro: my grandfather. AKA "Two Beers."

Ralph Cefaro: my great-grandfather, who ran a sham moving company on Manhattan's Lower East Side to transport bootleg whiskey during Prohibition for Lucky Luciano.

Pedro Charria: manager of Gerardo Moncada's operations in the northeast U.S.

Azizulah Chaudhry: general manager of Banque de Commerce et de Placements, based in Geneva and partially owned by BCCI.

Nelson Chen: Customs undercover agent in Manhattan. AKA "Chino."

Nazir Chinoy: regional manager of BCCI branches in Europe and North Africa.

Clark Clifford: former secretary of defense under President Lyndon Johnson; founding partner of Clifford and Warnke law firm, which represented BCCI; and chairman of First American Bank, a U.S. affiliate of BCCI.

Lynn Cole: former assistant U.S. attorney based in Tampa.

Steve Cook: Customs group supervisor based in Tampa.

George Corcoran: assistant commissioner of enforcement for Customs.

José Cordero: Customs undercover agent based in Tampa.

Paulyna de Quintero: launderer for the Medellín cartel based in Cartagena, Colombia.

Thomas Dewey: former U.S. attorney who spearheaded the prosecution of Lucky Luciano.

Carlos Díaz: Roberto Alcaíno's partner in operating a Buenos Aires anchovy packing plant as a front used to transport cocaine for the Medellín cartel to the U.S. and Europe.

Emilio Dominguez: see Emir Abreu.

Dominic: government informant and adviser.

Jack Dubard: convicted drug-money launderer and partner with Charles Broun in laundering funds for drug trafficker Bruce Perlowin.

Daniel Dunn: Customs group supervisor based in Tampa.

los duros: "the strong ones," code for the leaders of the Medellín cartel.

Dynamic Mortgage Brokers: undercover front company used to launder funds for drug traffickers.

Kathy Ertz: Customs undercover agent, playing the role of my girlfriend and fiancée. AKA Kathy Erickson.

Pablo Escobar: head of the Medellín cartel.

Samuel Escruceria: Colombian congressman involved with Roberto Alcaíno in drug trafficking.

Matt Etre: Customs agent in Miami.

los feos: "the ugly ones," code for U.S. federal agents.

Jean Figali: drug trafficker and money launderer aligned with the Medellín cartel. AKA John Nasser.

Financial Consulting: undercover front company used to launder funds for drug traffickers.

First American Bank: U.S. bank based in Washington, D.C., and secretly owned by BCCI.

Frankie: government informant and adviser

Urs Frei: Swiss magistrate and prosecutor.

Fernando Galeano: Pablo Escobar's associate entrusted, along with Gerardo Moncada, to operate Escobar's empire during the late 1980s.

Joe Gallo: member of the Profaci-Colombo crime family whacked at Umberto's Clam Bar in Little Italy in 1972.

José Gonzalo Rodríguez Gacha: a member of the Medellín cartel and Clara Tobón's uncle.

Jaime Giraldo: primary distributor of cocaine in Detroit, working with Gerardo Moncada for the Medellín cartel.

Norberto Giraldo: Jaime's brother, who also distributed cocaine in Detroit.

Rudy Giuliani: U.S. attorney in New York during Operation C-Chase.

Wilfredo Glasse: BCCI Colón officer in Panama.

Jim Glotfelty: Customs special agent in Detroit.

Harold Greenberg: one of several defense attorneys in California representing Roberto Alcaíno.

Leon Guinn: southeast regional commissioner of Customs.

Sibte Hassan: BCCI Paris officer.

Jesse Helms: U.S. senator from North Carolina and mentor to Commissioner von Raab.

Al Henley: DEA special agent in Tampa.

John Hensley: assistant commissioner of enforcement for Customs who succeeded William Rosenblatt.

Eleanor Hill: assistant U.S. attorney in Tampa, who became chief counsel to the Senate's permanent subcommittee on investigations.

Joe Hinton: IRS special agent in Manhattan who trained undercover agents.

Terrell Hodges: U.S. District Court judge in Tampa, who presided over the trial of BCCI officers and Rudolf Armbrecht.

James Hogan: Miami criminal defense attorney, who defended Syed Hussain.

Ian Howard: BCCI Paris officer.

Marta Cecilia Carvajal Hoyas: one of Alcaíno's girlfriends, who both supplied and distributed cocaine.

John Hume: defense attorney representing Amjad Awan in the Tampa trial.

José Hurtado: Chicago buyer of cocaine from Tuto Zabala and Roberto Alcaíno.

Pepe Hurtado: Chicago buyer of cocaine from Tuto Zabala and Roberto Alcaíno.

Syed Aftab Hussain: BCCI Panama City officer.

Lee Iacocca: CEO of the Chrysler Corporation.

Jessie Ibarra. Customs agent stationed in Los Angeles. AKA "Chewie."

IDC International: undercover front company in Panama used to launder funds for drug traffickers.

Mark Jackowski: assistant U.S. attorney in Tampa who provided legal consultation during Operation C-Chase and handled the criminal trials in Tampa.

Dieter Jann: examining magistrate for mutual assistance in criminal matters for the Canton of Zürich in Switzerland.

Craig Jantz: high school and college friend, and a broker at Merrill Lynch in Manhattan.

Linda Kadluboski: Customs undercover agent in New York who played the role of one of Emir Abreu's girlfriends. AKA Linda Kane.

Khairi Kalashol: head of Iraqi-based Chaldean mafia in Detroit in the late 1980s.

Stephen Kalish: drug trafficker in Tampa introduced to BCCI by Manuel Noriega.

Adnan Khashoggi: billionaire Saudi arms dealer and a BCCI client.

John Kerry: U.S. senator from Massachusetts who chaired the sub-committee on terrorism, narcotics, and international operations.

Bill King: assistant U.S. attorney in Tampa.

Joe Ladow: assistant special agent in charge of the Customs office in Tampa.

Bert Lance: former director of the Office of Management and Budget under President Jimmy Carter.

Brian Loader: FBI special agent in Washington, D.C., overseeing undercover operations.

Tommy Loreto: Customs group supervisor overseeing the New York portion of Operation C-Chase.

Frank Lucas: major heroin trafficker based in New York City.

Charlie Luciano: first head of the Genovese crime family and considered the father of the Sicilian mafia in America. AKA Salvatore Lucania.

John Luksic: Customs special agent assigned to the embassy in London.

Tony Macisco: Customs undercover agent in Chicago.

Franz Maissen: Banque de Commerce et de Placements officer in Geneva.

Robert Mangione: one of my undercover identities.

Daniel Manrique: Colombian in Boca Raton distributing cocaine supplied by the Medellín cartel and a BCCI client.

Eduardo Martinez Romero: chief lieutenant and financial adviser to members of the Medellín cartel, including Gerardo Moncada, and one of my laundering competitors. AKA *El Costeño Mama Burra*, "Donkey-Fucker from the North Coast."

George Meros: prominent attorney in St. Petersburg, Florida, convicted of laundering millions in drug proceeds for Florida-based drug traffickers.

Conrad Milan: Customs undercover agent assigned to Los Angeles.

Dayne Miller: BCCI Tampa officer.

Mike Miller: Customs agent in Tampa.

La Mina: a group of Argentinean money launderers, with offices in Los Angeles and New York City, who serviced the Medellín cartel through fraudulent precious metals transactions.

Saul Mineroff: president of Mineroff Electronics, a supplier of electronic equipment to U.S. government agencies.

Luís Carlos Molina: major money launderer for the Medellín cartel.

Gerardo Moncada: one of two members of the Medellín cartel entrusted by Pablo Escobar to manage cocaine routes in the late 1980s. Moncada reported directly to Escobar. AKA Don Chepe.

Gonzalo Mora: money broker for the Medellín cartel.

Jaime Mora: Gonzalo's brother, who distributed cocaine in Miami and Los Angeles for Roberto Alcaíno and the Medellín cartel.

Lucy Mora: Gonzalo's wife.

Craig Morgan: Customs undercover pilot.

Larry Mulkerns: assistant special agent in charge in Tampa, reporting to Bonni Tischler.

Robert Musella: one of my undercover identities.

Swaleh Naqvi: BCCI executive who succeeded Agha Hasan Abedi as president.

John Nasser: See Jean Figali.

Richard Nixon: thirty-seventh president of the U.S.

Manuel Noriega: military leader of Panama in the late 1980s.

Oliver North: Marine Corps lieutenant-colonel involved in the Iran-Contra arms scandal.

Orin Oakes: IRS special agent assigned to Tampa.

Paul O'Brien: Customs group supervisor in Tampa at the start of Operation C-Chase.

Fabio Ochoa Restrepo: Patriarch of the Ochoa crime family in Colombia. Father of Jorge Ochoa Vazquez, Juan David Ochoa Vazquez and Fabio Ochoa Vazquez, three notorious leaders within the Medellín Cartel.

Fabio Ochoa Vazquez: the youngest of Fabio Ochoa Restrepo's three sons. He, his brothers, and father were all sitting members of the Medellín cartel. He partnered with Roberto Alcaíno to import cocaine into the U.S. AKA Fabito.

Guillermo Ochoa: a relative of the Ochoa Vazquez family who attended the University of Medellín with Gonzalo Mora.

Jorge Ochoa Vazquez: another of Fabio Ochoa Restrepo's three sons.

Operation C-Chase: code name of the undercover Customs operation that brought down BCCI.

Operation Greenback: joint Customs and IRS task force in Florida in the early 1980s that targeted drug-money launderers.

Operation Pisces: DEA undercover operation based in Miami in 1987 that resulted in indictments of high-level drug traffickers and money launderers in Colombia.

Bentley Orrick: *Tampa Tribune* reporter who broke the news of my undercover identity.

Javier Ospiña: drug money broker for Gerardo Moncada and Fernando Galeano introduced to me by Gonzalo Mora. AKA "Javier *Mina.*"

Kevin Palmer: Customs undercover pilot.

Greg Passic: DEA special agent assigned to Zürich.

Alvaro Perez: New Jersey distributor of cocaine supplied by Roberto Alcaíno.

Angel Perez: DEA special agent in Santa Cruz, Bolivia.

Diego Perez: Juan Tobón's brother-in-law.

Bruce Perlowin: head of an international drug-trafficking group based in San Francisco, importing marijuana into the U.S. from Colombia and Thailand.

Gaith Rashad Pharaon: Saudi billionaire and major BCCI and Capcom shareholder.

Lynden Pindling: prime minister of the Bahamas.

Mike Powers: assistant special agent in charge of the DEA office in Tampa.

Sushma Puri: officer and shareholder of Capcom.

Charles "Bebe" Rebozo: Florida banker and confidant of President Nixon.

Sugar Rojas: super flyweight world champion from Colombia. AKA "Baby."

Gil Roman: super flyweight world champion from Mexico.

William Rosenblatt: assistant commissioner of enforcement for Customs.

Brian Ross: NBC *Nightly News* reporter.

Rita Rozanski: Florida National Bank officer authorized to help me establish bank accounts in undercover names.

Sheereen Asghar-Khan: Amjad Awan's wife and the daughter of Asghar Khan, the youngest head of the Pakistan Air Force.

Charles Schumer: congressman from New York during Operation C-Chase and now senior U.S. senator from New York.

Frank Serra: Customs special agent in Chicago.

Saad Shafi: manager of BCCI Nassau.

Laura Sherman: Customs special agent in Tampa and case agent for C-Chase after I assumed the lead undercover role.

Ira Silverman: chief investigative producer for NBC *Nightly News*.

Morris Skolnick: special agent with the IRS Intelligence Division in Manhattan.

Joe Slyman: owner of the Royal Casino in Las Vegas.

Samuel Sommerhalder: Credit Suisse officer in Zürich.

Tammey Jewels: costume jewelry outlet company operated by Eric Wellman that I used as a fake front.

Marcella Tasón : secretary to Manuel Noriega.

John Thomas: professional boxing referee.

Bonni Tischler: special agent in charge of the Customs enforcement office in Tampa.

Clara Tobón: Juan Tobón's wife and the niece of José Gonzalo Rodríguez Gacha.

Juan Tobón: trafficker from Medellín operating with Roberto Alcaíno and others to import and distribute cocaine in the U.S. and Europe.

Roger Urbanski: Customs special agent in Vienna who also covered Switzerland.

Santiago Uribe: attorney working with Pablo Escobar and other members of the Medellín cartel involved in the laundering of drug proceeds and other crimes.

Rogelio Vargas: colonel in the Bolivian National Police who led a raid on the clandestine lab in Bolivia manufacturing tens of thousands of kilograms of cocaine for Roberto Alcaíno, Fabito Ochoa, and other members of the Medellín cartel.

Juan Guillermo Vargas: Colombian stockbroker in Medellín involved in the laundering of drug proceeds for the Medellín cartel.

Guillermo Velásquez: Colombian trafficker supplying Roberto Alcaíno with shipments of cocaine.

Mauricio Vives Carrillo: a primary money launderer for José Gonzalo Rodríguez Gacha, based in Bogotá.

William von Raab: commissioner of Customs.

Tony Weda: Customs special agent assigned to the agency's Undercover Operations Unit in Washington, D.C.

Buddy Weinstein: DEA special agent in San Francisco.

Eric Wellman: former employee of Palm State Bank and owner of Tammey Jewels, which I used as a fake front.

Gail Wellman: Eric's wife.

Tony Wilson: DEA assistant special agent in charge of training at the DEA academy in Quantico, Virginia.

Andrew Young: former ambassador to the United Nations and mayor of Atlanta.

Carmin Zabala: Tuto Zabala's wife.

Tuto Zabala: Cuban-born associate of Roberto Alcaíno in Miami.

Sheik Zayed bin Sultan Al Nahyan: ruler of Abu Dhabi and founder of the United Arab Emirates.

Muhammad Zia-ul-Haq: president and military ruler of Pakistan.

ACKNOWLEDGMENTS

My thanks to:

Scott and Andrea — I pray you feel how much I love you. Even though there were times when I couldn't be there, I hope you understand and forgive me. Thank you for everything you are.

Mom and Dad — for your unfailing love and guidance.

Ed and Gail — for the help and love you provided in the toughest of times.

Emir — for teaching me. You are and will always be my brother. You're the best at what you did. It couldn't have happened without you.

Mark — for being the only prosecutor dedicated and talented enough to make this story possible. I'm proud to call you my very good friend.

Kathy, Linda, Adella, Millie, José, Nelson, Frank, and Tony — for taking your job so seriously. Your work undercover meant much more than many people knew, and you deserve to be known as the brave people you are.

Dan, Steve, Joe, Laura, and Dave — for your endless dedication to serving the public and fighting the many battles you did behind the scenes.

The many dedicated law-enforcement officers in the U.S., U.K., and France — for keeping all of us safe.

Robert Guinsler — for embracing this story with your extraordinary talent and making this book happen. You're the best agent any writer could have.

Kati Hall — for the special energy and talent you shared in the process of our crafting the proposal for this book.

James Jayo — for your unparalleled magic as an editor. Your patience and wisdom are greatly appreciated.

INDEX